TERRE à TERRE
The VEGETARIAN COOKBOOK

Amanda: for my makers, Sheila and Otto Powley.
Philip: for my family – they know who they are.

We dedicate this book to Caroline Nunneley: who is a part of our story.
Thank you for your tireless support, and your generous and erudite contribution.

TERRE À TERRE
The VEGETARIAN COOKBOOK

AMANDA POWLEY WITH PHILIP TAYLOR

A.

First published in Great Britain
in 2009 by

Absolute Press
Scarborough House
29 James Street West
Bath BA1 2BT
Phone 44 (0) 1225 316013
Fax 44 (0) 1225 445836
E-mail info@absolutepress.co.uk
Website www.absolutepress.co.uk

Text copyright
Amanda Powley and Phil Taylor

Photography copyright
Lisa Barber

Publisher Jon Croft
Commissioning Editor Meg Avent
Editor Diana Artley
Assistant Editor Lucy Bridgers
Designer Matt Inwood
Assistant Designer Claire Siggery
Indexer and Publishing Assistant
Andrea O'Connor
Photography Lisa Barber
Photography Assistant Neri Kamcili
Food Stylists Amanda Powley, Joss Davey
and Dino Pavledis

A catalogue record of this book is
available from the British Library

ISBN 9781906650049

Printed and bound by Butler, Tanner
& Dennis, Somerset

A note about the text
This book is set in Sabon MT. Sabon was
designed by Jan Tschichold in 1964.
The roman design is based on type by
Claude Garamond, whereas the italic
design is based on types by Robert Granjon.

{MENU}

MY FAMILY AND OTHER COMESTIBLES

My entire childhood revolved around food. My mother was a domestic science teacher with a wicked sense of humour: a sort of Fanny meets Nigella, with Heston tendencies. She was experimental, fabulously inspiring and cooked only industrial quantities. My father scoffed, quaffed and carved while we giggled (I am the youngest of three), and at the end of every meal he said, 'You've hit the jackpot this time, darling' – even if we were filling our pockets and the dog with it.

But it was when I was 15 years old and my family moved from Britain to Saint Paul de Vence in the south of France that my foodie fireworks really began. I was at school in Switzerland and had a holiday job in a restaurant close to my parents' house. Eating out and trips to the market were a large part of our lives and had a big early influence on my perception of food and its impact on the world. A number of places and people stand out for me but none more so than the daily market in Nice (just one of its divine pleasures). It was a bouillon of bustling excitement.

EAU DE MARCHÉ

I loved the very essence of the market, with its hot, sticky pavements, fresh-as-a-daisy food, rolling, spitting rotisseries and the theatre of its pantomime-sized pans piled with perfumed paella and socca. The atmosphere was loaded with delicious, curious aromas, sights and sounds: shiny-eyed fish displayed over glistening ice; skilfully balanced towers of fruit; lines of vivid, colourful vegetables arranged with military precision; bursting blooms; giant bowls crammed with herbs, olives, tapenades, pickles and peppers; stalls heaving with clouds of cheeses; bottles of wine from rich ruby red to rose-petal shades; oils the colours of cut grass; the scent of spices mingled with wafts of strong cigarette smoke and coffee; the clatter of cutlery on china and the chatter of customers in the cafés. All this mixed with the distant, salty whiff of the sea proved to be a powerful and heady concoction and remains a delicious, scented memory to this day.

We often arrived very late for the market. In fact our favoured time of arrival was just as it was beginning to wind down, but still with plenty of time left for lunch. We would crowd on to a tiny, packed terrace around kamikaze tables and wobbly chairs, beckoning the snake-hipped waiters, who expertly wove their way around tables, children, small dogs and the day's purchases. We ate and drank too much and, after much giggling, snapping and struggling with bags crammed with our carefully selected produce, made our way back to the car. Whoever got there first drove home. Still, we all survived. Our afternoons were a much more leisurely affair, as we prepared the evening meal, which was inevitably shared with neighbours, house guests and whoever my older brothers had picked up on their travels that day. They were such happy times and the embodiment of my world.

It all changed suddenly when we moved back to the UK, but my love affair with food continued. By day, I devoured cookery books and created havoc in the kitchen at home, while at night I washed up in a restaurant nearby. Luckily for me, the head chef was very encouraging, and within a year I had progressed from chief bottle washer to commis chef. By now I was also attending cookery school, which gave me a good, solid grounding in traditional and international cooking methods and a fundamental understanding of wines and spirits. My journey had begun.

I was desperate to learn and needed to earn, so I moved to London and cooked my socks off, undertaking almost every foodie job going: working in Harrod's food hall, cooking in restaurants, hotels and directors' dining rooms, and catering at events. As a result, I earned enough to pay the rent and to travel, cook and eat my way around the world. I spent the next ten years in and out of the UK on a culinary quest. I cooked barracuda in Brazil, caribou in Canada and an awful lot in between, but throughout this time there was something niggling at me that just wouldn't go away.

MEATY MADNESS

For years my brother, Roger, had been a herdsman on a dairy farm in Surrey. It had always been a traditionally run family farm but when it changed hands he found himself working in a very different environment. Profit and productivity were valued over good animal husbandry, and the farming methods became cruel and dispassionate. This started me thinking about the intensive meat industry and the state of farming, and my thoughts were fuelled by a book called *Diet for a Small Planet*, given to me by a friend. I was working overseas again and having many heated debates with people on the subject, including my head chef, who was less than impressed with my heretical thoughts. I became a big fat thorn in his side and after one particularly tricky night service I pushed him to the brink of meaty madness. He spat out the six words that were to change the course of my life: 'You are not paid to think.' A few days later I handed in my notice and headed back to England.

THINKING

This wasn't the first time I'd had an impassioned tête-à-tête with chefs and other foodie folk about vegetarians, but the response was almost always the same: no serious gourmand could be a vegetarian and expect to be treated with respect by their contemporaries. What's more, the vegetarian diet was perceived to be dull and about denial. That was not the way I saw it. In fact, I felt quite the opposite, but it left me in a bit of a culinary conundrum: this negative impasse could only ever be bridged with a positive deed.

It had become clear to me that much of the developed world had entrenched ideas about food and what constituted a good diet – ideas often based on traditions that were themselves changing, although our society's beliefs remained rigid.

EUREKA!

Through my travels I had garnered different ideas and developed a fairly individual style of cooking that led me to view meat and fish as secondary commodities, so it was as easy as a warm knife through butter to take the next step and ditch them altogether. Until that point the vegetarian lifestyle hadn't been on my radar, and I had never been squeamish or overly sentimental about animals – I had plunged my fair share of lobsters, chased foxes over ditches, blasted a few bunnies and taken piggies to market – but the brutality and insanity of intensive farming were a bombshell to me. The more informed about meat production I became, the more overwhelmingly concerned I felt. My deep mistrust about the provenance of the products I was cooking and serving left me with an all-consuming sense of responsibility. I was young, and probably very naïve, but I felt compelled to try to make a difference. I wanted to alter people's perceptions of vegetarian food and to demonstrate that far from meaning missing out on something, eating 'flesh free' was about adding another dimension.

That was my eureka moment. All my experiences before this, with my family, my travels, my many jobs, had turned me into a culinary conscientious objector, or a hot potato in some eyes!

BRIGHTON BECKONED

My reaction to the food industry and my desire to do something different came as little surprise to those who know me. I've always had a rebellious nature and a distrust of all things establishment. No surprise, then, that I found Brighton to be my spiritual home. Brighton and I went back a long way. I would often bunk off school and jump on a bus to Pool Valley in the town centre. During the journey, I'd change my clothes and apply my make up (badly) before heading to a steamy café, two paces from the bus stop. Here I idled away my truanting hours, hiding on the top floor, my back to the rattly dumb waiter, watching the comings and goings of Brighton's colourful life, while smoking Benson and Hedges and nursing a cup of frothy coffee.

It was 1984 when I returned, knowing no one, but I was instantly swept along, as visitors to Brighton often are, by its habit of adopting and accepting new blood. I worked in some great places, met some amazing characters, made lifelong friends, and fortuitously landed on my feet in a thriving vegetarian restaurant, where I met a comrade-in-arms, Philip Taylor: a lovely man, a truly inspirational chef, and now my friend of 20 years. We shared a lot of common ground: we'd both cooked our way round the globe and ended up in Brighton with the desire to find a platform for our culinary ideas. We were both inspired to push the boundaries of traditional cooking and to see what we could put on the table for Brighton.

After months of rumination, Philip called me to say that he had found rundown premises in Pool Valley. It had been a café years ago, he told me, was pretty derelict, had three floors and a rattly dumb waiter. Did I want to see it? I did, and sure enough, it was my 'café à la truant'! This made our venture a dead cert for me from then on. Despite the fact that the British economy was in a mess and no commercial banks would lend to us, we bit the bullet. Blind with passion and empowered by enthusiasm, we believed nothing mattered but our vision. So instead we begged, borrowed, but drew the line at stealing (well, I did – not sure about Phil), and signed the lease. We bought the *Reader's Digest Book of DIY*, and two balaclavas. During this time we received an immeasurable amount of support from family, friends and the brilliant Brighton community. It was overwhelming for both of us, and we will always be truly indebted to everyone who helped us. It has been an amazing journey and we are still on the road.

AMANDA POWLEY

FROM THERE TO HERE

And so it begins, as I'm sure it has for many a chef, at home in their mother's or father's kitchen, the warm heart of the house, helping when there are bowls to lick and treats to make, watching and participating in the whole seemingly magical process of taking disparate ingredients and chopping, mixing, beating, cooking and coaxing until the finished dish is ready for the table.

From there, a short jump into catering college and then out into the real world of professional kitchens: turns on the larder, the sauce, the veg section, a roasting on the grill, cooling down in the pastry kitchen. Hotels, restaurants, cruise ships, banquets and bakeries. Fresh foods, French food and whole foods.

On the London-to-Brighton train, intrigued by an advert for a pastry chef in a vegetarian restaurant and tempted by a summer by the sea, off to meet Simon, the founder of Food for Friends restaurant.

I take the job... I don't go back... a summer by the sea turns into a whole new life. Several summers and lives later, and now head chef, I meet Amanda, a kindred cheffy spirit with a similar take on food and a desire to push the boundaries of vegetarian cuisine and boldly go where no bean has been before.

Taking on the lease of a small, rundown café in need of repair and repaint, we swap our knives and pastry brushes for saws, sanders, paint brushes and rollers and, with much help from friends, families and partners, finally open Terre à Terre.

Welcoming our first guests, cooking in probably the smallest, hottest kitchen ever. Guests leave happy – phew.

We move on from the 28-seat café to more substantial premises and go from feeding 30 people a night to 130, but the lovely, ever-evolving Terre à Terre team more than copes and our guests leave happy – phew!

And so it carries on.

PHILIP TAYLOR

ALL THINGS BRIGHTON BEAUTIFUL

It is a cliché but, as is the way of clichés, it's founded on a bedrock of truth: Brighton accommodates pretty much anyone and anything. It has an all-embracing spirit that, even in the recession-hit 1980s, welcomed two driven individuals to the town (for those were the days before 'city' status), who truly had no pennies to rub together, but who were relatively young and had idealism aplenty, and a surfeit of amazingly generous and energetic friends.

Philip Taylor and I met in a subterranean kitchen in The Lanes and recognized in each other a kindred spirit. Although from completely different cooking backgrounds, we had very similar ideas about the type of food we wanted to create: food without meat but in a way that meant more taste and more possibilities, stretching the boundaries rather than being always curtailed by the missing element, and making 'less' a very definite 'more' (to steal from a very apt quotation). We wanted vegetarianism that had more to do with indulgence than with abstinence. We pretty soon found a half-derelict Georgian property, into which we, and our good friends, poured all our time and energies to see what would unfold.

It is a miracle that the restaurant ever got off the ground. We undertook a basic business course and borrowed from parents and sensible, fiscally minded friends. We couldn't afford to pay workmen for more than the structural work, so our mates worked their weekends, days and nights off, stripping wood, painting, plastering. They shared their skills, precious time and humour. It was great fun. We had a lot of laughs and quite a few disasters, we forged lifetime friendships and we made a restaurant!

Eighteen years on and we're still here. In fact, we still exist only in Brighton, which does indeed 'own' us. The restaurant has grown and evolved beyond our expectations but we still feel entirely part of the community. We might have upped sticks and moved around the corner to bigger premises (as you do when the family grows) but the core of our customers are those who supported us in the early days, when we were BYO, and the creaky food lift often didn't work, and we couldn't afford the fee to take credit cards, and we accidentally let a night's takings blow away in the wind from the back of a bicycle pannier! The babies who came in to the first Terre à Terre with exhausted parents are now young adults, and we've watched them grow (indeed, have fed them whilst they did), as the lovely people of Brighton have watched us grow (and been instrumental in the process).

We would never have got off the ground without our friends, but we would never have survived this long without our fabulous and committed staff. We've had so many along the way who have been dedicated and inspired, and brought so much with them, that it's impossible to name them all. Right now, we have Dino Pavledis as head chef: a skilful, hard-working, much-respected lovely bear of a man who brings much to the party. And there's our wonderful Joss Davey, an absolute genius of a pastry chef. If we have even the glimmer of an idea, Jossy works out how it can be done, and then does it. Pâtissièrs are truly scientists, with maybe a hint of magician in them. Olivia Reid is our rock. She keeps us shipshape, organizes just about anything that happens here, has brainwaves and slaves away in a tiny, airless office, making sure we run on time and that the world is kept up to speed with what we're doing. She is the drive and engine behind all that we do. And then there's gorgeous Christian Cotton. He came to us right at the very beginning, a long-haired young man with a cheeky sense of humour and the voice of an angel, now a lynch-pin in the business and a close-shorn father of three! And Chris Wales deserves a mention here; the most charming, professional and able general manager we could hope for. Also Wendy Jane Taylor, a bespoke painter and friend, whose inspired use of colour and design has helped us create an identity in the restaurant that entirely reflects what we're trying to achieve with the food. Just a few names out of the huge team that makes Terre à Terre happen.

One of the great privileges of being such a long-established business is that we've been able to watch other local businesses grow alongside us, whilst forging strong links with our local growers and suppliers. We buy cheeses from High Weald Dairy, 'Parmesan' from Bookham Fine Foods, juices from Oakwood Farm and fantastic organic produce from Stanmer Organics, just up the road. We are blessed to have award-winning wines grown in our county by Breaky Bottom and Ridgeview. This is just a handful of our local producers and suppliers. Sussex is teeming with independent, hard-working growers and makers, far too many to be able to mention them all here. So much being produced on our doorstep! We feel very honoured to be a part of their stories, too.

Whilst we're talking about the food, people sometimes take issue with us over the wording of our menus. This seems a good moment at which to issue a disclaimer. They are playful and fun, often full of homegrown words that sound right and fitting, and sometimes loaded with puns, jokes and wordplay (the staff always have a glossary to hand should it be required.) All too often, people dine in fine restaurants where the menus are in archaic French and are incomprehensible to the general public. Well, why should they have all the fun? We take food very seriously but, unashamedly, we can't resist a little playfulness too.

Supporting us both throughout it all have been our beautiful families, now much larger than when it all began. They've subbed us money (couldn't have done it without you, Dee), listened ad nauseam to our worries, eaten our experiments and supported and encouraged us in so many ways. Roger provided a huge shoulder to lean on when needed, and bought the original tables for the restaurant, as we reached opening night with no money left, plenty of chairs but nothing to sit at! Barry bailed us out and then bought the car that carried the endless builders' supplies, which then became the official Terre à Terre vehicle in which years of outside catering was delivered. Froukje bailed us out (again!) and Dee kept us solvent, and sane, when times got tough. Spike was our accountant with a twist (a dab hand with a paintbrush) and is still a great mentor and dear friend. David, Katie and Rosa provided a beautiful reason for Phil to keep bringing home the bacon (!) and gave fantastic culinary advice to their Dad. Handsome Tommy worked the bar and Jacqui worked the floor (and made the pots for the flowers). Without Caroline, this book would not exist, and neither would the beautiful Miriam and Reuben, feisty little critters who have eaten their way through the menus, all in the name of research of course.

To you all, we say the biggest, most heartfelt thank you.

Terre à Terre has been in all our lives for such a long time now. It's thanks to every one of you that we are still here, and hopefully, with your support, we will continue to grow and evolve, and to carry on feeding all you lovely people.

Now, we hope you enjoy your meal!

AMANDA POWLEY
AND PHILIP TAYLOR
SEPTEMBER 2009

ABOUT THE FOOD AND THIS BOOK

Enough about me and him, and on to the important stuff. Food. After all, that's what we are all here for. Whether you're a flesh-free devotee or a vegetarian virgin, we hope you find recipes in the following pages that will inspire your creativity and tantalise your taste buds. Because contrary to popular belief meat-free doesn't mean fun-free. At Terre à Terre we passionately believe that vegetarian food is vibrant, exciting and challenging, and our team of talented and committed staff have laboured with us to discover tastes and combinations that will satisfy and delight. We hope that you too will discover this when cooking our food in your home.

There may be some ingredients that you're not familiar with, or certain techniques you've not tried before, but don't let that put you off. The recipes aren't set in stone – they're simply a starting point and the finished product is entirely in your hands. Our food philosophy has always been to mix and match, and in the past we have been prolific culinary globetrotters with magpie gathering tendencies, bringing back ideas to hatch at Terre à Terre – the ideal recipe roost.

Now it's your turn to get creative in the kitchen, so don't be afraid to play around with the recipes, personalize them and create dishes that you will love to eat. Because that should be the ultimate goal when cooking. If it doesn't taste good, no one is going to want to eat it, it's as simple as that. This is all we ever have in our sights and it is what we hope you get from this book: the chance to find out new and delicious food combinations that will encourage you to experiment and tinker, as well as enjoying making your Terre à Terre favourites.

Happy cooking and even happier eating.

Opposite, top: the team at Terre à Terre; and below:
the mini team that produced the food that you see in this book
– head chef, Dino, me and pastry chef, Joss.

A NOTE ON MEASURES

Our recipes use level spoon measures and large eggs. For readers in the US, there is a list of conversion measures on page 226.

A FEW
BASICS

...

{white stock}

50g leek, white part only, chopped
250g white onions, chopped
150g celery, chopped
150g carrot, chopped
150g fennel, chopped
3 garlic cloves
12 black peppercorns
4 juniper berries
2 star anise
8 coriander seeds
1 bouquet garni (bay leaves, thyme and
   curly leaf parsley)
2.5 litres water250ml dry white wine
1 lemon, sliced

Put all the ingredients except the wine and
sliced lemon into a large pan, bring to the
boil, cover and simmer for 15 minutes. Add
the wine and lemon. Remove the lemons
before cooling. Chill overnight, if possible.
Strain the stock through a fine sieve. Keep
refrigerated, or split into smaller batches
and freeze.

{demi glace sauce}

50g dried porcini mushrooms
2 tablespoons olive oil
40g white onion, chopped 125g carrot,
   chopped
125g celery, chopped
1 tablespoon tomato purée
30g plain flour
1 litre hot White Stock (see opposite)
   or water
200ml red wine
200ml medium dry sherry
2 teaspoons tamari (gluten free soy sauce)
5g parsley
5g rosemary
5g thyme
2 bay leaves
5 peppercorns
5 allspice berries

Place the porcini mushrooms in a bowl,
pour over 500ml boiling water and leave
them to soak. Heat the oil in a large pan
and add the onion; it should sizzle noisily.
Cook over a medium to high heat, stirring
constantly, until the onion is an even nutty
brown; be careful not to let it burn. Add
the carrot and celery, and turn the heat to
low, then add the tomato purée and flour
and cook, stirring regularly, for 5 minutes.
Add the stock or water, wine, sherry,
tamari, the mushrooms and their soaking
liquid, and the herbs, peppercorns and
allspice. Turn up the heat to medium,
cover and simmer for 20 minutes. Strain
through a fine sieve, cool and refrigerate
until needed

{mayonnaise}

3 large eggs (preferably free range
   organic)
1 garlic clove, crushed
1/2 teaspoon sea salt
250ml olive oil (extra virgin essential)
2 teaspoons white wine vinegar
250ml grapeseed oil
freshly ground black pepper

to finish (optional) – choose one or more
of the following options
lemon zest or juice
wholegrain or English mustard
smoked paprika
finely chopped parsley, tarragon or basil

Combine the eggs, garlic and salt in a
large bowl, using a hand whisk, or use a
food processor. Start to whisk, or process
on medium speed, drizzling in 25-50ml of
the olive oil in a slow steady stream, until
the mixture starts to thicken. At this point
add the vinegar, which will thin the
mixture down again. Now continue to
drizzle in the rest of the olive oil and then
the grapeseed oil, each in a thin steady
stream, while whisking or running the
machine. When you have added both oils,
add seasoning to taste.

If the mix is too runny or separates, don't
panic! Just beat in another egg yolk, and
the mix will stabilize. If, on the other
hand, it's too thick, simply beat in a little
cold water to thin it down.

Once you have made the basic mayonnaise,
you can use it just as it is, or flavour it
with citrus, spice or herbs. Try adding
lemon zest or juice, wholegrain or English
mustard, smoked paprika, or finely
chopped parsley, tarragon or basil.

{herb oils}

200g herb leaves of your choice
100ml grapeseed or sunflower oil
100ml olive oil (extra virgin essential)

These vibrant, fragrant green oils are fabulous to drizzle over just about anything. You could stick with one type of herb but, once you get started, you may well become inspired to mix up various combinations.

Bring a large pan of salted water to the boil. Plunge the herbs into the boiling water for a few seconds, then instantly remove them and plunge into icy water. Leave until cold, then remove the chilled herbs from the water and drain well. Squeeze out any moisture with a clean tea towel or paper towels.

Place the herbs and oils in a blender and blitz for about 20 seconds, until well combined. Transfer to an airtight container and refrigerate for at least 12 hours, overnight if possible.

Place a sieve lined with muslin over a bowl, making sure the base of the sieve is well above the base of the bowl (if you don't have any muslin, a fine sieve will do; the oil might not be so clear but it will taste just as good). Strain the oil through the sieve, letting it drip through at its own speed without forcing it. In this way, the oil will retain the beautiful verdant green of the herbs. The finished oils can be stored in bottles or airtight containers in the refrigerator or a cool dark place, for up to 1 week. You can keep the leftover herb bits and add them to soups, stocks and other dishes.

{creamy mashed potatoes}

1kg potatoes (preferably Maris Piper), peeled and chopped
200ml double cream
50g salted butter
a pinch of ground mace, salt and freshly ground black pepper

Put the potatoes in a large pan of salted water and bring to the boil. Reduce the heat, cover and simmer until the potatoes are tender. Drain, then leave the potatoes to stand in the colander until dry, or put them back into the pan over a low heat to dry off any excess moisture.

Warm the cream, butter and mace in a separate pan. Mash the potatoes and add to the warm cream and butter. Season with salt and plenty of pepper (white looks nice here, but we prefer to use black).

For a vegan alternative, see Miso Mashed Potatoes, page 94.

{puff pastry}

400g strong flour
400g unsalted butter (or vegan pastry fat)
250ml water
1 teaspoon lemon juice
1/2 teaspoon salt

Sieve the flour into a large bowl, then rub in 50g of the butter. Mix the water, lemon juice and salt. Add this liquid to the flour mixture, either stirring in by hand or using a food mixer with a dough hook, to make a smooth firm dough. Cover with a clean cloth and leave to rest in a cool place for 20 minutes.

Take the dough and, using a sharp knife, cut a cross in the top about half way through. From the centre, pull out each cut quarter to form a rough star or cross. (The centre will remain fairly thick.) Roll out each corner of the star to a quarter of the thickness of the centre.

Shape the remaining 350g butter into a round the same thickness as the centre and place on top of the dough. Fold in the points of the star over the butter, applying light pressure on the joins to ensure that the flaps enclose the butter completely. Cover and leave to rest in a cool place for 30 minutes.

You will now give the pastry 4 'book turns'. Roll out the dough to a long rectangle about 10mm thick (the length should be about 4 times greater than the width). Next, fold both the short edges into the centre. Now, imagine you have a book in front of you. Close the book by folding the left side on to the right side. Cover and leave to rest in a cool place for 1 hour.

The dough requires 3 more book turns. Each time, roll out and fold as instructed above. Keep the closed 'book' edge on the same side every time. Allow 1 hour's rest between turns. When rolling, try to keep the corners square. The pastry must be rolled evenly and not too thin. Before folding, dust off all the flour.

If you are short of time, you can always substitute a bought, good quality, all-butter puff pastry.

{vanilla ice cream}

300ml milk
300ml double cream
1 large or 2 small vanilla pods, split and
    scraped
6 large egg yolks
185g caster sugar

Put the milk, cream, and vanilla pod and seeds in a heavy based pan and bring slowly to the boil, to allow the vanilla to infuse. Cover and remove from the heat.

Whisk the egg yolks and sugar together in a bowl until pale and creamy. Pour on about one third of the hot milk mixture and stir in well. Return the pan to a low to medium heat, pour the milk and egg mixture back in and cook, stirring constantly with a wooden spoon, until you have a custard that is thick enough to coat the back of the spoon. Do not allow it to boil or the eggs will scramble. As soon as the custard has thickened, pour it into a cool bowl (leaving in the vanilla pod). Stir every 5-10 minutes to release the heat, or place the bowl over iced water.

Once the custard is cool, strain it through a sieve, squeezing the vanilla pod to extract all the flavour. Refrigerate for at least 1 hour before churning in an ice cream maker. Freeze the ice cream in a sealed container.

{sugar syrup}

1 litre water
125g liquid glucose
375g caster sugar

Sugar syrup is an essential component of many sorbets and ices. Put all the ingredients in a pan and bring to the boil, stirring to dissolve the sugar. Simmer for 2 minutes, then leave to cool.

IN THE BEGINNINGS

Ruby Tang Thang

soft sheep's milk cheese wrapped in beetroot and damson leather, served with bannock biccies

Small but perfectly formed, these sweet little mouthfuls are extremely flexible: we decided to class them as a starter, but they could happily sit anywhere in a meal. On their own they make a cracking canapé; served with heaps of well dressed leaves they transform into a scrumptious small salad; and they are sweet enough to fill a pudding gap too.

The delicious biscuits can be celebrated all on their own for their easy to make, savoury loveliness. Pinhead oatmeal, contrary to what one would think, is actually the chunkiest grade of oatmeal, so it adds an interesting texture to your cooking. And, as it contains the whole grain including the bran, it is highly nutritious.

serves 6

{ruby tang thang}
for the fruit leather

14 damsons or 10 red plums, stoned and diced
30g fresh or frozen blackcurrants
80ml agave syrup
30g raw beetroot, peeled and grated

for the sheep's milk cheese filling
250g soft sheep's milk cheese (Sussex Slipcote is ideal)
70ml crème fraîche
grated zest and juice of 1 lemon
salt and pepper

First prepare the filling. Crumble the cheese into a bowl with the crème fraîche, lemon zest and juice, and season to taste. Mix everything together well.

Put the fruit into a medium sized saucepan with the agave syrup and beetroot and bring to the boil. Simmer for 10 minutes, then remove from the heat. Blend the mix in a jug blender until smooth, then strain it.

Preheat the oven to 70°C/Gas Mark 1/4. Line a large baking tray with baking parchment and pour the mix in until it spreads out to the sides. Place in the oven and leave for 6 hours until it has dried out and set.

This fruit leather can be made in advance and rolled up in clingfilm to store in an airtight container for 2 months, the refrigerator for 4 months or the freezer for 1 year.

When you are ready to fill the fruit leather, cut it into three 30 x 10cm rectangles and place each one on a piece of clingfilm. Carefully spoon the cheese mix lengthways down the centre of each rectangle, dividing it equally between the 3. Bring one edge of the fruit leather over the filling and tuck it in around the cheese. Now roll up to form a sausage shape. Roll firmly in the clingfilm and refrigerate for at least 2 hours before assembling the dish.

{bannock biccies}

120g pinhead oatmeal
a pinch of salt
20g unsalted butter, melted
about 3 tablespoons boiling water

Mix the oatmeal, salt and melted butter, stirring well. Pour in the boiling water to form a sticky dough, adding a drop more if the mixture looks too dry. Cover the dough and leave to rest for 30 minutes.

Roll out the dough to a 5mm thickness and cut out rounds with a 5cm cutter. You should have about 30 rounds. Bake at 180°C/Gas Mark 4 for about 25 minutes until crisp. Cool on a wire rack and store in an airtight container. (You will have plenty left over after asssembling this dish, but they will soon disappear!)

{to assemble}

Remove the chilled sausages from the clingfilm and, with a very sharp, thin bladed knife, cut each one into 6 slices (discarding the end pieces), making 18 slices altogether. Gently place each slice cut side down on to a bannock biccie and garnish with something pretty – tiny flowers, if available.

Dunkin' Doughnuts

parmesan doughnuts rolled in porcini dust, served with chestnut soup with
frothy mace bay cream and frozen pear shavings

This lovely autumnal dish is screaming crackling fires and comfy sofas.... Absolutely delicious doughy delights, loaded with lashings of Parmesan and heady hits of intensely pungent porcini – the perfect dunking partner to the velvety chestnut and bay cappuccino. If you don't avail yourself of the readily obtainable tinned chestnuts, you will need to brace yourself for tackling the prickly process of removing fresh chestnuts from their spiky jackets. In the woods they start to hit the ground from October but be warned, the squirrels are early risers and sneaky little devils, and can clear a forest floor in no time: half and half is a good compromise, so get there early!

serves 4–6

{parmesan doughnuts}

250g strong flour
3g dried yeast
125ml warm water
30g soft unsalted butter
50g Parmesan cheese, freshly grated
10g caster sugar
1 teaspoon salt
1 egg, beaten
oil for deep frying

for the Parmesan porcini dust
10g dried porcini mushrooms
100g Parmesan cheese, freshly grated
salt and freshly ground black pepper

First prepare the Parmesan porcini dust. Blitz the dried porcini in a liquidizer or food processor until they resemble fine dust. Mix with the Parmesan cheese, season lightly with salt and pepper and spread out thinly on a large plate. Leave at room temperature for about 1 hour, to dry. Then keep in an airtight container.

Next, prepare the dough for the doughnuts. Sieve the flour into a bowl and make a well in the centre. Dissolve the yeast in 60ml of the warm water and pour this liquid into the well. Combine the flour with the liquid and leave to ferment in a warm place, until bubbles start to break through the flour (about 10 minutes).

Now add the remaining water, the butter, Parmesan, sugar, salt and egg. Either by hand or in a food mixer with a dough hook, knead the mix to form a soft dough that is smooth and pliable without being sticky. Cover the bowl with a clean tea towel and leave in a warm place to prove for 1 hour.

Turn out the dough on to a lightly floured surface and pull off pieces weighing about 25g. Roll these into tight balls and arrange on a lightly oiled tray, leaving a 5cm gap between each one, so they do not stick together as they prove. You should end up with 18–20 pieces. Cover them with a clean tea towel and leave to prove for about 30 minutes until they have doubled in size. They are now ready to cook.

Heat the oil in a deep fryer or deep pan to 180°C. Lower the doughnuts carefully into the oil, 4 at a time. Fry for about 4–5 minutes until golden brown. Drain on paper towels, then roll in the Parmesan porcini dust.

{chestnut soup}

25g unsalted butter
100g shallots, finely chopped
1/2 teaspoon chopped thyme
1/2 teaspoon chopped rosemary
1 bay leaf
1 garlic clove, finely chopped
200g cooked chestnuts, roughly chopped
  (fresh are best, but tinned will do)
1 litre White Stock (see page 18) or water
250ml whipping cream
salt and ground white pepper

Melt the butter and cook the shallots, herbs and garlic until they are soft and translucent, taking care not to brown them. Add the chestnuts to the pan and cook gently for another 5 minutes, then add the stock and bring to the boil. Simmer for a further 10 minutes. Remove the pan from the heat, stir in the cream, and blitz the mix in a food processor or liquidizer. Strain through a fine sieve, season to taste, and set to one side until needed.

{frozen pear shavings}

4 ripe Williams pears
1 tablespoon lemon juice

Peel the pears, cut in quarters lengthways, remove the cores and toss the quarters gently in lemon juice. Carefully lay out on silicone paper and freeze. When frozen, remove from the freezer and, using a large knife, slice as finely as possible. Place back in the freezer until ready to use.

mace bay cream
50g shallots, finely chopped
10g unsalted butter
150ml white wine
25ml whipping cream
a pinch of ground mace
2 bay leaves
salt and ground white pepper

Cook the shallots in the butter until soft, then pour the wine into the pan and carry on cooking until the liquid has reduced by half. Add the cream, mace and bay leaves and simmer for another 10 minutes. Remove the bay leaves and season the sauce. Set aside until needed.

{to assemble}

good quality cocoa powder to dust

Arrange the hot doughnuts on serving plates and dust with a little cocoa powder. Heat the chestnut soup and pour it into warmed coffee cups, leaving a space at the top for the mace bay cream. Gently warm this now and, if you like, froth it with a small whisk or hand blender, then spoon it on to the chestnut soup, dust for a cappuccino effect. Have the remainder of the mace cream in a jug on the table for top-ups. We like to serve this in the restaurant with frozen pear shavings, hot to cold in 5 seconds (a bit like the weather...).

Turtle and Tostones

{VEGAN} {WHEAT FREE}

turtle bean soup with smoky spice dusted plantain fritters, avocado lime salsa and guava tamarind ice

This dish is a little bit like a South American festival: there is a whole load going on....It's fun, feisty and full of crackers! Delicious smooth swallows of dark savoury packed soup, with lasting chilli heat; just perfect with sizzling spice dusted tostones (fried plantain), either for dipping or to be loaded with generous heaps of creamy avocado lime salsa. The ideal cool companion is the refreshingly sweet and sour guava and tamarind ice. (A small shot of tequila is optional but adds another little cracker to the display.)

This soup recipe uses a combination of three contrasting chillies. Chipotles are smoked and dried jalapeños. With tastes of tobacco and dried fruit, these little devils pack a punch too – not a killer heat, but a lingering zing. Guajillo means 'little gourd': these chillies have a sweet sharpness and a relatively gentle heat. Habaneros have an interesting fruity flavour but are incredibly hot, so approach with caution. And if you're wondering what the black turtle bean has in common with its namesake, it's merely the shiny shell! With a firm texture and mushroomy taste, this bean is an extremely good source of antioxidants, and therefore a healthy and useful addition to meat free cooking.

Plantains look like massive bananas but with thicker skin. They are eaten all over Africa and the Americas. A hugely versatile fruit, they can be boiled, roasted, grilled or fried – and for this recipe they need to be still green, which is when they are starchy and pretty neutral in flavour. They can also be fermented to make an alcoholic drink, but we haven't got round to trying that out yet!

serves 6

{guava and tamarind ice}

1 guava (about 280g), peeled and cut into chunks
60g tamarind paste (see page 152)
4 tablespoons lime juice
75ml Sugar Syrup (see page 21)
grated zest of 1 lime

Blend all the ingredients together and then strain into a freezerproof container. Place the mix in the freezer and bring it out when it is slushy. Now whisk until the icy lumps are broken up and the mixture is smooth. Return to the freezer and repeat this chilling and whisking process once more. Now freeze the ice until 15 minutes before you plan to use it. (If you are lucky enough to have an ice cream maker, refer to the manufacturer's instructions.)

{avocado lime salsa}

2 tablespoons lime juice
280g ripe avocados, peeled, stoned and finely chopped
50g tomato, diced
50g red pepper, diced
50g coriander, chopped
4 garlic cloves, crushed
1 tablespoon finely chopped red chilli pepper
1/2 teaspoon cumin seeds, toasted
salt and freshly ground black pepper

Add the lime juice to the chopped avocado and mix with all the other ingredients, adding seasoning to taste. Refrigerate in an airtight container until needed.

{turtle bean soup}

10g dried chipotle chilli
10g dried guajillo chilli
1g dried habanero chilli
150g turtle beans, soaked overnight in cold water
3 tablespoons olive oil
1 1/2 teaspoons cumin seeds, toasted
1 teaspoon coriander seeds
2 bay leaves
1 1/2 teaspoons chopped thyme
300g onions, finely diced
75g celery, finely diced
75g carrot, finely diced
75g red pepper, finely diced
3 litres White Stock (see page 18) or water
150ml medium dry sherry
salt

Pour boiling water on to the dried chillies and leave to soak for 20 minutes, then drain, reserving the soaking liquid. Deseed and chop the chillies. Rinse the turtle beans, cover with fresh cold water and bring to the boil. Allow to boil rapidly for 10 minutes, then drain.

Heat the oil in a large pan and cook all the dry spices, the chillies, bay leaves and thyme, stirring constantly. Add the onions, celery, carrot and red pepper and cook, covered, for 10 minutes, until the vegetables have softened. Now add the turtle beans, the stock or water, and the reserved chilli liquid. Cover and simmer for 45–60 minutes until the beans are very soft.

The soup now needs to be blended, so half fill a jug blender and liquidize for about 3 minutes until smooth, then strain into a clean pan. Repeat with the remaining soup.

Just before serving, season to taste with salt, bring the soup to a simmer and pour in the sherry.

{tostones (plantain fritters)}

2 green plantains
200ml sunflower oil

for the spice dust
1 teaspoon cumin seeds
1/4 teaspoon smoked paprika
1/4 teaspoon sea salt
8 black peppercorns
1/2 teaspoon chopped thyme

First prepare the spice dust. Toast the cumin seeds in a dry pan or under a grill, taking care not to let them burn as this would make them bitter. Put all the ingredients in a mortar or spice grinder, then grind to a rough powder. Store the dust in an airtight container until you are ready to use it.

Plantains are hard to peel, so begin by cutting the skin from top to bottom in 3 places, then peel. Now chop them widthways into 3cm chunks: you want 2 chunks per person, and will probably get about 6 from each fruit. Heat the oil in a skillet or deep frying pan and blanch the chunks evenly over a medium heat for 3–4 minutes, so that they become soft enough for a knife to sink easily into their flesh. Remove from the oil with a slotted spoon and drain. Now squash each plantain chunk flat (cut side up) between 2 sheets of greaseproof paper; apply pressure (the palm of your hand will do) and then put them aside to cool.

Only start cooking the tostones just before you are ready to eat. Reheat the oil and fry the tostones in small batches on both sides, for 4–5 minutes until brown and crisp. Drain on paper towels and then sprinkle with the spice dust.

{to assemble}

10g coriander leaves, torn
6 tablespoons tequila (optional)
a pinch of salt (optional)

Ladle the soup into 6 warmed bowls and garnish with the coriander. Pile all the hot tostones on to a large serving platter and heap the avocado lime salsa to the side, for communal dipping in. Give everyone their own frozen glass of guava and tamarind ice. If you like, pour tequila over the ice and sprinkle with salt.

Chilly Bristols

fat green olives, filled with soft ricotta, rolled in rosemary crumbs,
deep fried and served with sherry granita

Very simple, very rewarding, very Abigail's Party, not to mention bordering on food porn in the flavour department too! Call me old fashioned, but I do find a chubby olive and a dry sherry hard to resist, and this easy, unfussy grouping of hot and cold, sweet and salty sensations is inexplicably good. Don't just take my word for it: try it! If you have a go at just one recipe in this book, let it be this one...you won't be disappointed. It hits the spot at the beginning of a meal, and is pleasingly presented as a tapas style plate or small, but perfectly formed, starter.

Serve these sizzling hot, fat olives, crammed with creamy ricotta and rolled in rosemary crumbs, cut with boozy, icy mouthfuls. And remember, a bottle of sherry is not just for Christmas....

serves 4–6

{sherry granita}

50ml water
50mg caster sugar
350ml fino sherry
175ml cream sherry (preferably Harvey's Bristol Cream)
about 2 teaspoons lemon juice

Bring the water and sugar to the boil in a pan, and simmer for 5 minutes. Transfer to a cold bowl and leave to cool. Add both the sherries, and lemon juice to taste. Pour into a shallow container and place in the freezer. When the mixture is almost frozen, break it up with a fork and put it back into the freezer. Keep in the freezer until you are ready to serve it.

{deep fried olives}

36 queen green olives, stoned
150g ricotta cheese
grated zest of 1 lemon
25g Parmesan cheese, freshly grated
3 eggs, beaten
100ml whole milk
100g plain flour, seasoned with salt and pepper
125g focaccia breadcrumbs (preferably rosemary focaccia)
oil for deep frying

Rinse the olives in cold running water and drain them. Mix the ricotta, lemon zest and Parmesan until blended. Spoon this mix into a piping bag and fill each olive with it. Beat together the eggs and the milk. Roll the olives in the flour (shake off any excess), dip quickly into the egg mix (again, shake off any excess) and finally roll in the breadcrumbs. (The olives are best if totally coated so, if they have not covered well, put them back in the refrigerator for 10 minutes and then once again dip in the egg mix and roll in the breadcrumbs.) Keep in the refrigerator until you are ready to cook them.

Just before the meal, heat the oil in a deep fryer or deep pan to 180°C and cook the olives for 2–3 minutes until golden brown. Remove and drain them on paper towels.

{to assemble}

chopped parsley and basil

Generously fill wide-mouthed chilled glasses with the sherry granita and place in the freezer while you fry the olives (see above). Serve the olives immediately, with cocktail sticks or skewers (they are hot tricky little beggars!), garnished with parsley and basil and accompanied by glasses of chilled sherry granita.

Blond Chick Frits

white leek soup with braised leek shred, served with chickpea and cashew fritters, harissa, and argan oil

{VEGAN} {WHEAT FREE}

We are big on soups at Terre à Terre, especially with a bit on the side, so this is perfect all round! Delicious creamy white leek soup with a mild onion taste and tender braised shredded leaves ... just the right host for the aromatic blend of chillies and spices loaded into our fiery harissa and served with delicious little sizzling fritters, savoury with crushed cashews, chickpeas, basmati, fresh mint and chives. Pile these into the soup or put them on the side for dipping and noisy slurping – either way, this dish is great as either a starter or light meal.

However you serve our line-up, don't forget the argan oil with its fresh and nutty flavour. Rich in vitamin E, it's been used for centuries by Berber women in Morocco to nourish their skin, hair and nails. But here we suggest it just for the extra dimension it adds to the taste combination – extremely Moorish on every level!

serves 4–6

{chick frits}

150g chickpeas
250g basmati rice
100g cashew nuts, toasted
2 tablespoons soya yogurt
4 teaspoons lemon juice
1 teaspoon lemon zest
4 tablespoons chopped mint
2 tablespoons chopped chives
$1/2$ teaspoon baking powder
$1 1/2$ teaspoons sea salt
freshly ground black pepper
gram flour for coating
250ml sunflower oil

Cook the chickpeas and basmati rice according to packet instructions. Put all but the last 2 ingredients in a food processor and pulse quite roughly until they are combined but are not a smooth mix. With a dessertspoon, scoop out the mixture and mould into your preferred shape. Roll the fritters in the gram flour and lay them on a lined baking sheet. Cover with clingfilm and refrigerate until needed.

Just before you are ready to eat, heat the oil in a deep fryer or deep pan to 180°C. Lower the frits gently into the oil and cook for about 2 minutes or until golden. Drain on paper towels.

{braised leeks}

100ml dry white wine
200ml White Stock (see page 18) or water
50ml olive oil
1 bay leaf
$1/2$ teaspoon chopped rosemary
salt and freshly ground black pepper
300g finely shredded leeks (green part only)

Reserve the unused, white parts of the leeks for the Leek Soup (see below). Place all the ingredients in an ovenproof dish, cover and bake at 180°C/Gas Mark 4 for 20 minutes or until the leeks are tender. Strain off 100ml of the braising liquid and reserve for making the soup. Set aside the dish of braised leeks for when you come to assemble the dish.

{leek soup}

3 tablespoons olive oil
500g finely chopped leeks (white part only)
200g finely diced potatoes
1 bay leaf
2 teaspoons finely chopped preserved lemon peel
800ml White Stock (see page 18) or water
100ml leek braising liquid (see Braised Leeks, above)

Heat the olive oil in a saucepan and add the leeks, potatoes, bay leaf and lemon peel. Cover and cook gently for 5 minutes. Add the stock or water and the leek braising liquid, cover again and simmer for a further 10 minutes or until the potatoes are soft. Allow to cool slightly, then blend the soup in a jug blender, half a jug at a time: blend for about 3 minutes per batch or until the soup is very smooth. Strain through a fine sieve and refrigerate until ready to use.

{harissa hotty}

5g dried chipotle chilli
5g dried guajillo chilli
20g fresh jalapeño chilli, deseeded
1 red pepper, roasted, peeled and deseeded
8 garlic cloves
1 teaspoon coriander seeds, toasted
3 teaspoons cumin seeds, toasted
3 teaspoons caraway seeds, toasted
2 teaspoons sun dried tomato paste
4 tablespoons olive oil
3 tablespoons red wine vinegar
$1/4$ teaspoon cracked black pepper
$1/4$ teaspoon salt

Pour boiling water on to the dried chillies and leave to soak for 20 minutes, then drain and deseed. Put all the ingredients into a blender and blend until smooth. Taste and adjust seasoning. Beware, it is very hot!

This is more sauce than you will need here, but it will keep well in the refrigerator if covered in oil (so not exposed to air).

{to assemble}

75ml double cream or soya cream
1 tablespoon lime juice
3 tablespoons argan oil (or olive oil)
salt and freshly ground black pepper
chopped mint leaves

Warm the braised leeks in the oven at 160°C/Gas Mark 3 for about 10 minutes. Gently heat the soup in a pan and, once it is hot, stir in any remaining braising liquid from the leeks, and the double cream or soya cream. Heat through again. Ladle the soup into warm bowls and spoon some of the braised leeks on top. Mix 1 tablespoon of harissa hottie with the lime juice and argan oil, and top each bowl of soup with a little of this fiery mix – but beware, it is not for the faint hearted! Serve each bowl with a scattering of frits, sprinkled with salt, pepper and chopped fresh mint.

Number Seventy One

kohlrabi blankets filled with beansprout, micro leaf and
yuzu salad, served with cucumber, pickled ginger and
wasabi granita, and tamari sesame

{VEGAN} {WHEAT FREE}

Kohlrabi might look as if they have just arrived off the latest Harry Potter set but, after a minimum of trimming and tarting up, they reveal a refreshingly delicious and adaptable flesh. The success of this deceptively simple dish is largely due to the freshness of the ingredients. The flavours are clean, the textures snappy, and the temperature chilly, with surprising wasabi heat in the icy granita. This is an ideal starter to have before Miso Pretty as a main course.

And 'Number Seventy One'? Remember the days of ordering your takeaways by numbers? Those days are now back, and you can order this in the restaurant and avoid any embarrassment that the waiter might think you cannot pronounce the real name of the dish!

Kohlrabi is often thought of as a root vegetable (the name means 'German turnip'), but it is in fact a bulbous stem that grows just above the ground; once trimmed of its somewhat curious but beautiful exterior, it is delicious either raw or cooked, and is high in vitamin C and dietary fibre.

serves 6

{tamari sesame}

25g sesame seeds
1 tablespoon tamari (gluten free soy sauce)

Pour the sesame seeds on to a small baking tray and roast in the oven at 160°C/Gas Mark 3 for about 5 minutes until golden brown. Now add the tamari to the seeds, coating them well. Return the seeds to the oven for about another 5 minutes until they are dry and crispy.

{cucumber granita}

350g cucumber, peeled and deseeded
1 tablespoon best quality sushi ginger juice (pickled ginger)
2 teaspoons mirin (sweet rice wine)
$1/2$ teaspoon wasabi paste (Japanese horseradish)
a pinch of salt

Blend all the ingredients together in a food processor until smooth. Pour into a container, seal and freeze. Once completely frozen, grate the granita and spoon into frozen shot glasses. Place the glasses on a tray in the freezer until you are ready to serve them.

{kohlrabi pickle}

100ml cider vinegar
1 teaspoon mirin (sweet rice wine)
25g caster sugar
3 star anise
50g finely diced kohlrabi

Put the vinegar, mirin, sugar and star anise in a pan and bring to the boil, then cook until the sugar has dissolved. Meanwhile place the diced kohlrabi in a non-metallic bowl. Strain the vinegar mixture on to the diced kohlrabi, cover and leave to cool. Keep in an airtight container in the refrigerator.

{beansprout and yuzu salad}

150g beansprouts
5g shiso shoots
5g daikon shoots
50g coriander, leaves picked and stalks chopped

for the yuzu dressing
1 tablespoon yuzu juice (Japanese citrus fruit) – or use lime juice
1 tablespoon grapeseed oil

First make the yuzu dressing by mixing the yuzu juice with the grapeseed oil. Keep refrigerated until needed.

Next, prepare the salad. Mix the beansprouts, shiso and daikon shoots, and coriander in a bowl. Once you are ready to assemble the whole dish, toss the salad in the yuzu dressing.

{kohlrabi blankets}

2 large kohlrabis, peeled
juice of 1 lemon
pinch of salt

The kohlrabi blankets are best made shortly before you assemble the dish. Use a mandolin to slice the kohlrabis as thinly as possible. Alternatively, do it by hand but try to make the slices thin enough to see through. Put the lemon juice in a shallow dish, season with salt, then dip the slices into the juice. Now make the blankets by arranging kohlrabi slices on sheets of clingfilm, overlapping them quite a bit to make 10cm squares. Allow one square sheet of kohlrabi slices for each person. It is best to complete the blankets now but, if you are not quite ready, place the sheets, still on their clingfilm, on layers of silicone paper in the refrigerator.

{to assemble}

15g best quality sushi ginger (pickled ginger), shredded

Remove the kohlrabi blankets from the refrigerator. Place one sheet, still on its clingfilm, on your worktop. Spread a thick layer of freshly dressed salad on to the kohlrabi sheet, followed by a sprinkling of drained pickle. Now roll up the sheet by rolling it away from you, quite tightly, off the clingfilm. It will hold together so that you can stand each one up on a serving plate.

Remove the frozen granita glasses from the freezer and stand one next to each blanket, garnishing it with the shredded sushi ginger. Add a heap of the remaining salad to each plate. Sprinkle with the tamari sesame and finish off with a smudge of the kohlrabi pickle.

Wild Side

Wonderful wobbly rich custard cups, laced with the spring scent of woodland garlic, are beautifully balanced with succulent strands of salty samphire tangled with peppery watercress,and doused with sweet nutty, buttery yellow linseed dressing. And to dunk into the custards, crispy cheese twists, peppered with mustard seeds. This is great as a starter and it makes a lovely light lunch, too.

Watercress is now accepted as a real superfood, packed full of essential vitamins, minerals and antioxidants. This semi-aquatic plant is grown in a number of counties in the UK, although Alresford near Winchester is considered to be the watercress capital of Britain – even the steam railway line there is named after the local crop. Linseed is another food attracting attention: people are only just discovering its delicious taste, health benefits and versatility. We buy ours from Flax Farm, a local producer in Horsham. It is gluten free, low GI, low carbohydrate and suitable for diabetics, and we like to use it – and linseed oil – for its unique mild nutty taste. Be careful not to cook it at high temperatures as this destroys the more important properties.

Samphire is one of those plants beloved by foragers. It can be gathered in abundance from May to June. It has distinctive bright green stalks, similar to young asparagus, and may be eaten raw or lightly blanched and tossed in a delicious dressing. Many people like to soak it in cold water before cooking, as this removes some of the sea saltiness.

Wild garlic is a beautiful, fragrant herb that grows in woodlands and hedgerows, blooming with tiny white flowers in May and June. We like to collect it while taking a favourite walk in Ditchling, just 15 minutes out of Brighton. It's much milder than cultivated garlic and the stalks, leaves and flowers can all be eaten and enjoyed.

serves 6

{cheddar and mustard straws}

400g Puff Pastry (see page 20)
1 tablespoon coarse grain mustard
1 teaspoon milk
75g Cheddar cheese, grated
freshly ground black pepper

for the glaze
1 egg
1 tablespoon milk
1 tablespoon black mustard seeds

Place the pastry on a floured surface and roll out into a rectangle about 3mm thick, then cut in half. Blend the mustard with the milk and spread over one half of the pastry, then sprinkle the grated Cheddar and freshly ground pepper on top. Place the other pastry half over this, pressing down gently. With a sharp knife, cut into 5mm strips (there is enough pastry to make about 20–30 straws). Now twist each strip at both ends in different directions, to make corkscrew shapes. Lay them out on 2 lined baking sheets with spaces in between each straw. Beat the egg with the milk, and brush on to the straws to glaze. Sprinkle with the mustard seeds.

Bake at 180°C/Gas Mark 4 for 25–30 minutes until the straws are puffed up and golden brown. Transfer to a wire rack (they need to cool down a little to firm up). Serve warm or cold.

{wild garlic custards}

50g wild garlic
5g chives
50ml whole milk
2 eggs
2 egg yolks
200g full fat soft cream cheese
salt and freshly ground black pepper

Finely chop the garlic plants and chives and add them to the milk in a food processor. Blend together on a high speed until smooth and vibrantly green. Strain the mixture through a fine sieve, pressing firmly with the back of a spoon to extract all the essence possible, leaving just the fibres.

Mix the eggs and egg yolks with a fork and stir them into the cream cheese, then add the garlic and chive liquid mix. Beat together until smooth, then season to taste. Butter the insides of 6 ramekins (or ovenproof coffee cups) and divide the mixture between them.

Place the custards in a roasting tin and pour in boiling water to reach halfway up the sides of the ramekins. Place in the oven at 160°C/Gas Mark 3 and cook for 15–20 minutes. When the custards are ready the edges should be set, but the middles should still be a little wobbly. Remove the ramekins from the roasting tin and leave them to cool a little. The custards are best served straight after cooking, but warm rather than boiling hot.

{samphire and linseed salad}

25g samphire
50g watercress, trimmed
25g spring onions, chopped

for the dressing
$1/2$ teaspoon linseeds, toasted and crushed
1 tablespoon linseed oil
2 teaspoons lemon juice
salt and freshly ground black pepper

First prepare the dressing: combine the
linseeds, linseed oil and lemon juice,
season to taste, and mix thoroughly.
Next blanch the samphire: plunge it into a
large pan of boiling water for 1 minute,
drain and cool. Mix the samphire with the
watercress and spring onions. Wait until
you are ready to serve before you pour on
the dressing.

{to assemble}

This could not be easier. Place a warm
garlic custard on each plate, no need to
decant it. Toss the samphire salad in the
linseed dressing and serve a bundle of this
to one side of each custard. Stack the
straws in the middle of the table for
sharing. Make sure you get yours first!

Idli Pom

{VEGAN} {WHEAT FREE}

steamed idlis served with chilli tamarind tomatoes and
curry leaf mustard seed coconut chutney

A real 'roll up your sleeves' kind of dish: soft, spongy, spicy buns, perfectly porous, so well designed for mopping up purposes. They are just the ticket for soaking up plump, juicy, chilli tomatoes, sticky with sharp tamarind, and the contrasting cool coconut chutney.

Idlis are an ancient and traditional savoury cake, mainly popular in southern India, and most often eaten for breakfast. We've made ours vegan and added some baking powder to make the mix quicker and less temperamental to cook.

serves 6

{coconut chutney}

1 teaspoon mustard seeds
2 tablespoons sunflower oil
5 curry leaves, finely shredded
250g freshly grated coconut (or coconut powder)
about 500ml soya milk (or thin yogurt for non-vegans)
grated zest and juice of 2 limes
salt and freshly ground black pepper

In a small heavy based pan, heat the mustard seeds until they start to pop. Add the oil and, when it has heated up, drop in the shredded curry leaves so they sizzle and stiffen. Remove the pan from the heat. Add the coconut, soya milk or yogurt, lime zest and juice, and seasoning to taste, and mix well. You may need to add a little more soya milk or yogurt to achieve a creamy consistency. This chutney can be made a day in advance and kept in the refrigerator.

{pom toms}

2 tablespoons sunflower oil
2 teaspoons black onion seeds, toasted and ground
1 teaspoon cardamom seeds, toasted and ground
1 teaspoon coriander seeds, toasted and ground
2 teaspoons chopped chilli pepper
3 garlic cloves, chopped
200g onions, sliced
25g tamarind paste (see page 152)
200ml water

½ teaspoon grated lemon zest
¼ teaspoon salt
freshly ground black pepper
1kg big fat juicy tomatoes

Heat the oil in a heavy based pan and lightly fry the spices. Throw in the chillies, garlic and onions and cook them until they look opaque. Add the tamarind paste and water, lemon zest, salt and pepper, and simmer gently for 5 minutes. Cut the tomatoes in half widthways and place them cut side up in a baking dish. Pour the tamarind mix over them and bake at 180°C/Gas Mark 4 for 20 minutes. It is good to make this dish a day in advance to allow the flavours to permeate the tomatoes.

{steamed idlis}

200g fine rice flour
110g gram flour
50g potato flour
25g cornflour
½ teaspoon coriander seeds, toasted and ground
½ teaspoon cumin seeds, toasted and ground
½ teaspoon cardamom seeds, toasted and ground
¼ teaspoon ground turmeric
¾ teaspoon salt
1 teaspoon finely diced fresh ginger
2 garlic cloves, crushed
50ml soya yogurt
1 tablespoon lime juice
400ml warm water
2 teaspoons toasted sesame oil
1½ teaspoons gluten free baking powder
soya margarine or sunflower oil for greasing

To make idlis you will need an idli steaming stack and moulds, which can be purchased from specialist suppliers. This quantity of batter will make about 12 idlis.

Mix together the rice flour, gram flour, potato flour, cornflour, coriander, cumin, cardamom, turmeric and salt. Add the ginger, garlic, soya yogurt and lime juice to the warm water. Thoroughly incorporate the wet mix into the dry mix and leave overnight in a warm place to ferment. When the mix is looking active, add the sesame oil and baking powder.

To prepare the idli moulds, grease each one with soya margarine or sunflower oil. Heat 5cm of water in a large saucepan with a tight fitting lid. (You will need to keep checking the water level just in case it boils dry.)

Place 2–3 of tablespoons batter into each idli mould. Assemble the moulds in the tiered rack and place in the steaming pan. Cover and steam for 10–15 minutes. To check if the idlis are ready, insert a fine knife. If it comes out sticky, they need more cooking. If it comes out clean, they are ready. When they are cooked, they have a soft rounded surface.

Allow the idlis to cool a little before removing from the moulds. They may need a little prising out with a spoon.

Idlis can be made up to 2 days in advance and then reheated and assembled with the other components as below.

{to assemble}

chopped pickled or fresh chilli peppers
torn mint and coriander
lemon wedges

Idlis are best served straight away but, if they are made in advance, they can be wrapped in foil and reheated in the oven at 180°C/Gas Mark 4 for about 10 minutes. Alternatively, they are delicious deep fried, which leaves them crispy on the outside with fluffy middles.

Present the warm idlis in a big covered basket to keep them hot, or piled on to a plate. Heap the coconut chutney into a bowl to share. Reheat the tomatoes and and serve steaming hot on individual plates, generously scattered with the chillies, mint, and coriander, with lemon wedges on the side.

Cauliflower Pots

warm cauliflower and cumin creams served with cheddar, mustard and crème fraîche sauce, a salad of fried florets, dressed with turmeric and ginger oil, tarragon and dill, and roasted spiced almonds

{WHEAT FREE}

Forgive us our fun with a British classic. It's possible that people all over the country will now demand that their childhood favourite has a makeover, after discovering how delicious cauliflower cheese can really be (though with some swanky additions). It still remains a comforting combination of tastes, textures and colours, a bumper dish if ever there was one....

Another bonus is that all the elements can be prepared well in advance, making it an easy starter for a dinner party. Slight hints of cumin mingled with warm creamy cauliflower marry well with the turmeric and ginger drenched, tarragon and dill tossed, seared floret salad. A light crème fraîche mustardy Cheddar sauce helps to bring all the flavours together, and roasted spiced almonds add a final crunch.

serves 4–6

{cauliflower pots}

50g unsalted butter
600g cauliflower florets, finely chopped
1/2 teaspoon cumin seeds, toasted and
   ground
a little freshly grated nutmeg
1 bay leaf
salt and freshly ground black pepper
300ml White Stock (see page 18) or water
100ml dry vermouth or dry white wine
300ml double cream
4 eggs
30g Parmesan cheese, freshly grated
1 tablespoon chopped chives

Melt the butter in a saucepan and add the cauliflower, cumin, nutmeg, bay leaf and seasoning and cook until the cauliflower begins to soften. Add the stock or water and the vermouth or wine and simmer until the liquid has almost evaporated, then add the cream and reduce by half. Remove the bay leaf.

Turn the mixture on to a flat baking tray and allow it to cool a little. Once cooled, place in a food processor with the eggs, blend until smooth, then add the Parmesan cheese and chives and check the seasoning.

Divide the mixture between 6 buttered 100ml dariole moulds or ramekins, and place in a bain-marie. Cook the cauliflower creams at 160°C/Gas Mark 3 for 20–30 minutes until they feel firm to the touch with a slight wobble to them.

{cheddar and crème fraîche sauce}

250ml crème fraîche
125g mature Cheddar cheese, grated
1/2 teaspoon Dijon mustard
a pinch of ground mace
salt and ground white pepper

Heat the crème fraîche in a pan without letting it boil, then add the cheese and mustard, whisking continuously until the cheese has melted. Remove the pan from the heat and season to taste with mace, salt and pepper. Set the sauce to one side until you need it.

{turmeric and ginger oil}

15g fresh root ginger, chopped
1/2 teaspoon chopped fresh turmeric root
   or 1/4 teaspoon ground turmeric
100ml sunflower oil

Place all the ingredients in a blender and blitz on a high speed for 5 minutes or until the oil is orange and slightly emulsified. This is best done the night before, to get the most potent results from the spices. Strain the oil through a fine sieve or a piece of muslin and keep the amber liquid in a sealed container until needed.

{cauliflower, ginger and turmeric salad}

600g cauliflower, cut into small florets
2 tablespoons Turmeric and Ginger Oil
(see 20)
2 tablespoons chopped tarragon
2 tablespoons chopped dill

for the turmeric and ginger dressing
2 tablespoons Turmeric and Ginger Oil
(see above)
2 tablespoons lemon juice
salt and ground white pepper

First prepare the turmeric and ginger dressing. Mix all the ingredients together and store in an airtight container in the refrigerator until needed.

Heat a non-stick frying pan to very hot, coat the cauliflower in the turmeric and ginger oil and then toss into the hot pan and cook over a high heat until it becomes a nutty brown colour. Remove from the heat and, once cooled, drench with the dressing and add the chopped herbs. Set to one side until required.

{roasted salt spice almonds}

1 teaspoon yellow mustard seeds, toasted
1 teaspoon black mustard seeds, toasted
1 teaspoon black peppercorns, toasted
2 teaspoons sea salt
1 teaspoon smoked paprika
200g whole blanched almonds
1 teaspoon olive or almond oil

Pound the seeds and peppercorns in a pestle and mortar with the salt and paprika. Roast the almonds in the oven at 150°C/Gas Mark 2 for 15 minutes or until they turn a light golden colour. Toss the nuts in the oil then coat them with the ground spices and put them back in the oven for 5 minutes. Once cooled, store the almonds in an airtight container.

{to assemble}

If the cauliflower pots were made in advance, heat them up on a baking tray in the oven at 150°C/Gas Mark 2 for about 15 minutes. If not, let them sit for few minutes after cooking before turning them out of their moulds. Serve on plates with a heap of salad on one side, some warmed up sauce on the other, and a few of the salted spiced almonds.

It's a Quacker

creamy celeriac soup, wilted sea spinach, soft duck eggs and oaty soda bread

We are big fans of the gruff looking celeriac. Its gnarled rugged exterior, once cut away, leaves you with a surprisingly light and versatile, delicately fragrant flesh. Team it with sage, mace and cream, for a smooth, aromatic mouthful, which enhances the lush, robust, slightly sea salty spinach leaves, and the warm, yellow duck yolks. What better to soak up the lovely rich soup than the slightly sweet sour tang of the easy to make wholemeal, treacly, oaty loaf.

For the foragers and 'food for free' people among you, get out to your local shingle beaches and cliffs, and start looking for Beta vulgaris maritima, otherwise known as sea spinach. A distant relative of cultivated beetroot and spinach, it is (unsurprisingly) packed full of iron, and incredibly easy to cook. With lovely glossy dark green leaves and often reddish stems, the small leaves can be thrown into salads and the larger ones steamed, boiled or sautéed.

And just a word about duck eggs: as they have a lower water content than hens' eggs, they are much more gelatinous so tend to be rubbery if overcooked. Stick religiously to the tried and tested recipe and you'll get gloriously sunny runny yolks every time!

serves 4–6

{soda bread}

125g plain flour
125g wholemeal flour
40g oats
40g wheatgerm
1 teaspoon bicarbonate of soda
1/2 teaspoon cream of tartar
1/2 teaspoon salt
1 tablespoon runny honey
1 tablespoon black treacle
250ml buttermilk
oats to sprinkle

Preheat the oven to 190°C/Gas Mark 5 and line a baking tray with greaseproof paper. Mix all the dry ingredients together in a bowl. Heat the honey, black treacle and buttermilk together in a pan, just until the honey and treacle melt, then add this to the bowl. Mix everything together well; the dough will feel a little wet, so keep your hands floured and mould the dough into a round. Place it on the baking tray, cut a deep cross into the top and sprinkle with some oats. Bake for about 50 minutes or until the base sounds hollow when tapped.

{celeriac soup}

2 tablespoons olive oil
50g salted butter
500g celeriac, finely diced
150g onions, finely diced
150g potato, finely diced
2 bay leaves
1/2 teaspoon ground mace
1 tablespoon finely chopped sage
175ml White Stock (see page 18)
100ml dry white wine
sea salt and ground white pepper
250ml double cream

Heat the oil and butter together in a pan and add all the diced vegetables, and the bay leaves, mace and sage. Cover with a lid and cook gently for 10 minutes. Now add the stock and wine, bring to the boil and cook for a further 15 minutes.

Remove from the heat and allow to cool slightly. Half fill a jug blender with the celeriac mix and blend for 3 minutes or until very smooth. Strain through a fine sieve and continue with the remaining soup until it is all blended and strained in this way. Unless serving the soup immediately, allow to cool completely, then refrigerate. Only mix in the cream before reheating the soup to serve.

{wilted sea spinach}

3 tablespoons olive oil
350g sea spinach (use regular spinach or spring greens if sea spinach is unavailable)
sea salt and freshly ground black pepper

This is best cooked just before serving. Heat the oil in a pan and add the sea spinach. Cook until tender (this will take only 1–2 minutes). Strain off any excess liquid, season to taste, and serve.

{duck eggs}

4 or 6 free range duck eggs

Place them in a pan of cold water, bring to the boil and cook for 5–6 minutes. Take off the heat, remove the shells and serve immediately.

{to assemble}

salted butter to spread

Once you have mixed the cream into the soup, bring the soup to a simmer and ladle into warm bowls. Divide the sea spinach between each bowl, then cut the just cooked eggs in half over each bowl (so you don't lose any of the delicious runny yolk) to sit on top of the spinach. Serve with chunks of warmed soda bread and salty butter.

Golden Globe

whole braised globe artichokes, served with tomato bouillabaisse, haricot brandade and fennel seed bread

This is a terrific dish. Bold as brass, impressive looking, big on the flavour stakes and vegan, too! Gorgeous globes, sitting perfectly proud and perky, surrounded by fresh, rich, ripe tomato and saffron soup, laced with brandy and pastis: very satisfying! They're a heavenly match when stuffed with a well oiled haricot and garlic brandade, and served with hearty slices of fennel seed bread – perfect for soaking up the juices.

The globe artichoke is the antithesis of fast food. It's quite a job to prepare, but your patience will be amply rewarded when you reach the subtly flavoured leaves and mouthwatering heart. June to November is the best time to buy artichokes – look for ones with tightly packed crisp green or purple leaves, and a slight bloom. They should feel heavy and their leaves should squeak when the bud is squeezed gently. Once you've mastered the art of preparing them, they'll become a delicious summer constant. Now all we need is a bit of Mediterranean sunshine, some straw hats and a few finger bowls!

serves 4–6

{tomato bouillabaisse}

100ml olive oil
150g onions, sliced
3 garlic cloves, finely chopped
1/2 teaspoon coriander seeds
2 bay leaves
1 teaspoon saffron strands
1kg tomatoes, roughly chopped
150ml dry white wine
35g parsley, chopped
salt and freshly ground black pepper

Heat the olive oil in a saucepan and add the onions, garlic, coriander seeds, bay leaves and saffron. Cook until the onions are just softened. Add the tomatoes, wine, parsley and seasoning to taste, then cook for a further 15 minutes. You now need to half fill a jug blender with the soup mix and blend it for 3 minutes, or until very smooth. Continue until you have blended it all, then strain through a fine sieve into a clean pan.

{fennel seed bread}

300g rye flour
300g strong flour
1/2 teaspoon salt
1 teaspoon caster sugar
12g dried yeast
1 tablespoon fennel seeds
310ml warm water
3 tablespoons olive oil

Sift together the flours, salt and sugar and stir in the yeast and seeds. Add the water and oil to the flour mix and start working the dough together with a fork or spoon then, using your hands, work the mix into a firm but slightly sticky dough. If the dough seems tough just add a splash of water. Knead the dough for 5–6 minutes, then place in a bowl, cover with clingfilm and leave to prove until doubled in size.

Now turn out the dough on to a lightly floured surface and knock back. Knead again for 2–3 minutes, then form the required loaf shape. Place the dough in a lightly oiled 1kg loaf tin, cover with clingfilm and leave to prove again until it has nearly reached the top of the tin.

Bake at 180°C/Gas Mark 4 for 30–40 minutes until the top of the loaf is golden brown. To check if the loaf is cooked through, remove it from the tin and tap the bottom. A hollow sounds means the loaf is ready. Allow the loaf to cool down on a cooling rack.

{braised globe artichokes}

4–6 small globe artichokes
lemon juice or vinegar
2 bay leaves
1/4 teaspoon fennel seeds
1 star anise
20g parsley sprigs
20g basil sprigs
100g fennel, chopped
1 medium onion, chopped
6 garlic cloves
1 large tomato, chopped
125ml olive oil
125ml dry white wine
125ml White Stock (see page 18) or water

Wash the artichokes in cold running water and discard any small or discoloured base leaves. Cut off the stems close to the base and slice off the top quarter of the leaves, then plunge the artichokes into acidulated water to maintain their colour (add 2 tablespoons of lemon juice or vinegar per 200ml water).

(Continued on page 46)

Golden Globe

(Continued from page 44)

Peel away the fibrous outer layer to reach the tender part of the stem, which is edible and delicious. It is important you also remove the fuzzy choke from the centre – artichokes don't have that name for nothing! Spread the centre leaves until you reach the middle cone, then pull away the purple or thorny centre leaves. With a stainless steel spoon, scrape out the remaining purple tipped leaves and fibrous fuzz. Rinse the artichokes and keep in acidulated water until you are ready to cook them.

Put the prepared artichokes and all the other ingredients into a large heavy based pan, cover and bring to the boil. Simmer for 30 minutes, remove from the heat and leave to cool in the liquor. Refrigerate until ready to use.

{haricot brandade}

50ml olive oil
50g onion, finely sliced
$1/2$ teaspoon chopped sage
1 bay leaf
5 garlic cloves, finely chopped
250g cooked haricot beans
50ml dry white wine
salt and freshly ground black pepper

Gently heat the olive oil and add the onions, sage, bay leaf and garlic. Cover and cook gently for 5 minutes. Add the haricot beans and the wine and cook, uncovered, until most of the wine has evaporated. Taste and season. Now blend the mixture in a food processor until smooth, and refrigerate until needed.

{to assemble}

2 tablespoons brandy
3 tablespoons pastis

Bring the bouillabaisse up to a simmer, add the brandy and pastis and stir well. Gently heat the artichokes in their liquor, drain (reserving the liquor) and put into warmed bowls. (The liquor is much too good to waste and can form the basis of another lovely soup.) Now heat the brandade in a small pan and spoon it into the centre of the artichokes. Pour the hot bouillabaisse into the bowls around the artichokes, and place a chunk of fennel bread beside each bowl, ready for mopping up the delicious juices. Serve with finger bowls and giant serviettes: messy, but well worth it!

Arepas Mojo

corn cakes rolled in spice dust, stacked and served with tamarillo salsa, oregano mojo and avocado lime salsa

{VEGAN} {WHEAT FREE}

This dish makes excellent relaxed party food or, as our picture shows, precise plating can elevate it to à la carte heights! You can choose which way to go: posh presentation, or colourfully loaded party platters and brimming bowls; nice and neat, or rough and ready. Either way, the flavours always deliver and, as this dish is best prepared well in advance, it's a breeze to serve at the last minute.

Arepas are a staple food of Venezuela and Colombia: corn cakes that can be grilled or fried, and either topped with pretty much anything, or cut open and filled like baps. They are traditionally made from masarepa, a precooked cornmeal, but, to make things easier, we have substituted quick cook polenta and added sweetcorn kernels. We've also strayed from the true arepa path by omitting cheese and making a vegan version, but you can easily add cheese if you want to be authentic.

Tamarillo is a wonderfully juicy fruit, native to central and south America but now grown commercially in New Zealand. The flavour can range from bland to rather sweet with a tart edge, but its vitamin C levels are unarguable. We have mixed it with fresh tomatoes and gastrique, a classic French sauce made from a reduction of vinegar, sugar and fruit.

serves 4–6

{oregano mojo}

$1/2$ teaspoon cumin seeds, toasted
25g oregano leaves
25g flat leaf parsley leaves
$1/2$ green chilli pepper, deseeded
10ml lime juice
$1/4$ teaspoon salt
$1/4$ teaspoon freshly ground black pepper
200ml grapeseed oil

Place all the ingredients in a blender and blitz for 1–2 minutes until the mixture thickens and has the consistency of pesto. Refrigerate in an airtight container until needed.

{arepa corn cakes}

1kg canned sweetcorn
330ml coconut water (fresh or canned)
330ml White Stock (see page 18) or water
100g finely diced onion
200g quick cook polenta
zest of 2 limes
65ml lime juice
3 tablespoons chopped coriander
$1 1/2$ teaspoons salt
$3/4$ teaspoon freshly ground black pepper
150g mature Cheddar cheese, grated
   (optional, for non-vegans)
200ml sunflower oil

for the arepa spice dust
25g cumin seeds, toasted
25g coriander seeds, toasted
50g sesame seeds, toasted
2g dried caribe chilli

First make the arepa spice dust. Place all the ingredients in a grinder or pestle and mortar, and grind them until powdery. Keep in an airtight container until required.

Next, start preparing the corn cakes. Put the sweetcorn in a food processor or blender and pulse for 5–10 seconds or until the corn is broken down but not puréed. In a heavy based pan bring to the boil the coconut water, stock or water, and onion. When the liquid is boiling, reduce the heat to low and steadily pour in the polenta, gently beating as you do so, to produce a smooth consistency. Stir for 2 minutes and then add the lime zest and juice, chopped coriander, salt and pepper. Cook for another 8 minutes, stirring continuously, then remove from the heat. (At this point, non-vegans may wish to stir in grated cheese.)

Now spread the mixture evenly into a lined and lightly oiled 23 x 15cm baking tray. Smooth over with a flat implement, and cover with another sheet of greaseproof paper. Leave in the refrigerator for 1 hour to firm up.

Remove the chilled corn slab from the tray, lay it on a work surface and slice into 18 equal portions (6 long strips each cut into 3). Put the spice dust into a large shallow tray and roll each corn cake gently in it, patting each side firmly to ensure even coating. Refrigerate until you are ready to start frying.

Just before you are ready to eat, heat the oil in a deep fryer or deep pan to 180°C and fry the corn cakes in small batches for about 3 minutes until they are crisp and golden. Drain on paper towels.

(Continued on page 49)

Arepas Mojo

(Continued from page 47)

{tamarillo salsa}

300g tomatoes, peeled, deseeded and
 chopped
150g tamarillos, peeled, deseeded and
 chopped
salt and freshly ground black pepper

for the gastrique
50g caster sugar
100ml red wine vinegar
1 teaspoon finely chopped dried caribe
 chilli

First prepare the gastrique. Place all the
ingredients in a heavy based pan and
bring to the boil. Reduce the heat and
simmer until the mixture has reduced by
half, then remove from the heat and allow
to cool.

Now put the prepared tomatoes and
tamarillos in a bowl and add about
2 tablespoons gastrique, to taste. It has
a very piquant flavour so go easy at first,
then add salt and pepper. Keep the salsa
in the refrigerator until you need it.

{avocado lime salsa}

2 tablespoons lime juice
1 large ripe avocado, peeled, stoned and
 chopped
50g diced tomato
50g diced red pepper
50g chopped coriander leaves
4 garlic cloves, crushed
1 tablespoon finely chopped red chilli
 pepper
1/2 teaspoon cumin seeds, toasted
salt and freshly ground black pepper

Pour the lime juice on to the avocado,
then stir in all the other ingredients and
season well. Store in an airtight container
in the refrigerator.

{to assemble}

lime wedges
chopped coriander leaves
sliced spring onions

Make a stack of the hot corn cakes in the
centre of the plates. Spoon a good heap of
the tamarillo salsa on one side of them
and a heap of the avocado lime salsa on
the other, and a smudge of the mojo in
between. Scatter the plate with the
coriander and spring onions.

You Say Tomato

{VEGAN}

warm tomato consommé with thyme jelly and basil fritters
– or chilled tomato consommé with thyme ice

Two ways tomatoes... The success of this dish is largely dependent on the time of year and on the variety and condition of the tomatoes you use. They have to be juicy, ripe and full of flavour. Don't be conned into that 'very expensive because they're on a vine' malarkey. Prod and sniff your produce if you can. My lovely greengrocer up the road positively encourages it, but he is a man who knows his onions, and tries his best to source more unusual products for customers who bring him requests.

Don't be fooled by this lightly blushing liquid: it may look pale and meek but, if you get it right, it will knock your socks off. I have had great success using the September ripening Brandywine tomato (an heirloom variety which takes a bit longer to mature). It's tricky to decide between the two ways of serving this, but the hot version with the jelly cubes and crispy fragrant fritters is the obvious choice for a winter starter, whereas the chilled option with the thyme ice cubes works well as an aperitif on a scorchingly hot day. Either way, it's a little rosy beauty, so enjoy.

serves 6

{tomato consommé}

2kg ripe tomatoes
2 teaspoons sea salt
2 teaspoons icing sugar
a small pinch of finely ground black
  pepper

Roughly chop the tomatoes and sprinkle them with the sea salt, icing sugar and pepper. Leave this to macerate for 1 hour. Place the tomato pulp mix in a blender and purée until smooth. Line a colander with muslin and suspend it over a large bowl with enough room for the liquid to drip through. (You need to balance the colander on a couple of big objects – I use my bread bin and mixer!) As the clear liquid drips into the bowl, tighten the muslin parcel and elevate it further, without forcing the liquid out (as this would add sediment to the consommé and make it cloudy).

Leave to drip overnight and, when it has drained right through, carefully pour the clear consommé into a clean container, leaving any sediment behind in the muslin. Place in the refrigerator until needed.

{tomato and thyme jelly}
(for hot version only)

250ml Tomato Consommé (see above)
1/2 teaspoon finely chopped thyme
1/2 teaspoon finely chopped parsley
1 tablespoon agar agar

Place the cold consommé in a pan and add the chopped herbs. Sprinkle the agar agar over the consommé, but do not stir at this point. Place the pan over a medium heat and simmer for 4 minutes, stirring occasionally. Pour the warm jelly mix into ice cube moulds, cool and refrigerate. You should have about 12 cubes. (You could use a small, clingfilm lined baking tray if you prefer, and cut the jelly into cubes when set.) Keep refrigerated until needed.

{tomato and thyme ice}
(for cold version only)

250ml Tomato Consommé (see above)
1/2 teaspoon finely chopped thyme
1/2 teaspoon finely chopped parsley

Mix the consommé with the chopped herbs, pour into ice cube moulds and place in the freezer. You should have about 12 cubes. Leave in the freezer until needed.

{basil fritters}
(for hot version only)

200ml sunflower oil
20g basil sprigs

for the batter
120g plain flour
2 teaspoons nori seasoning (dried seaweed)
  – or use 1 nori sheet, toasted and crumbled
1/4 teaspoon baking powder
salt and freshly ground black pepper
1 tablespoon white wine vinegar
about 165ml ice cold water

First prepare the batter. Mix together the flour, nori seasoning, baking powder and salt and pepper. Then whisk in the vinegar and water until you have a smooth batter. It should have the consistency of double cream, so add the water slowly as you might not need all of it (the amount required may vary according to the brand of flour used). Keep the batter in the refrigerator: it needs to be very cold when you come to use it.

Now all you have to do is to fry the delicate fritters. (Leave this until the last moment.) Heat the sunflower oil to 180°C, in either a deep pan or a wok. Dip a few basil sprigs at a time into the batter and lay them gently in the hot oil, turning them once and making sure they brown evenly (frying will take no longer than 1 minute). Drain on paper towels.

{to assemble}

6 lemon wedges (optional)

The consommé can be served either hot or cold. If serving hot, gently heat it in a pan. Place a couple of cubes of tomato and thyme jelly at the bottom of each soup bowl, and pour the hot consommé over the top. Serve immediately with the basil fritters and a wedge of lemon. If serving cold, omit the basil fritters and lemon: place a couple of frozen tomato and thyme cubes at the bottom of each large chilled glass, then top up with chilled consommé.

Pea Shooter

baked goat's cheeses and roast whole violet garlic, with minted pea soup topped with lemon thyme cream, served with onion seed parchment shards

I love this dish: it's beautiful and packed with textures and flavours. Try to find the fattest crowns of garlic that you can. When you've baked them, it's pure bliss to squeeze out the perfectly soft, sticky filling from the papery coats – messy, but most definitely worth it. They are perfect with glorious gulps of velvety minted pea soup (hidden under a luscious layer of chilled fragrant cream) and deliciously crispy, salty, seeded parchment to scoop up the yielding thymey goat's cheese.

There was a time when you could only get this wonderful violet garlic by travelling to the Mediterranean, but thankfully old Blighty has now accepted glorious garlic in its many forms into the national store cupboard, so it shouldn't be too hard to find (and certainly can be bought on the internet). Considered by the French to be the ultimate 'ail de cuisine', it now has 'appellation contrôlée' status and, once you've tried it, you can't help but recognize its superior creamy smooth flavour. It stores well without going soft and is packed full of antioxidants, so never mind what it does to your breath!

serves 4–6

{baked goat's cheeses}

4–6 individual goat's cheeses
4 tablespoons olive oil
2 teaspoons chopped thyme
grated zest of 1 lemon

Ideally, use Crottin de Chavignol, the famous goat's cheese of the Loire valley. Marinate the cheeses overnight in the olive oil, thyme and lemon zest. Just before you are ready to eat, place the cheeses on a baking tray lined with greaseproof paper and bake at 160°C/Gas Mark 3 for 5–7 minutes until the outsides are just starting to melt.

{black onion seed crackers}

150g strong flour
a pinch of salt
1 teaspoon black onion seeds
1 teaspoon celery seeds
100ml water
oil for deep frying (optional)

Place all the dry ingredients in a bowl (or a food mixer with a paddle attachment). Add the water, but do not overwork the mix or it will become tough. Wrap the dough in clingfilm and refrigerate for 1–2 hours.

Cut the dough in half and roll out on a floured surface. Roll as thin as possible (paper thin) to achieve the best cracker effect. Quarter turn the dough each time you roll it so it does not stick, and sprinkle flour every time. You can now cook the dough in one of two ways.

To bake: place the 2 pieces of thinly rolled dough on to dry baking sheets and bake at 180°C/Gas Mark 4 for 15 minutes. Once cooled, break into shards and store in an airtight container.

To fry: cut the thinly rolled dough into any shapes you like. Deep fry at 180°C, moving them about during cooking, until they are golden brown. Drain, cool and store in an airtight container.

{lemon thyme cream}

200ml low fat crème fraîche
2 tablespoons finely chopped lemon thyme
1 teaspoon lemon juice
salt and freshly ground black pepper

Gently heat the crème fraîche and lemon thyme together. Take the pan off the heat as soon as the mixture starts to bubble and leave it to cool. Strain through a fine sieve, add the lemon juice and seasoning, and chill in the refrigerator.

{pea shooter soup}

75g dried split green peas
100ml olive oil
200g onions, finely diced
2 tablespoons chopped mint
2 tablespoons chopped parsley
1 bay leaf
150ml dry white wine
500ml White Stock (see page 18) or water
salt and freshly ground black pepper

for the pea purée
500g fresh peas (or frozen peas, defrosted)
50g mint, chopped
50g parsley, chopped
100ml olive oil
100ml White Stock (as above)

First make the pea purée. If using fresh peas, blanch in boiling salted water for 2 minutes. Place all the ingredients in a

(Continued on page 54)

Pea Shooter

(Continued from page 52)

blender and blitz them until you have a smooth purée. Refrigerate until needed.

To make the soup mix, rinse the dried peas in cold water, cover with fresh cold water, bring to the boil, then skim. Cover and simmer for 30 minutes, then drain. Now gently heat the oil in a pan and add the onions, peas, mint, parsley and bay leaf. Cover and cook slowly for 5 minutes, then add the wine and stock or water. Simmer, covered, for a further 15 minutes.

Now stir the pea purée into this soup mix. Start blending the soup, half a jug at a time, for about 3 minutes or until smooth. Then strain through a fine sieve into a clean pan. When the soup is all blended and strained, bring to a simmer and season carefully.

{baked violet garlic}

2 fresh bay leaves
4–6 violet garlic crowns
2 tablespoons olive oil
salt

You can bake any variety of garlic you like, but our favourite (when it's in season) is violet garlic – it has papery white skin, deep purple cloves and a delicate flavour. Baking the garlic mellows the taste and brings out its creamy sweetness.

Rinse the bay leaves in water and lay them on a baking sheet while still wet (as this imparts a subtle flavour to the garlic). Cut the tops off the garlic crowns and coat them in the oil, then place them on the bay leaves, sprinkle with salt and bake at 180°C/Gas Mark 4 for 30 minutes, or until the garlic has softened.

{to assemble}

Heat the pea and parsley soup and pour it into heatproof glasses. Top this with a spoon of the chilled lemon thyme cream. Place the glasses of soup on plates and serve with a pile of craggy black onion seed crackers, some hot baked garlic and a melting goat's cheese.

Carrot or Stick

carrot, spring onion and sancerre terrine with goat's cheese yogurt, celery melba, chervil and macadamia mayonnaise

This is such a lovely light dish, perfect for sharing. The creamy bright white blend of goat's cheese and yogurt has a slightly sharp edge to it, an ideal contrast to the aromatic, sweet mouthfuls of soft, intensely flavoured carrot terrine. You can stop there if you will but, to tie the tastes together, celery seeds in snappy slices of Melba toast and little wisps of refreshing chervil are cracking companions for cheese and carrots. For a vegan dish, omit the goat's cheese and yogurt sauce.

This is surely giving away my age but any fine restaurant dining in my 1970s childhood (and I'm talking Britain here) involved deliciously thin, crispy and highly breakable Melba toast, to be spread with butter curls or pâtés, or whatever the Seventies concocted for our delight. The reason we loved it is because it was a fantastic vehicle for something richer or fuller – but here it carries a subtle flavour of its own, to marry with the star of the show, the brightly coloured, spring fresh terrine.

Macadamia nuts have a delicious, creamy flavour, so make a perfect vegan alternative to dairy mayonnaise. Although they are not cheap, their taste and crunch justify their cost.

serves 4–6

{macadamia mayonnaise}

150ml rice milk, soya milk or White Stock (see page 18)
20g chives, chopped
2 tablespoons lemon juice
225g macadamia nuts
salt and ground white pepper

Place all the ingredients, apart from the macadamia nuts, salt and pepper, in a blender and blend until smooth. Add the macadamia nuts, in 2 or 3 batches, and carry on blending until you have a thin mayonnaise. Season to taste and keep in the refrigerator until needed. If the mixture is too thick, just add a little water to thin to the required consistency.

{carrot and spring onion terrine}

1 tablespoon olive oil
$1/2$ teaspoon cumin seeds
$1/2$ teaspoon coriander seeds
2 bay leaves
1 vanilla pod, split and scraped, seeds reserved
200g large spring onion bulbs or shallots
500g long thin baby carrots
salt and ground white pepper
1 litre White Stock (see page 18) or water
200ml carrot juice
600ml Sancerre or similar Sauvignon based white wine
2 tablespoons agar agar

Heat the olive oil in a heavy based pan to a medium heat, then add the cumin and coriander seeds, the bay leaves and the vanilla pod and seeds, and warm them for 1 minute. Add the spring onion bulbs (or shallots) and baby carrots, add seasoning, and coat them in the spice and herb infused oil. Add the stock, and cook over a medium heat until the vegetables are tender. Now add the carrot juice and wine and cook for about 45 minutes until the liquid has reduced enough just to cover the vegetables.

Let the vegetables cool in their cooking liquor and then drain them, reserving the liquor. Place the cold liquor in a pan and sprinkle with agar agar. Bring to a simmer and cook for 3 minutes, stirring occasionally.

Line a 1 litre terrine mould with clingfilm, slice the onions in half, and press them into the bottom of the mould to create a pretty base. Lay the carrots in layers on top of the onions until the mould is three quarters full, then pour in the agar agar liquor. Cover the top with clingfilm and refrigerate until set.

{celery seed bread}

300g rye flour
300g strong flour
$1/2$ teaspoon salt
1 teaspoon caster sugar
12g dried yeast
1 tablespoon celery seeds
310ml warm water
3 tablespoons olive oil

Sift together the flours, salt and sugar and stir in the yeast and seeds. Add the water and oil to the flour mix and start working the dough together with a fork or spoon. Then, using your hands, work the mix into a firm but slightly sticky dough. If the dough seems tough just add a splash of water. Knead for 5–6 minutes, then place in a bowl, cover with clingfilm and leave to prove until doubled in size.

(Continued on page 57)

Carrot or Stick

(Continued from page 55)

Now turn out the dough on to a lightly floured surface and knock back. Knead again for 2–3 minutes, then form the required loaf shape. Place the dough in a lightly oiled 1kg loaf tin, cover with clingfilm and leave to prove again until it has nearly reached the top of the tin. Bake at 180°C/Gas Mark 4 for 30–40 minutes until the top of the loaf is golden brown. To check if the loaf is cooked through, remove it from the tin and tap the bottom. A hollow sounds means the loaf is ready. Allow the loaf to cool down on a cooling rack.

{celery melba toast}

Celery Seed Bread (see page 55)

Slice the bread evenly and toast it. While still warm, cut off the crusts and, using a bread knife, cut the slices in half horizontally so you have 2 thin slices of bread, both toasted on one side only. Now cut each of these slices into halves or quarters (depending on their size). Put the slices on a baking sheet, untoasted side up, and bake at 150°C/Gas Mark 2 for about 30 minutes, until golden on both sides.

If time is limited, you can make Melba toast using a plain uncut white loaf rather than the celery bread.

{to assemble}

150g soft goat's cheese (optional)
50ml goat's milk yogurt (optional)
2 tablespoons chopped chervil

If you are serving the goat's cheese and yogurt sauce, cream together the cheese and yogurt and chill in the refrigerator. Turn out the terrine and slice it with a very sharp, serrated knife and divide between the serving plates. Depending upon whether you want the dish to be vegan or not, spoon a smudge of either the vegan macadamia mayonnaise on to the plate, or the creamy goat's cheese sauce. Or maybe a bit of both if you can't decide. Scatter each plate liberally with chervil, and place the celery Melba toast to the side.

Soba Salad

chilled soba noodles, piled with crisp raw vegetable spaghetti, beansprouts and mizuna leaves in a miso and mirin plum dressing, served with skewered smoked {VEGAN} {WHEAT FREE} tofu, pickled ginger, pomegranate seeds and wasabi cashews

This dish has been on the menu in the restaurant almost since day one, so is virtually a tradition. It's a constant customer favourite, withstanding many a change in food trends and fulfilling the gluten free and vegan option with ease. Delicious lightly charred cubes of tamari coated smoked tofu, slippery with warm toasted sesame oil, secure crispy strings of vegetables, knitted together with soft soba noodles, all bathed in piquant miso, mirin, plum and ginger dressing. A scattering of wasabi spiced cashews and pomegranate seeds adds texture and sweetness to the savoury smoothness of the noodle tangle.

It might take a few goes to perfect the twist of the wrist to assemble the salad stacks with precision, but it's worth being patient because they look gorgeous and striking. And please don't let the more unfamiliar ingredients put you off trying this dish: it's surprisingly easy to put together. In Japanese cooking there are soba noodles, which are thin and made from buckwheat flour, and udon noodles, which are thick and made from wheat. Soba noodles are considered the noodle of choice in Tokyo and are ubiquitous – on street corners as fast food, in serious restaurants, and of course at home. Traditionally, good manners dictated much slurping and noisy consumption of the noodles, however these days it's not imperative!

serves 4–6

{wasabi cashews}

300g whole unsalted cashew nuts
2 tablespoons wasabi powder (Japanese horseradish)
20g caster sugar
30ml water
salt and freshly ground black pepper

Bake the cashews on a roasting tray at 160°C/Gas Mark 3 for 15–20 minutes until they are golden brown. Make up 1½ tablespoons of the wasabi powder into a paste, according to the packet instructions. Bring the sugar and the water to the boil in a small pan, remove from the heat and add the wasabi paste, mixing it in thoroughly. Add the cashews to this

wasabi syrup and coat them well, turning them over with a spoon. Then sprinkle in the remaining ½ tablespoon wasabi powder, add seasoning to taste, and stir again. Return the coated cashews to the roasting tray and bake at 110°C/Gas Mark ¼ for about 45 minutes, until they are dry and crunchy. Allow the nuts to cool down, then store in an airtight container.

{miso and mirin dressing}

50g white miso (soy paste)
50ml mirin (sweet rice wine)
25ml toasted sesame oil
2 teaspoons umeboshi purée (pickled plum)
125g best quality sushi ginger (pickled ginger)
1 tablespoon rice wine vinegar
2 tablespoons yuzu juice (Japanese citrus fruit) – or use lime juice
75ml grapeseed oil
about 20ml water

Put all the ingredients together in a blender and blitz on high until the mixture has a smooth coating consistency. (You need to add just enough water to thin the mixture.)

{soba salad}

250g soba noodles
1 tablespoon toasted sesame oil
35g carrot, peeled
35g daikon (Japanese white radish or mooli), peeled
35g courgette
35g mangetout
100g pomegranate seeds
35g mizuna (Japanese greens)
35g beansprouts

Bring a large pan of water to the boil and submerge the noodles. Bring straight back to the boil, then reduce to a medium heat and cook for 5–6 minutes. Drain the noodles in a colander, then refresh under cold running water. When they are cold, drain thoroughly then toss them in a bowl with the sesame oil, making sure each strand is well coated, otherwise they will stick together. Now chill.

Slice the carrot, daikon and courgette through a Japanese mandolin (also known as a vegetable spaghetti machine), or hand slice them as finely as possible. Thinly slice the mangetout by hand. Set aside half the pomegranate seeds and a few of the mizuna leaves for garnishing, and gently mix all the other ingredients with the cold noodles.

The salad will be dressed just before you are ready to serve it.

{smoked tofu}

250g smoked tofu
1 tablespoon toasted sesame oil
1 tablespoon tamari (gluten free soy sauce)

Cut the tofu into 16 cubes and fry in the oil for 2 minutes until the cubes are brown on all sides. Add the tamari, coating all of the tofu, and continue to fry for 2 minutes until the tofu is glazed. Remove the cubes from the pan and keep hot.

{to assemble}

20g best quality sushi ginger (pickled ginger), finely shredded

Gently mix the bowl of salad and noodles with three quarters of the miso and mirin dressing. Twist up little piles of the dressed mix, and heap them on to big serving plates. Splash each plate with the remaining dressing. Thread the smoked tofu cubes on to wooden skewers with the shredded sushi ginger and reserved mizuna leaves. Top each noodle pile with a smoked tofu skewer and scatter the reserved pomegranate seeds, the wasabi cashews and any remaining sesame oil artistically around the plate.

Tikka Kachumber

{WHEAT FREE}

halloumi kebabs marinated in tandoori yogurt spice,
served with kachumber salad and cumin lassi

Even lovelier to eat than it is to say!
A wonderfully spicy kebab of yielding
halloumi, not quite at melting point, and
sweet lemony onions, wonderfully offset
by the revitalizing cooler and the chilli
kicking, yet subtly piquant leafy salad.

Halloumi is a firm white cheese,
originating in Cyprus but widely used in
Greece and the Middle East. Traditionally
made from goat's and sheep's milk, it
holds its shape well during cooking.
The cumin cooler is really a simple lassi,
a popular Indian drink that is remarkably
refreshing in the heat. Lassis are usually
salty when served with a meal, or sweet if
served afterwards. The plain yogurt is a
perfect foil for spicy food, even here with
its own subtle cumin flavour.

serves 4–6

{yogurt cumin cooler}

2 teaspoons cumin seeds, lightly toasted
175ml yogurt
1/4 teaspoon salt
cold water to taste (optional)

Crush the cumin seeds in a pestle and
mortar, put them in a bowl with the yogurt
and stir well. Leave to marinate for 2 hours,
then strain. Stir in the salt and refrigerate
until needed. To thin to a smoothie like
consistency, you can add a little water.

{halloumi kebabs}

750g halloumi cheese (3 packs of 250g)
150g red onions
5 tablespoons lemon juice
1/4 teaspoon salt
1/4 teaspoon caster sugar
6 cherry tomatoes
1 tablespoon sunflower oil

for the halloumi marinade
2 tablespoons sunflower oil
3 teaspoons ground coriander
3 teaspoons ground cumin
3 teaspoons paprika
2 teaspoons garam masala
1 teaspoon ground ginger
1 teaspoon chilli powder
2 teaspoons garlic purée
3 teaspoons chopped mint leaves
2 tablespoons lime juice
150ml yogurt
50ml water

Cut each pack of halloumi into 6 cubes,
rinse in cold water and drain well.

Next prepare the marinade. Heat the oil in
a small stainless steel saucepan and warm
all the ground spices together, stirring
constantly and taking great care that they
do not burn. Now put this spice mix in a
bowl and stir in the garlic purée, mint, lime
juice, yogurt and water. Mix together well.

Add the halloumi cubes to the marinade
and make sure every piece is fully coated.
Cover and refrigerate for 24 hours to
allow the halloumi to absorb the flavours.

Segment the onions, first by cutting in half
crossways. Now put the onion halves flat
side down and cut each half into 4 chunks.
Take each chunk and separate out the
onion layers into individual pieces.

Bring a pan of salted water to the boil and
plunge in the onion pieces. Boil for about
5 minutes until they become soft.
Meanwhile mix the lemon juice, salt and
sugar in a bowl. Remove the onions from
the heat, drain and, while still hot, toss in
the seasoned lemon juice. Leave to
marinate for 15 minutes, then drain.

Have 6 skewers ready. Drain the
marinated halloumi. Take a skewer and
thread on a cube of halloumi, pushing it
right down, then thread on 3 slices of
onion. Alternate this pattern, using 3
halloumi cubes for each kebab and
finishing off with a tomato. Cover the
kebabs and refrigerate until needed.

Just before you are ready to eat, heat a
griddle or non stick frying pan and brush
with the sunflower oil. Place the kebabs
on the griddle or in the pan and gently
brown the cheese without melting it, then
turn the kebabs over and brown the other
side. It does not take long – no more than
about 30 seconds on each side.

{kachumber salad}

$1/2$ cucumber, deseeded
1 red pepper, deseeded
1 yellow pepper, deseeded
1 tomato, deseeded
10g red chilli pepper, deseeded
1 red onion
3 tablespoons lemon juice
$1/4$ teaspoon salt
$1/4$ teaspoon caster sugar
$1/2$ teaspoon black mustard seeds, toasted
5g mint leaves
5g flat leaf parsley leaves
10g coriander leaves

for the lime dressing
3 tablespoons olive oil
2 tablespoons lime juice
salt and freshly ground black pepper

First prepare the lime dressing. Put the olive oil and lime juice in a lidded container and season to taste. Cover, give it all a good shake and refrigerate until needed.

Slice the cucumber, peppers, tomato and chilli into strips as thinly as possible.

Slice the onion in the same way. Now repeat the same process as for the onions in the Halloumi Kebabs (see opposite page). Bring a pan of salted water to the boil and plunge in the onion strips. Boil for about 5 minutes until they become soft.

Meanwhile mix the lemon juice, salt and sugar in a bowl. Remove the onions from the heat, drain and, while still hot, toss in the seasoned lemon juice. Leave to marinate for 15 minutes, then drain.

Put the onions in a bowl with all the other vegetable strips, the mustard seeds and the herb leaves. Wait to dress the salad until you are just about to serve it.

When you are ready, pour the dressing over the salad and toss to coat.

{to assemble}

1 teaspoon cumin seeds, lightly toasted
thick lime slices

Fill chilled shot glasses with the chilled yogurt cooler and sprinkle over the toasted cumin seeds. Heap the freshly tossed salad on to one side of the plates. Put the hot halloumi kebabs on the other side, so they do not wilt the salad. Add a glass of the cooler and a slice of lime.

This is also a cracking dish to share, served on a big platter for communal feasting.

Skordalia and Sesame Discos

sesame sumac coated fried aubergine, served with a garlic and bread purée,
and pomegranate, radish and fenugreek mint salad

{VEGAN}

A feast of flavours! Crispy coats of sizzling sesame sumac cornmeal encase succulent soft aubergine; perfect for decadently scooping up liberal amounts of unashamedly garlicky skordalia. They're teamed with the terrific textures and tastes of popping pomegranate seeds, fresh crunchy radishes, firm sweet grapes, salty plump olives and piquantly dressed leaves.

Sumac is a useful spice for us in the restaurant. A key ingredient in Arab cooking, it has a sour lemony flavour, and is often used as a substitute for fresh lemon. The berries of the sumac bush are harvested in late summer, dried out, then ground to a fine powder. This is used to season salads and stews, as a rub before grilling, and as a medicinal tea.

Skordalia is a traditional Greek dip or sauce, which often accompanies fried food. It can be made with either potato or breadcrumbs, but always with masses of fresh garlic and good quality olive oil. Very usefully, it can be made well in advance and kept in the refrigerator.

serves 6

{sesame discos}

2 medium sized aubergines
1 tablespoon sea salt
50g sesame seeds
1 tablespoon sumac
100g fine cornmeal
100ml soya milk
100ml sunflower oil
2 tablespoons toasted sesame oil

Slice the aubergines into rounds (you should have about 18 rounds or 'discos', to allow 3 per person). Put them in a colander, sprinkle with the salt and let them drip for at least 1 hour to remove any bitterness. Mix the sesame seeds, sumac and cornmeal together on a flat tray, ready to coat the aubergines. Pour the soya milk into another tray ready for the coating process. Rinse the salt off the aubergines in cold water, then drain and pat dry on kitchen towels. Dip the aubergines into the soya milk and then into the cornmeal mixture, carefully checking that they are evenly coated. Lay the coated aubergines on a lined tray, making sure they're not touching each other by layering with more greaseproof paper. Chill for at least 1 hour before cooking.

Just before you are ready to eat, heat the oils in a frying pan. Fry the discos for about 3 minutes on each side until golden and crispy. Drain on paper towels.

{skordalia}

150g breadcrumbs from stale white bread (crusts removed)
125ml soya milk
4 tablespoons lemon juice
2 tablespoons white wine vinegar
5 garlic cloves, crushed
100ml olive oil
salt and freshly ground black pepper

Soak the breadcrumbs in the soya milk, lemon juice and vinegar for 30 minutes. Put the mixture into a blender with the garlic. While blending, slowly pour in the olive oil as if you were making mayonnaise. If the mixture becomes too sticky, add a little water or stock. Season to taste and refrigerate until needed.

{pomegranate, radish and fenugreek salad}

120g radishes, trimmed and halved
50g Kalamata olives, halved and stoned
50g white grapes, halved
125g pomegranate seeds
50g fenugreek leaves
10g mint leaves
10g flat leaf parsley leaves
for the pomegranate dressing
1 tablespoon balsamic vinegar
1 tablespoon grapeseed oil
1 tablespoon pomegranate molasses
salt and freshly ground black pepper

First prepare the pomegranate dressing. Combine all the ingredients together and keep in an airtight container. (You could mix and store in a jam jar.)

Prepare the salad ingredients shortly before you are ready to eat. Mix the radishes, olives and grapes with the pomegranate seeds and all the leaves. Wait until you are ready to serve before you dress the salad.

{to assemble}

Lightly toss the salad in the dressing. Arrange the fried aubergine discos on serving plates, with spoonfuls of chilled skordalia and little heaps of glistening salad.

Roquefort Trifle

riesling pickled pears served with roquefort rounds, rosemary and black pepper digestive biscuits and cox's orange pippin hazelnut salad

So versatile and fabulously fragrant, this is equally good at the beginning or end of a meal. The most delicious crumbly digestive biscuits, packed with warm flavours of black pepper and rosemary, go beautifully with smooth smudges of salty blue Roquefort cream and scrumptious slivers of pungent pickled pears, all brought together with a tart crisp combination of Cox's Orange Pippin, hazelnut, celery and spring onion salad.

Roquefort is a crumbly, moist, tangy, bluey green veined sheep's milk cheese which is made only in a designated part of France where the local caves produce a mould that creates the distinctive veins and flavour (although this has now been recreated in a laboratory). Eating it takes you through a range of taste sensations, from mild and creamy to sweet, then on to an almost smoky saltiness. Set it against all the other elements of this dish – pepper, nuts, pears and pickling spices – and you'll discover inspiring taste combinations.

We leave it up to you to choose your pear variety for the pickle, as it's best to use what's in season. In the restaurant we've made it with large firm varieties such as Conference or Comice, and these have been absolutely delicious.

serves 6

{riesling pickled pears}

250ml pear juice
25ml cider vinegar
250ml dry Riesling wine
4 allspice berries
1 cinnamon stick
2 bay leaves
5 peppercorns
2 juniper berries
2 tablespoons caster sugar
350g pears, peeled, cored and sliced

Place all the ingredients in a large pan and cook over a medium heat until the pears becomes soft and opaque. Remove from the heat and allow to cool, then store in an airtight container in the fridge.

{rosemary and black pepper digestive biscuits}

100g oatmeal
100g wholemeal flour
45g soft light brown sugar
$1/2$ teaspoon bicarbonate of soda
$3/4$ teaspoon salt
75g butter, diced
3–4 tablespoons whole milk
2 teaspoons lemon juice
$1/2$ teaspoon finely chopped rosemary
1 teaspoon cracked black pepper

Mix all the dry ingredients with the butter in a food processor until the mixture resembles breadcrumbs. Add 3 tablespoons milk, the lemon juice, rosemary and pepper, and process for a little longer. (If the mixture seems too stiff, add a further 1 tablespoon milk – you need just enough to make it pliable.) Press the mixture into a ball, wrap in clingfilm and refrigerate for 1 hour.

Roll out the dough on a floured surface to 5mm thick. Using a biscuit cutter, cut out 6cm circles (or whatever other shape you want). Lay these on a lined and buttered baking tray, prick with a fork and bake at 200°C/Gas Mark 6 for 15 minutes. They need to be crisp, but watch that they don't overcook. Cool on a wire rack and store in an airtight container.

{cox's orange pippin hazelnut salad}

200g Cox's Orange Pippin apples (or other tangy apples), peeled, cored and sliced
100g spring onions, peeled and trimmed
200g celery, trimmed and cut into thin matchsticks
100g watercress
65g hazelnut slivers, toasted

for the dressing
100ml toasted hazelnut oil (or walnut oil)
50ml cider vinegar
salt and freshly ground black pepper

To prepare the dressing, put all the ingredients in a jar, cover and give it a good shake. Refrigerate until needed.

Mix all the salad ingredients together in a bowl and cover with clingfilm. Wait until you are ready to serve before you dress the salad.

{roquefort cream}

200ml crème fraîche
2 tablespoons agar agar
150ml double cream or whipping cream
350g Roquefort cheese, crushed until
    smooth

Put the crème fraîche in a pan, sprinkle over the agar agar and simmer for 3 minutes, beating vigorously all the time. Gently whip the cream (but not so far as to make soft peaks) and fold the smooth Roquefort into it. Blend the crème fraîche mix in a blender and, once smooth, fold into the creamy Roquefort mix.

Line six 100ml ramekins with clingfilm. Spoon the mixture into the ramekins to three-quarters full, fold the clingfilm over the tops and refrigerate until set. Remove from the refrigerator 1 hour before serving, to allow to come to room temperature.

{to assemble}

Place a digestive biscuit on each plate and spoon some of the pickled pears neatly on top, smoothing them down to make a flat surface. Carefully turn the Roquefort creams out on to the pear topped biscuits. Dress the salad and arrange a neat bundle next to each biscuit tower. Present the remaining biscuits for sharing out.

Polenta Plumps

{WHEAT FREE}

fried parmesan and polenta plumps served with toy box tomatoes and olive cassoulet

Simply delicious big flavours, vivid colours, happy guests! This is an easy going starter to share, or it could be a main course served with a generous leafy salad.

Hot, plump, Parmesan packed balls, with hints of cinnamon and bay, accompanied by tiny juicy tomatoes (we prefer to use 'toy box' for a riot of colour), loaded with heaps of fragrant basil, the sticky tang of balsamic vinegar and lemon, and little studs of pine nuts. The polenta plumps are perfectly formed for scooping up the succulent salty olives and chunks of fleshy pepper and the deliciously aromatic winey sauce.

Polenta, made from golden yellow Italian cornmeal, is a staple food in northern Italy. Making it from scratch requires time and effort (there is quite a ritual to it in Italy) but quick cook polenta (though some might say it's cheating) removes the bother of it all. It can be used hot and soft or, if left to cool, may be sliced and then fried or grilled. It can accompany pretty much anything.

serves 6

{olive cassoulet}

2 tablespoons olive oil
1 teaspoon fennel seeds
1/2 teaspoon coriander seeds
150g green peppers, diced
150g onions, diced
200g mixed stoned olives
15g garlic cloves, chopped
1 bay leaf
300ml dry white wine
240g cooked borlotti beans
1 tablespoon lemon juice
salt and freshly ground black pepper

Heat the oil in a pan and add the fennel and coriander seeds. Heat them gently, then add the peppers, onions, olives, garlic and bay leaf. Leave to cook on a low heat until soft. Add the wine and cook until the mixture reduces by one third, then add the borlotti beans and simmer for a further 3 minutes. Stir in the lemon juice and seasoning. Serve hot.

{polenta plumps}

250ml whole milk
250ml White Stock (see page 18) or water
75g onion, chopped
1 bay leaf
3 cloves
1/2 cinnamon stick
1/3 teaspoon grated nutmeg
125g quick cook polenta, plus extra for coating
75g Parmesan cheese, freshly grated
salt and freshly ground black pepper
50ml sunflower oil

Pour the milk and stock or water into a thick based pan and add the onion, bay leaf, cloves, cinnamon and nutmeg. Bring to the boil, turn off the heat, cover and leave to infuse for 15 minutes. Strain the infused liquid, pour back into the pan and bring up to simmering point. Now add the polenta and, stirring all the time, cook for about 5 minutes until the mixture thickens. Now stir in the Parmesan and add seasoning to taste. Spread more dry polenta on a flat baking tray and, when the cooked mix is cool enough to handle, scoop out random amounts, rather like big marbles, and roll them in the dry polenta. Keep the polenta shapes on a lined baking tray in the refrigerator until needed.

Just before you are ready to eat, heat the oil in a non-stick pan and fry the polenta shapes for 2–3 minutes until golden. Drain on paper towels.

{toy box tomatoes}

1 tablespoon olive oil
18 cherry tomatoes
1 tablespoon balsamic vinegar
1 tablespoon lemon juice
salt and freshly ground black pepper
25g basil leaves, torn
25g flat leaf parsley, roughly chopped
2 tablespoons pine nuts, toasted

Heat the oil in a frying pan until very hot, then scorch the tomatoes on one side, turn the heat off and add the vinegar, lemon juice and seasoning. Transfer the tomatoes to a bowl, spoon the warm oily dressing over them and scatter with the basil, parsley and pine nuts. Serve warm.

{to assemble}

Load a big platter with the freshly fried plumps and warm, shiny basil-coated tomatoes, and place a bowl of hot aromatic olive cassoulet in the centre. Give your guests side plates, spoons and napkins and just let them dig in.

Walnut Whip

griddled bruschetta loaded with soft sticky spiced red onions
and melting beenleigh blue cheese, served with seared
radicchio, warm garlicky lentils and walnut whip

Of all the many bruschetta topping combinations you could pick, this is an exceedingly satisfying choice. Simple, slightly charred griddled garlic oil bread is piled first with soft sweet cinnamon stewed onions, and then with ivory blue barely melting cheese. Seared radicchio with its bitter zesty flavour and deep red fleshy leaves is the perfect partner, alongside little heaps of warm Puy lentils dressed in wine and fresh herbs, and – to crown it all – walnuts, whipped into a cooling nutty cream. Bliss....

Beenleigh Blue is a sheep's milk cheese from a farm in Devon, one of only three blue sheep's milk cheeses made in Britain today. It has a moist and crumbly texture, and a rich, slightly sweet taste, similar to Roquefort but less salty.

To make the best bruschetta, get a good quality firm loaf with a decent crust. First choice is pane pugliese. Failing that, pain de campagne or even ciabatta, but nothing too doughy. It can be either white or brown and needs to be a bit stale (preferably two days old) and cut into 1.5cm thick slices. Traditionally, bruschetta was cooked over charcoal, but today it is more often toasted on a ridged cast iron griddle, giving each slice toasty tiger stripes and an unmistakable charred flavour. We periodically have a bruschetta on the menu, and this combination is without doubt the most popular and most requested.

serves 6

{walnut whip}

50g walnuts, toasted
50g fresh white breadcrumbs
100ml whole milk or soya milk
1 tablespoon lemon juice
200ml olive oil
2 teaspoons walnut oil
salt and freshly ground black pepper

Rub the skins off the toasted walnuts. Soak the walnuts and breadcrumbs in the milk and lemon juice for at least 1 hour (preferably longer). Blend this mix at high speed, dribbling in the olive oil and walnut oil a little at a time, as you would for mayonnaise. If the whip looks too thick, add a little warm water to slacken it. Add seasoning to taste and refrigerate until needed.

{soft spiced red onions}

1 tablespoon olive oil
250g red onions, finely sliced
1/2 cinnamon stick or a good pinch of
    ground cinnamon
2 allspice berries, cracked
1 bay leaf
150ml red wine (Merlot is ideal)
75ml White Stock (see page 18) or water
1/2 teaspoon soft dark brown sugar
2 tablespoons balsamic vinegar
salt and freshly ground black pepper

Heat the oil in a pan. Add the onions, cinnamon, allspice and bay leaf and fry lightly together. Pour in the wine and stock or water, cover and cook over a medium heat for 35 minutes, stirring regularly so the mixture does not stick to the bottom of the pan. Remove the lid and add the sugar, vinegar and seasoning. Cook for a further 15 minutes or until the onions are sweet, soft and sticky. Don't let the mixture become too jammy: there should be a good bit of juice. Once cooled,

it will keep in an airtight container in the refrigerator for a week.

{warm puy lentils}

20g flat leaf parsley
2 tablespoons olive oil
65g onion, finely diced
1 garlic clove, chopped
2 teaspoons chopped thyme
1 bay leaf
1/3 teaspoon cracked black pepper
100g Puy lentils
100ml dry white wine
600ml White Stock (see page 18)
    or water
salt and freshly fround black pepper
1 tablespoon balsamic vinegar

Remove the leaves from the parsley and reserve as a garnish (see assembly notes opposite); chop the stalks. Heat the olive oil in a large deep pan and add the onion, garlic, parsley stalks, thyme and bay leaf. Cook over a medium heat until the onion becomes soft and looks opaque. Add the lentils, wine and stock or water. Turn up the heat and cook at a hard boil for 10 minutes, then turn down the heat to a simmer, cover and cook the lentils for a further 35 minutes. Add seasoning to taste. This can be made a day in advance and, once cooled, stored in the refrigerator. Reheat before serving, and only stir in the balsamic vinegar at the last moment.

{seared radicchio}

3 radicchio heads (preferably Treviso)
4 tablespoons olive oil
2 tablespoons balsamic vinegar
salt and freshly ground black pepper

Remove the outer layers from the radicchio and cut in half lengthways. Lay out flat on a baking tray, cut side up, pour over the olive oil and vinegar, and season to taste. Leave to marinate for at least 30 minutes.

Heat a dry frying pan or griddle until very hot and smoky. Cook the radicchio cut side down for 2 minutes, then for another 2 minutes on the other side. Keep in a cool place until needed.

{toasted bruschetta}

6 slices of bread, 1.5cm thick
2 large garlic cloves, halved
2 tablespoons olive oil
sea salt

Toast the bread on a griddle until it is slightly charred, then rub with the raw garlic and sprinkle with the olive oil and sea salt. All this preparation is best done just before serving, so the bruschetta is still warm and garlicky.

{to assemble}

150g blue cheese (preferably
   Beenleigh Blue)
6 walnuts, toasted
10g marjoram leaves

Warm the onions and heap them on to the just griddled slices of bruschetta. Crumble the cheese over the top and gently warm the loaded bruschetta under the grill. Don't worry about melting the cheese completely, as it is perfect just warm. Once you have reheated the lentils and stirred in the balsamic vinegar, heap on to the plates with the radicchio. Top each bruschetta with a swirl of walnut whip and a toasted walnut. Scatter the marjoram and reserved parsley leaves liberally over the plates.

Congee Puff Cluster

seaweed and miso risotto served with deep fried chive rice clusters, sherry and {VEGAN} {WHEAT FREE} shiitake sauce and shiso beansprout salad with yuzu dressing

This is a distant relative of the traditional Chinese dish, congee, although closer to the Japanese version, okayu – we've done a bit of tweaking, but think it fits the bill on many levels. We wanted a dish on the menu that was vegan and gluten free, and which would satisfy the risotto urge. This is quite a tall order, but I think we cracked it... you can never replace cheese and it's best not to try, but this risotto has its own unique salty tang and creaminess. It's one of my favourites from our menu – full of different textures and strong flavours, and impressive looking too. We think it's definitely worth the effort.

Puffed rice is usually made by heating rice kernels under high pressure in the presence of steam. It's used in various breakfast cereals, and is a familiar street food in many parts of the world. An ingredient of bhel puri, a popular Indian snack, it's readily available in Asian and Middle Eastern shops.

We are obviously being a bit cheeky with our terminology here – congee is really more of a watery rice gruel, savoury or sweet, which many Chinese eat for breakfast – but it's the rice element we've borrowed. Shiitake mushrooms (Chinese xiang gu) are common in Chinese as well as Japanese dishes, and are an obvious addition: they have been used medicinally in Asia for centuries for their immune boosting powers, and are now commonplace in Western cooking. Chinese chives taste more garlicky and less oniony than our regular chives, and you can use the flowers as well as the stalks.

serves 4–6

{puffed rice clusters}

50g unsweetened puffed rice

for the batter
75g rice flour
120ml water
2 tablespoons sushi vinegar
1 teaspoon finely chopped chives (ideally Chinese chives)
1 teaspoon gluten free baking powder
a pinch of salt
1/4 teaspoon freshly ground black pepper
1/4 teaspoon ground Szechuan pepper

to finish
sunflower oil for deep frying

Start by preparing the batter. Mix the rice flour with the water, then add the rest of ingredients and combine well. This can now be refrigerated until you are ready to start frying the clusters. When you are ready, heat the oil in a deep sided pan to 180°C, using a thermometer. Working in small batches, add spoonfuls of puffed rice to the batter mix and then drop into the hot oil. Fry until golden brown, lift out with a slotted spoon and drain on paper towels.

{congee stock}

2 litres water
50g kombu (dried seaweed)
25g wakame (dried seaweed)
6 dried shiitake mushrooms
1 teaspoon roughly chopped fresh root ginger
1 teaspoon roughly chopped chives (ideally Chinese chives)

Put all the ingredients into a large pan, bring to the boil, cover and simmer for

20 minutes. Remove from the heat and strain, discarding the seaweed, ginger and chives. Reserve the shiitake mushrooms for the Congee Garnish (see below). Once

cooled, keep the stock refrigerated until required.

{congee garnish}

75g daikon (Japanese white radish or mooli), peeled and cut into ribbons
6 shiitake mushrooms (see Congee Stock, above), sliced
10g shiso shoots (or any preferred micro leaves)
150g beansprouts

for the yuzu dressing
2 tablespoons yuzu juice (Japanese citrus fruit) – or use lime juice
2 tablespoons grapeseed oil

for the rice garnish
1 tablespoon risotto rice

First, prepare the rice garnish. Toast the rice in a dry frying pan until golden, then remove from the heat and grind until it is powdery. Put to one side for finishing the dish.

Next, make the dressing. Blend together the yuzu juice and grapeseed oil and refrigerate until ready to use.

Mix together the daikon, shiitake mushrooms, shiso shoots and beansprouts. Put aside.

When you are ready to serve the congee garnish, dress the salad with the yuzu dressing, but keep the rice garnish separate.

(Continued on page 72)

Congee Puff Cluster

(Continued from page 70)

{sherry and shiitake sauce}

500ml Congee Stock (see page 70)
1½ tablespoons tamari (gluten free soy
    sauce)
2 teaspoons ground kuzu (gluten free
    starch thickener)
2 teaspoons water
1 tablespoon medium dry sherry

Put the stock in a pan, bring to the boil and cook until it has reduced by half. Add the tamari, then bring back to the boil. Mix the kuzu with the water to make a thick paste and stir this into the boiling reduced stock. Return to the boil and cook for only 1 minute, stirring, then remove from the heat and add the sherry. Put to one side until required.

{congee risotto}

1 tablespoon sunflower oil
1 small onion, finely diced
1 bay leaf
250g risotto rice
800ml hot Congee Stock (see page 70)
25g white miso (soy paste)
20ml mirin (sweet rice wine)

In a thick based skillet or sauté pan, heat the sunflower oil then add the onion and bay leaf and cook until the onion is soft. Add the rice and continue cooking, stirring, until the rice becomes opaque. Gradually ladle the hot stock into the rice, stirring constantly. Now, whisk the white miso and mirin together until the mixture acquires the consistency of double cream. When the rice is cooked and most of the liquid has been absorbed, take the pan off the heat. Slowly add the white miso mix, a little at a time, taking great care not to add too much at once or the risotto will become too loose. Keep checking the consistency and stop adding the miso mix when you are satisfied with the results. This risotto is best served a few minutes after it is cooked.

{to assemble}

shiso shoots

Heap the hot risotto on to warmed serving plates and place a handful of congee garnish (salad) on top. Place the freshly fried puffed rice clusters around the risotto. Heat the sherry and shiitake sauce and pour around the edge of each plate. Scatter some shiso shoots over the whole dish and add a sprinkling of toasted rice powder.

Whistlestop Tomatoes

fried green tomatoes served with little gem lettuce, caesar dressing and deep fried capers

This simply prepared salad dish is a genuine crowd pleaser. Crunch through the piping hot crumb coats into succulent fleshy tomatoes, bursting with juice and full on flavour, followed by crisp lettuce leaves dressed with rich, salty, Caesar dressing, and bites of pucker-up deep fried capers.

There are myriad tomato varieties to choose from: if you don't fancy the green version, go for something with a firm flesh and robust flavour, or try mixing the colours. The Elizabethans might have believed the red colouring indicated that tomatoes were highly poisonous, but we know better. They are incredibly good for us, and are partly why the Mediterranean diet, rich in tomatoes, is considered one of the healthiest in the world. The reason for this is their high level of vitamin C and a secret weapon, lycopene, which has scientists scratching their heads in disbelief at its benefits. And they are incredibly easy to grow: just stick a few plants in an organic grow bag, remember to water them and distract the snails – and start harvesting!

serves 6

{fried whistlestop green tomatoes}

25g fresh basil
400g focaccia bread
6 green tomatoes (or use firm red tomatoes if green are unavailable)
200g plain flour
3 eggs, beaten
salt and freshly ground black pepper

Chop the basil, keeping back 12 nice leaves for the salad.

Roughly dice the bread, divide it into 4 batches, and in a food processor or jug blender turn it into breadcrumbs, 1 batch at a time. This is important as if too much is processed at once, it is likely to get too doughy. When each batch is nearly finished, add a quarter of the basil to the jug and the crumbs will turn a beautiful shade of green.

Cut a thin slice from both ends of the tomatoes then slice into halves through the middle.

Put the flour, beaten eggs and breadcrumb mix into 3 separate bowls and season each one.

Coat each tomato half by dipping first into the flour (shaking off any excess), then into the beaten egg and finally into the basil breadcrumbs. Lay the evenly coated tomatoes on a lined tray and refrigerate until you are ready to cook them.

The final step is to deep fry the tomatoes, and this is described in the assembly instructions below.

{caesar dressing}

$1/8$ teaspoon wholegrain mustard
$1/8$ teaspoon Dijon mustard
$1/4$ garlic clove, crushed
1 egg yolk
1 teaspoon vegetarian Worcestershire sauce
1 tablespoon lemon juice
100ml grapeseed oil
10ml warm water
50g Parmesan cheese, freshly grated
freshly ground black pepper

Whisk together the mustards, garlic, egg yolk, Worcestershire sauce, lemon juice, oil and water until they emulsify. Stir in the Parmesan and some freshly ground pepper to taste. Refrigerate the dressing until required.

{to assemble}

250ml sunflower oil
18 large capers, rinsed and dried
4 little gem lettuces
basil leaves, torn

Heat the oil in a deep fryer or deep pan. Fry the capers for 10–15 seconds until they are crisp and starting to open up. Drain on paper towels.

Now fry the prepared whistlestop tomatoes, turning them once in the oil, until they are golden brown and crisp on both sides. Drain on paper towels.

Pull off the outer leaves of the lettuce and cut the heart into quarters. Toss the leaves and hearts in the Caesar dressing and arrange them, either on a large sharing platter or on individual plates. Put the tomatoes on the dressed lettuce and scatter the capers and torn basil leaves all over.

Cool as a Cucumber

cucumber mousses and sesame egg toasts, served with kicking ketchup and salad of tomatoes and nasturtium leaves sprinkled with wasabi salt

This is a lovely dish on a summer's day. It's not exactly cucumber and egg sandwiches, as the concept began, but it's not a million miles away and the flavours are equally as recognizable and more than delicious. Sizzling hot eggy toasts with salty caper centres and deep fried crunchy sesame seed coats are the perfect foil for the fresh, delicate little cucumber creams. Try smudging them together with some piquant ketchup and a few peppery leaves.

Adding home grown flowers to your cooking is such a simple but transforming thing to do. You don't even need a garden, as a number of edible flowers such as nasturtiums, marigolds and borage can be grown in a window box. Not only do they look beautiful, they also add subtle or more distinct flavours to food. Nasturtiums have a strong peppery taste, and their seed heads, pickled, can be used as a substitute for capers. Gone are the days when it was polite to leave the garnish on your plate!

serves 6

{cucumber mousses}

650ml double cream
2 cucumbers, peeled, deseeded and cut
    into chunks
50g ground kuzu (gluten free starch
    thickener)
4 tablespoons water
1/4 teaspoon celery salt

Line six 125ml dariole moulds (or eight 100ml moulds) with clingfilm. Put 500ml of the cream in a heavy based pan, bring to the boil and cook until reduced by half, then pour into a measuring jug.

Liquidize the chunks of cucumber in a jug blender, or using a hand blender, until you have a smooth juice. Sieve to remove any final lumps. Add enough of this juice to the reduced cream to make 650ml of total liquid, then pour this mixture back into the pan. Mix the kuzu with the water to form a smooth paste. Stir this into the cucumber cream and heat, still stirring, until the cucumber mixture thickens and bubbles.

Remove the pan from the heat and transfer the mixture to a bowl, placing it over iced water to speed the cooling process. Stir the mixture with a spatula until it cools and thickens, then remove from the iced water.

Put the remaining 150ml cream in a bowl and whip to soft peaks, then fold into the cool cucumber mix. Sprinkle in the celery salt and mix well. Spoon the mousse into the lined moulds, fold the clingfilm over the top and refrigerate until you are ready to assemble the dish.

{kicking ketchup}

450g ripe tomatoes, chopped
150g red peppers, deseeded and chopped
175g white onions, chopped
100g apple, chopped (preferably Braeburn)
1 red chilli pepper, deseeded and chopped
1 star anise
15 Szechuan peppercorns
1 tablespoon umeboshi purée (pickled plum)
40ml white wine vinegar
salt

Put all the ingredients in a heavy based pan and bring to a simmer. Reduce the heat and cook, barely bubbling, for $1 1/4 - 1 1/2$ hours or until all the vegetables are soft and the liquid has evaporated. Remove from the heat and take out the star anise. Pour the ketchup into a jug blender and blitz until smooth. Strain through a fine sieve, add salt to taste, cool and refrigerate until required.

{sesame egg toasts}

20g capers, rinsed and dried
oil for deep frying
4 eggs, beaten
6 slices of white bread, crusts removed
3 nori sheets (dried seaweed)
100g sesame seeds

Deep fry the capers in hot oil at 170°C, for 10–15 seconds. Drain on paper towels.

Pour the beaten eggs into a shallow dish and dip the bread slices into them, coating each side well and soaking thoroughly. You need to dip 2 slices at a time, ready for the next stage. Reserve any leftover beaten egg for later in the recipe.

Lay 2 sheets of clingfilm on the worktop, one on top of the other (for extra strength). Put 2 slices of egg soaked bread on to them, overlapping the bread by 2–3cm, and press down to seal the slices. (They need to make a long rectangle, one short edge nearest you.) Cover the whole surface of the bread with pieces of nori and sprinkle the capers on top. Tightly roll the bread into a sausage shape, like a Swiss roll, using the clingfilm to help you. Seal the ends of the clingfilm by twisting them. Repeat this whole process twice more so that you have 3 short, fat sausages. Chill them in the refrigerator for at least 2 hours.

Gently remove the sausages from the clingfilm and carefully slice each one into 6 pieces, giving a total of 18 pieces. Dip the slices in the remaining beaten egg, then dip in the sesame seeds until completely coated. Put on a tray lined with clingfilm and refrigerate until needed.

Just before you are ready to eat, deep fry the sesame toasts at 170°C for about 2 minutes until brown and crispy, then drain on paper towels. (They may also be shallow fried.)

{nasturtium salad}

12 ripe cherry vine tomatoes
6–8 nasturtiums, leaves and flowers
2 teaspoons grapeseed oil

for the wasabi salt
1 teaspoon wasabi powder (Japanese
    horseradish)
1 teaspoon salt

Prepare the wasabi salt by mixing the wasabi powder with the salt.

Shortly before serving, cut the tomatoes in half and combine them with the nasturtium leaves and flowers. Pour over the oil and sprinkle on a small pinch of the wasabi salt. (Keep the remaining wasabi salt for the final assembly.) Gently toss the salad.

{to assemble}

Turn out the cucumber mousses on to serving plates. Next to each mousse, arrange a little nasturtium salad, 3 hot sesame toasts and a good splodge of the ketchup. Add a tiny mound of wasabi salt to each plate.

MAINS
AWAY

Colada Toddy

coconut, kaffir and lemon basil fragrant rice sausages rolled in dry spices, fried and served with thai red relish, charred aubergine and umeboshi plum hash, lime scented gazpacho and a colada toddy

{VEGAN} {WHEAT FREE}

Just the name gets you in the mood for a shot of something to warm your heart and stoke your appetite! This dish is absolutely rammed full of potent flavours, spot on if you want some wheat free sustenance. The hot, smoky, spice-laden sausages, with a touch of refreshing mint and a scattering of nutty black rice, are ideal companions for the punchy charred aubergine hash, sharp but creamy, beautifully balanced with the cool crunch of revitalizing green gazpacho and the shock of fiery sweet shallot relish. Then comes a taste of the sweet-sour umeboshi plum dressing, followed by the comforting, warm coconut and rum toddy, to sip while contemplating the party your taste buds are having!

We love to use fresh, fragrant, citrusy galangal in the restaurant. Used as a root, it looks almost exactly like ginger (sometimes it's referred to as Chinese ginger), but the taste is far removed. Galangal supplies the distinctive flavour of Thai food, and some of the complex undertones here.

serves 6

{gazpacho}

8 chives (ideally Chinese chives)
2 teaspoons finely chopped green chilli pepper
1 teaspoon wasabi paste (Japanese horseradish)
salt and freshly ground black pepper
1 tablespoon grapeseed oil
75g fennel, finely diced
75g green pepper, finely diced
35g onion, finely diced
2 teaspoons finely diced galangal
30g celery, finely diced
juice of 1 lime

In a blender blitz together the chives, chilli and wasabi and season the mix. Add the oil while still mixing, until a purée is formed. Turn the purée out into a bowl and add the diced vegetables. Combine well and your gazpacho is made. Stir in the lime juice just before serving.

{thai red relish}

3 cloves
1 teaspoon cumin seeds
3 cracked cardamom seeds
½ cinnamon stick
250g Thai pink shallots
125ml clear distilled vinegar (or malt vinegar)
1 tablespoon finely chopped red chilli pepper
50g caster sugar

Tie the cloves, cumin, cardamom and cinnamon in a piece of muslin. Put the shallots in a stainless steel pan with the muslin wrapped spices and all the other ingredients and bring slowly to a simmer. Cover and cook gently until the shallots are tender, then take off the heat, remove the spice bundle and leave the relish to cool.

This will keep for several weeks in the refrigerator, but it's unlikely there'll be much left after the first serving!

{colada toddy}

1 lemongrass stick
800ml coconut water
25ml white rum

Trim the lemongrass: keep the stick end for the garnish and crush the bulbous end. Put the coconut water and crushed lemongrass into a saucepan and heat gently to release the flavour. Remove the pan from the heat, strain through a fine sieve and stir in the rum.

{umeboshi plum dressing}

50ml umeboshi purée (pickled plum)
50ml grapeseed oil
juice of ½ lemon
2 garlic cloves, crushed to a paste
salt and freshly ground black pepper

Put all the ingredients in a jar, cover and give them a good shake. Keep the dressing refrigerated, but let it come back to room temperature before use.

{charred aubergine and umeboshi plum hash}

500g aubergines, cut into 1cm slices
25ml olive oil
juice of 1 lemon
2 teaspoons chopped red chilli pepper
20 mint leaves
2 garlic cloves, chopped
salt and freshly ground black pepper
2 tablespoons umeboshi purée

Season the aubergines, brush them with the oil, then griddle them until they are scorched and tender on both sides. Put half the grilled aubergine in a blender or food processor with the lemon juice, chilli, mint and garlic. Blitz until puréed, then season with salt and pepper.

While the remaining aubergine is still hot, chop it into 1cm batons, then marinate these in the umeboshi plum purée. When the batons are cool, fold them into the aubergine purée. Refrigerate until required.

(Continued on page 80)

Colada Toddy

(Continued from page 78)

{sausage spice mix}

4 tablespoons dried caribe chilli flakes
50g sesame seeds, toasted
1 teaspoon black peppercorns
2 tablespoons ground ginger
1 teaspoon ground star anise
1 teaspoon allspice berries
1 teaspoon cloves
1 teaspoon ground cinnamon
½ teaspoon salt
75g almonds, toasted and ground

Grind all the spices to a powder, then add the almonds and stir well. This mix will keep for several weeks in an airtight container. Leftovers can be used as a spice rub or seasoning; try it sprinkled over rice, roast vegetables or yogurt, or into salads and soups. It can also be added to breadcrumbs or polenta as a coating.

{rice sausages}

200g jasmine rice (or Thai fragrant rice)
250ml water
a pinch of salt
grated zest and juice of 1 lemon
50g black rice, boiled until tender, then
  cooled
125g freshly grated coconut
1 tablespoon finely chopped shallots
8 lemon basil leaves, chopped
16 mint leaves, chopped
5 kaffir lime leaves, finely chopped
200g smoked tofu mince, finely chopped
Sausage Spice Mix (see above)
sunflower oil for deep frying

Rinse the jasmine rice in a fine sieve under cold running water for about 5 minutes, until the water runs clear, then drain well. Put in a pan with the water, salt, lemon zest and juice and bring to the boil. Cover with a tight fitting lid, reduce the heat to low and simmer until all the water has evaporated. Remove from the heat, cover and leave to steam for 15 minutes, then spread the rice out on a tray to cool.

Stir in all the remaining ingredients except the spice mix and sunflower oil and work to a malleable but nicely textured mixture – this will take a good bit of effort. Shape into 12 sausages, roughly 4 x 2cm, and coat generously with the spice powder. You might want to roll them several times in the powder to achieve a good coating. Refrigerate until required.

Shortly before you are ready to serve, heat the oil to 170°C in a deep fryer or deep pan (if you don't have a thermometer, drop a small piece of bread into the oil; if it goes golden brown within a minute, the oil is hot enough). Deep fry the sausages until crisp and golden, then drain them on paper towels.

{to assemble}

lemongrass stick (see Colada Toddy, above)

Reheat the toddy. Cut the lemongrass stick lengthways into 6 and trim into long strips. Place each in a shot glass as a stirrer and pour the delicious toddy hot on its heels.

Place 2 sausages on each plate, upended if possible. Warm the aubergine hash in a small pan and place a heap of it next to the sausages, then divide the cold gazpacho between each plate, with a little of the bright Thai relish alongside. Spoon the umeboshi plum dressing between each of the elements and serve with a glass of hot toddy.

Sin Sin Salad

rice noodle, green mango and toasted ground rice salad, loaded with lemongrass, lime leaf and ginger dressing and finished with garlic, chilli and peanut frizzle

{VEGAN} {WHEAT FREE}

No light hiding under a bushel here. These flavours leap out and grab you, whether you like it or not! Sin sin salad will sharpen your appetite and tease your taste buds and and it's a real treat to make. With simple, fresh, clean flavours, packing a chilli kick, and full of terrific textures, it looks pretty darn dandy, too. Serve as a lunch or light supper – it's open to offers....

Heaps of sesame-drenched noodles with thin strips of crunchy, revitalizing green mango and papaya are mixed with toasted ground rice, then doused with an unmistakably fragrant lemongrass, lime leaf and ginger dressing. The toasted rice imparts its own interesting flavour and texture and also soaks up the zesty dressing, distributing it through the whole dish. The noodle salad stack is topped with the crispy, salty, sizzling peanut frizzle.

Mangoes and papayas are often used green and unripe. Green mangoes are commonly eaten with salt or chilli, and have a refreshing, acidic taste that is quite different from the intensely sweet and perfumed flavour of the ripe fruits, which are soft and yielding and beautifully orange.

serves 6-8

{lemongrass, lime leaf and ginger dressing}

3 lemongrass sticks
5 lime leaves, spines removed
20g fresh root ginger, finely grated
6 Thai pink shallots, finely chopped
100ml lime juice
25ml lemon juice
100g coriander, chopped
50g basil, chopped
1 teaspoon finely chopped garlic
2 teaspoons finely sliced green chilli pepper
1 teaspoon finely sliced red chilli pepper
3 teaspoons toasted sesame oil
50ml olive oil
15g palm sugar, chopped (or dark muscovado sugar)

Remove the outer layer of the lemongrass, cut off the hard, thinner ends and then crush and chop it. Put it in a jug blender with the lime leaves, ginger, shallots, lime and lemon juices, and blend to a smooth paste. Add the herbs, garlic, chillies, oils and sugar and blend again until you get a beautifully green, smooth, thick dressing.

{rice noodle and green mango salad}

20g jasmine rice (or Thai fragrant rice)
150g vermicelli rice noodles
1 tablespoon toasted sesame oil
175g red pepper, finely sliced
175g yellow pepper, finely sliced
150g cucumber, peeled, deseeded and cut into long, thin strips
150g long, thin celery sticks, finely sliced
6 spring onions, cut into long, thin strips
275g green mango, peeled and finely sliced
275g green papaya, peeled and finely sliced
Lemongrass, Lime Leaf and Ginger Dressing (see above)
salt

Put the jasmine rice on a baking tray and toast in the oven at 150°C/Gas Mark 2 until it starts to colour. Grind in a pestle and mortar or a blender.

Soak the noodles in boiling water for 3 minutes, then refresh under cold water. Drain well, sprinkle with the sesame oil and refrigerate until needed.

To finish the salad, put the peppers, cucumber, celery, spring onions, mango, papaya and ground jasmine rice in a large bowl. Add the dressing and mix well, ensuring that everything is coated. Now mix in the chilled noodles and season to taste.

{garlic, chilli and peanut frizzle}

50ml sunflower oil
4 large garlic cloves, finely sliced
2 Thai pink shallots, cut into long, thin strips
20g red chilli pepper, deseeded and finely sliced
salt
70g roasted peanuts, chopped

Heat the oil in a frying pan, then flash fry the garlic, shallots and chilli until brown and crisp, then season with plenty of salt. Add the peanuts.

{to assemble}

Sprinkle the garlic, chilli and peanut frizzle over the tangy salad stack. Missing ingredients: cold plates... cold beers. Now pile into both!

Saltimbocca

mushroom duxelles in parmesan polenta sausages, wrapped in tomato paper,
seared and served with cavolo nero, fennel butter, roast barley water,
garlic confit mash and big red sauce

{WHEAT FREE}

Saltimbocca is an ancient dish, typically featuring escalopes, prosciutto and sage, rolled up and pan fried. We say yes to the name and packaging idea, but no to hamming it up, thank you very much! Our version has intensely flavoured, seared tomato skins that taste a little bit cured and salty; it's a crafty way to encase the deliciously soft Parmesan polenta sausages, with their rich, earthy mushroom core. A perfect plush package, only enhanced by the aromatic, buttery, fennel-laced, crinkly cavolo nero leaves, with their added barley bits for texture; fresh, creamy, parsley barley water and then the dark, velvety, big red sauce. This is another flexible dish in terms of presentation – run wild with your artistic imagination, or just big it up in bowls. Barley is a wonderfully versatile cereal. As a whole grain, it has undisputed health benefits, the greatest being its considerable fibre content. The rich, nutty flavour and somewhat chewy texture make it a great addition to wintry, wholesome soups and stews, and it gives a real sense of having eaten well. Fermented barley is used to produce alcoholic drinks such as beer and whisky.

serves 6

{fennel butter}

75g soft salted butter
2 teaspoons fennel seeds, toasted and ground
1 tablespoon finely chopped fennel fronds
1 tablespoon lemon juice
freshly ground black pepper

Beat the butter with all the remaining ingredients. Refrigerate until you are ready to serve.

{roast barley water}

100g pearl barley
100ml white wine
100g onions, diced
50g celery, diced
1 bay leaf
¼ teaspoon celery seeds
800ml White Stock (see page 18) or water
salt and freshly ground black pepper
1 tablespoon finely chopped parsley

Spread the pearl barley out on a baking tray and roast in the oven at 180°C/Gas Mark 4 until it turns a nutty brown colour. Put it into a saucepan with all the ingredients except the parsley, bring to the boil and simmer for about 45 minutes, until the barley puffs up and becomes soft. Remove half the barley water and set aside: this will be used with the Cavolo Nero (see page 84).

Using a hand blender, blend the remaining mixture, check the seasoning and then pass it through a sieve to remove any lumps. If it seems too thick, thin it with a little water. Store in the refrigerator until required.

Just before serving, reheat the blended barley water and stir in the chopped parsley.

{mixed mushroom duxelles}

1 tablespoon olive oil
50g onion, finely diced
1 large garlic clove, finely chopped
1 bay leaf
100g mixed mushrooms, finely chopped
 (chestnut, pied bleu and shiitake are ideal)
25ml fino sherry
25ml red wine
1 tablespoon chopped basil
½ teaspoon chopped thyme
½ teaspoon chopped rosemary
salt and freshly ground black pepper

Heat the oil in a saucepan, add the onion, garlic and bay leaf, and cook gently until soft. Add the mushrooms and cook, stirring constantly, until all the liquid they release has evaporated. Pour in the sherry and wine and simmer for a few minutes until the mixture is dry. Stir in the herbs and seasoning. Remove the bay leaf later.

{parmesan polenta sausages}

570ml whole milk
1 tablespoon olive oil
1 onion, peeled
2 bay leaves
1 cinnamon stick
125g quick cook polenta
50g Parmesan cheese, freshly grated
salt and freshly ground black pepper
Mixed Mushroom Duxelles (see above)

To make the sausages you will need 2 piping bags, or plastic bags each with a corner snipped off. First put the milk, olive oil, whole onion, bay leaves and cinnamon in a pan and heat gently for 15 minutes, then remove the flavourings. Bring the infused milk to the boil and gradually add the polenta, stirring continuously. When the mixture has thickened, cook for 5 minutes. Stir in the Parmesan and season with salt and pepper.

Load the polenta into a piping bag, taking great care not to burn yourself. This needs to be done while the polenta is still hot, so we suggest wrapping the piping bag in a tea towel. You now need to make 3 polenta sausages. Lay a sheet of clingfilm on a work surface and pipe a line of polenta, roughly 24cm long, along the middle of it, horizontal to you. With wet fingers, make a groove along the middle of the polenta. Put the mushroom duxelles into another piping bag, then pipe a much thinner line of mushroom into the groove of the polenta.

Using wet fingers and gently tugging one side of the clingfilm, seal the sausage with the mushroom mix in the centre; the filling should be completely enclosed. Then roll the whole thing up and twist the ends of the clingfilm until you have a tightly rolled and sealed 'sausage'.

Repeat twice with the remaining polenta and duxelles, then refrigerate the 3 sausages so that they harden; this will make it easier to wrap them in the tomato paper.

(Continued on page 84)

Saltimbocca

(Continued from page 83)

{tomato wrapped parmesan polenta sausages}

Parmesan Polenta Sausages (see page 83)

for the tomato wraps
300g sun dried tomatoes
1.5 litres water
75ml sherry vinegar
1 cinnamon stick

for finishing the sausages
3 tablespoons quick cook polenta
2 tablespoons olive oil

First prepare the tomato wraps. Put the sun dried tomatoes, water, vinegar and cinnamon into a pan and bring to the boil. Cover and simmer for 20 minutes. Remove from the heat and strain off the liquid, reserving it to use in the Big Red Sauce (see below). Leave the tomatoes to cool, then wring them in a cloth or paper towels to make them as dry as you possibly can.

You now need to roll out a sheet of the tomatoes, about 30cm square, that will form the skin for the sausages. This is not an easy thing to do but we promise it gets easier with practice. Lay the tomatoes on a large sheet of silicone paper, slightly overlapping them so there are no gaps. Cover this with another sheet of silicone paper, then work at it with a rolling pin, tapping it, rolling it, bashing it, and continually checking there are no holes. When you have a continuous, reasonably thin sheet, you can roll up the sausages.

Take the chilled polenta sausages from the refrigerator, remove the clingfilm and cut each sausage in half. With sharp scissors, cut the tomato sheet in half lengthways and then across twice, creating 6 skins. Place a polenta sausage near the bottom edge of one sheet and roll it up. When it is fully covered, and hopefully has an overhang at each end, wrap it tightly in clingfilm, twisting the ends to make sure they are fully sealed. Repeat with the remaining polenta sausages. These are now ready to cook or can be refrigerated until required.

Cook the sausages shortly before serving. Remove the clingfilm and pat the sausages gently with paper towels to remove any liquid. Roll them lightly in the polenta. Heat the olive oil in a non-stick frying pan, add the sausages and cook until coloured all over. Transfer the sausages to a preheated non-stick roasting tin and place in the oven at 160°C/Gas Mark 3 to heat through while you assemble the dish.

{big red sauce}

1 litre Demi Glace Sauce (see page 18)
500ml sun dried tomato liquid (see Tomato Wrapped Parmesan Polenta Sausages, above)
200ml Marsala or cream sherry
salt and freshly ground black pepper

Pour the demi glace sauce, sun dried tomato liquid and Marsala or sherry into a heavy based pan, bring to the boil and simmer for about 45 minutes, skimming the surface occasionally to remove the froth. When the liquid has reduced by about one third, pass it through a fine sieve and season with salt and pepper. The resulting rich, dark sauce can be stored in the refrigerator until required.

{garlic confit mash}

100g garlic, peeled
2 teaspoons chopped rosemary
150ml olive oil
400g potatoes (Desiree or other waxy variety)
15g unsalted butter
1 tablespoon double cream
salt and freshly ground black pepper

Put the garlic in an ovenproof dish, add the rosemary and oil, then cover and bake at 180°C/Gas Mark 4 for about 30 minutes. Meanwhile, cook the potatoes in boiling salted water until tender, then drain thoroughly. Mash well. When the garlic is completely soft, cream it into the rosemary oil with a fork, then tip it into the potatoes, along with the butter, cream and seasoning. Stir everything together thoroughly.

{cavolo nero}

500g cavolo nero (or other dark green cabbage), sliced
½ quantity barley water (see Roast Barley Water, page 83)
Fennel Butter (see page 83)

Cook the cavolo nero in a pan of boiling salted water until tender. Drain well, then return to the pan and add the barley water and fennel butter. Toss well so that every leaf is coated.

{to assemble}

250g wild mushrooms (optional)

Gently reheat the big red sauce and garlic confit mash, if necessary. Place a spoonful of buttery cavolo nero on each plate and spoon the herby roast barley water over it, letting it spill out on to the plate. Lay a good smudge of mash to one side of this, prop the polenta sausage across the vegetables and then spoon liberal amounts of the rich, dark sauce around the plate. If you have the energy, wild mushrooms would go deliciously with this dish (briefly seared in a lightly oiled, very hot pan).

Fancy Nancy

fried coconut spiced rice with peanuts, spring onions, chilli sizzled shallots and beansprout egg foo yung

Nasi goreng is Indonesian and Malay for fried rice, while 'Fancy Nancy' is Terre à Terre for fabulous fried rice. This is delicious, simple and satisfying, a lovely dish for supper or lunch (traditional nasi goreng is often eaten for breakfast). It looks lush and is ludicrously easy to pull together, as the rice can be prepared in advance. Fragrant, nutty grains, sticky with spices, rich with egg and loaded with crunchy, raw and fried ingredients. Perfect alongside soft, pillowy sesame omelettes, crammed full of snappy beansprouts and fresh coriander; the whole lot steaming hot, wonderfully colourful and aromatic, and not far off the original version bar a few happy prawns that got to swim away!

We favour jasmine rice here (also known as Thai fragrant rice), for its delicate scent and because it does not become sticky after cooking, allowing the grains to remain separate. It is a long-grain rice that needs to be steamed rather than boiled, and the aroma varies according to when the rice was harvested. The spring crop, with its more subtle flavour, is considered superior.

serves 6

{beansprout egg foo yung}

3 eggs
1 teaspoon soy sauce (preferably tamari)
40ml water
1 tablespoon toasted sesame oil
100g beansprouts
25g coriander, chopped

Beat the eggs with the tamari and water. Heat a non-stick frying pan or wok and add the oil. When the oil is smoking, add a small ladleful of the egg mix and tilt the pan quickly so that it forms a pancake. Cook for 1 minute. Remove the pan from the heat, add a third each of the beansprouts and coriander, then roll up

the omelette so that the beansprouts are inside. Turn out of the pan. Make 2 more omelettes with the remaining ingredients. If you are feeding 6 people this will give them half a roll each, but if you want to be more generous, double the quantities.

{fried coconut spiced rice}

500g jasmine rice (or Thai fragrant rice)
800ml cold water
6 cardamom pods
400ml coconut milk
½ tablespoon five spice powder
2 tablespoons vegetable or peanut oil
80g fresh root ginger, finely chopped
100g shallots, finely chopped
2 garlic cloves, finely chopped
8 spring onions, finely sliced (green tops reserved for garnishing)
200g beansprouts
2 eggs, beaten

for the soy dressing
60ml ketjap manis (Indonesian sweet soy sauce) – or other good quality soy sauce
75ml light soy sauce
25ml Chinese chilli sauce

Rinse the rice in a fine sieve under cold running water for about 5 minutes, until the water runs clear. Drain off the excess water, then put the rice into a heavy based pan with the cold water and the cardamom pods. Bring to the boil, stir once and cover tightly with the lid. Remove the pan from the heat and leave to stand for 15 minutes. Do not remove the lid. After 15 minutes, stir in the coconut milk and five spice powder.

Now heat the oil in a wok and fry the ginger, shallots and garlic until lightly coloured. Add the spring onions and beansprouts, then the rice, and fry for about 2 minutes until piping hot. Meanwhile, mix together the ingredients for the soy dressing. Spoon two thirds of

the dressing into the wok and stir well. Make a well in the rice and add the eggs. Cook them in the centre of the wok for 30 seconds, then stir into the rice. Cook for 1 minute more, then it's ready to serve.

{chilli sizzled shallots}

50ml sunflower or peanut oil
25g garlic cloves, finely sliced
75g banana shallots (or Thai pink shallots), cut into long, thin slices
2 small red chilli peppers, deseeded and finely sliced

Heat the oil in a pan, add the garlic, shallots and chillies and fry until soft. Keep turning them while they fry so they cook evenly, then drain on paper towels.

{to assemble}

reserved green spring onion tops, cut into strips
80g unsalted dehusked peanuts, chopped and roasted
60g coriander, chopped

Cut the foo yung rolls in half. Liberally spoon the rice mixture on to a big serving plate, arrange the foo yung rolls randomly on top, and scatter the sizzling hot shallot garnish over the fiery fried rice. Top with the green spring onion strips and plenty of peanuts and coriander, then dig in.

Chana Chaat

chana chaat spice fried cumin biscuits layered with smashed potato and chickpea salad, served with turmeric and coriander rice muffins, {VEGAN} fresh coriander dressing, tamarind glaze and coconut and lime dressing

This truly terrific triple decker has been a regular favourite on the menu at Terre à Terre since we opened. The spice combinations set it apart in the taste test: the distinctive flavours of black salt and mango powder rub shoulders agreeably with 'panch phoron' and other like-minded spicy friends, making it an explosive day out for your taste buds. Hot fried cumin crackers are loaded with pungent chana chaat spice, stacked with generous layers of mouthwateringly delicious marinated chickpeas and potatoes, dressed with chilli and coriander, and drizzled with cool coconut lime and sweet and sour tamarind. Hot, fluffy, spicy rice muffins, straight from the oven, are the finishing touch – absolutely spot on for scooping up any runaway sauces.

The chana chaat spice is our version of panch phoran, an Indian spice mix that is sometimes called Bengali five spice. Although it is usually a mixture of fenugreek, nigella, mustard, fennel and cumin seeds, blended in equal proportions, there's always room for experimentation. And, by way of explanation, 'chaat' derives from a Hindi word, meaning (among other things) 'tasting' or 'delicacy', which we rather like. It's often used for savoury snacks, especially those sold from street stalls to be consumed on the move, and particularly snacks made from fried dough. We like to chop and change with our versions, and they've always gone down extremely well! Again, you will need to visit an Asian grocery store to find some of the ingredients used here. For more on tamarind paste, see page 152.

serves 6-8

{chana chaat spice}

1 teaspoon each cumin, mustard, fenugreek, coriander and fennel seeds
1 teaspoon mango powder
½ teaspoon black salt
1 teaspoon paprika
1 small dried chilli pepper

Toast the five spices in a dry pan until they release their aroma, then grind to a fine powder with the mango powder, black salt, paprika and dried chilli. This mix will keep in an airtight container for 1 week.

{tamarind glaze}

300g caster sugar
125ml red wine vinegar
300g tamarind paste
300ml water

Put the sugar and vinegar in a stainless steel pan and heat gently, stirring to dissolve the sugar. Add the tamarind paste and water and simmer for 4–5 minutes, until the mixture becomes sticky. Leave to cool. The glaze will keep for 2 weeks in the refrigerator.

{coconut and lime dressing}

75g creamed coconut
150ml soya cream
100ml sunflower oil
125ml lime juice

Put the creamed coconut and soya cream into a blender and whiz on a medium speed. Slowly pour in the oil and lime juice alternately. You are aiming for a thin mayonnaise consistency, bearing in mind that the mixture will thicken if chilled.

{fresh coriander dressing}

50g coriander, roughly chopped
1 small green chilli pepper, deseeded and roughly chopped
¼ teaspoon cumin seeds, toasted
150ml sunflower oil
salt and freshly ground black pepper

Place the coriander, chilli and cumin in a blender or food processor and gradually blend in the sunflower oil until the mixture is smooth. Season with salt and pepper.

{chana chickpeas}

250g dried chickpeas, soaked overnight in cold water
peel of 2 limes
2 bay leaves
1 onion, peeled
1 teaspoon Chana Chaat Spice (see above)
juice of 2 limes
2 tablespoons sunflower oil
salt

Rinse the chickpeas, cover with fresh cold water and bring to the boil. Allow to boil rapidly for 10 minutes, skim off any foam, then add the lime peel, bay leaves and onion. Cover and simmer for 1-1½ hours until the chickpeas are tender, then leave to cool. Drain the chickpeas, discarding the lime peel, bay leaves and onion. Toss the chickpeas with the spice, lime juice, oil and salt, ensuring that they are well coated. Refrigerate until needed.

{chana potatoes}

4 potatoes (Desiree or other waxy variety), peeled and cut into 1cm cubes
¼ cinnamon stick
5 cardamom pods, cracked
3 tablespoons sunflower oil
juice of 2 limes
2 teaspoons Chana Chaat Spice (see above)
salt

Put the potatoes, cinnamon and cardamom into a pan with plenty of generously salted cold water and bring to the boil. Simmer until the potatoes are tender, then drain thoroughly. Mix with the sunflower oil, lime

(Continued on page 88)

Chana Chaat

(Continued from page 86)

juice and chana chaat spice. Spread out on a tray to cool and soak up all the flavours.

{chana chickpea and potato mix}

Chana Chickpeas (see page 86)
2 tablespoons lime juice
1 tablespoon Chana Chaat Spice (see page 86)
3 tablespoons sunflower oil
15g mint, shredded
25g coriander, shredded
Chana Potatoes (see above)
salt and freshly ground black pepper

In a bowl, roughly crush the marinated chickpeas, then mix in the rest of the ingredients, checking the seasoning. Do not worry if the potatoes break up a little, as this gives a lovely texture.

{turmeric and coriander rice muffins}

300g basmati rice, soaked in cold water
  for at least 2 hours
soya margarine for coating
plain flour or fine semolina for dusting
280ml tepid water
½ teaspoon sugar
2 teaspoons dried yeast
½ teaspoon turmeric
¼ teaspoon salt
a small pinch of asafoetida
a small pinch of fenugreek
½ teaspoon black mustard seeds
¼ teaspoon fennel seeds
¼ teaspoon coriander seeds

Generously coat eight 100ml ramekins or dariole moulds with soya margarine, then dust them with flour or semolina, tapping them to shake off any excess.

Mix the water with the sugar and yeast and set aside for 10–15 minutes, until frothy. Drain the rice and place in a blender, then add the yeast mixture, turmeric, salt, asafoetida and fenugreek and blend on high speed.

Meanwhile, place a small pan over the heat and add the mustard, fennel and coriander seeds. When they start to crackle, add to the blender and continue blending for 4–5 minutes, until the mixture is smooth.

Pour the mixture into the moulds and leave at room temperature for 15–20 minutes until it starts to puff up. Place the moulds in a fairly deep roasting tin and fill the tin with enough boiling water to come half way up the sides of the moulds. Bake in the oven at 180°C/Gas Mark 4 for 20–30 minutes, until firm to the touch. A skewer inserted in the centre should come out clean.

{cumin biscuits}

150g plain flour
75g gram flour
½ teaspoon cumin seeds, toasted and
  ground
2 pinches of salt
75ml water
40g soya margarine, melted
sunflower oil for deep frying
Chana Chaat Spice (see above)

Put the flours, ground cumin and salt in a mixing bowl and gradually add the water, stirring well. When you have a smooth paste, add the melted soya margarine and work to a soft, silky dough. Wrap the dough in clingfilm and chill for at least 30 minutes.

Remove the dough from the refrigerator and roll out on a lightly floured surface to just 1mm thick. Prick all over with a fork and cut out rounds with a 7cm cutter. Chill for another 30 minutes.

Heat the oil to 170°C in a deep fryer or deep pan (if you don't have a thermometer, drop a small piece of bread into the oil; if it goes golden brown within a minute, the oil is hot enough). Fry the biscuits until golden brown, then drain on paper towels. Sprinkle with the chana spice and a little salt while they are still hot.

{to assemble}

2 limes, sliced into thick wedges

Make triple-decker spicy sandwiches by placing a cumin biscuit on each plate, then topping with some chana chickpea and potato mix, then spoonfuls of the coconut and coriander dressings. Top with another cumin biscuit, repeat the layers of chickpea and potato mix and dressings and add a third cumin biscuit.

Pour some coconut dressing around each plate and add a hot rice muffin. Tip a little tamarind glaze over the top of the muffin and spoon some more on the plate. Finally, dust the plate with a sprinkling of chana chaat spice and serve with lime wedges.

This is how we serve this in the restaurant but it is a pretty versatile dish so, if you don't have the time or inclination to fiddle around too much, you could present it more simply. It's great served in a rough and ready style. Just load the potato and chickpea mix into the centre of a serving plate, scatter with torn mint and coriander leaves and use the dressings as dips, serving the biscuits and muffins warmed and sprinkled with chana chaat spice – never too posh to party!

Better Batter

buttermilk soaked halloumi in crispy chip shop batter, topped with lemony yemeni relish, served with minty mushy peas, vodka spiked grape tomatoes, pickled quail's eggs and sea salad tartare sauce

This is one we were thinking about keeping under wraps, but we decided to be grown up and share! It's one of the most successful and best loved dishes we've ever had on our menu, and its success is chiefly due to our lovely, gifted head chef, Dino, who ran with the idea and nurtured it to fruition. We have a lot to thank him for.

This is a rather fitting tribute to the 'kiss me quick' kitsch Brighton seaside, although there's nothing fishy here! Only hot, light batter encasing soft, fleshy halloumi, with the fiery, zesty fresh foil of lemony Yemeni pickle, terrific and tart, with a smudge of comforting, familiar minty mushy peas, followed by the most 'adult' tomatoes you could hope for. Do they still count as one of your five a day if drenched in spirits? Then delicate, cooked-to-perfection quail's eggs and accompanying sea salad tartare sauce, a celebration of piquant, salty, straight-from-the-sea tastes. You begin to think you know where you are until a new flavour pairing throws you off course. Best just to go with the ebb and flow....

Nori is Japanese edible seaweed, prepared in thin, dried sheets. It is used to wrap sushi, and for flavouring and garnishing. The taste is distinctive, with an instantly recognizable sea saltiness. Rich in calcium and iron, too, and with a high vitamin content, nori is almost too good to be true! Before using the sheets, it's usually best to toast briefly over a naked flame, to bring out their full flavour. We use them in several recipes in this book, and here their flavour ties in beautifully with the ersatz fish and chips theme. Nori is available in Asian supermarkets.

serves 6

{pickled quail's eggs}

24 quail's eggs
500ml malt vinegar
500ml cider vinegar
30g sea salt
2 teaspoons caster sugar
3 chilli peppers
6 garlic cloves
1 teaspoon white peppercorns
4 bay leaves
4 blades of mace

These eggs must be prepared 2 weeks in advance. Place the eggs carefully in a pan, cover with cold water and bring to the boil. Instantly put the lid on the pan, turn off the heat and leave for 4 minutes. Transfer immediately to ice cold water, to halt cooking, and leave for 15–20 minutes. Drain again and place in a bowl. Cover completely with the malt vinegar (this may be an old wives' tale, but we find it makes them easier to peel). Leave for 2 hours. Meanwhile, bring all other ingredients to the boil and simmer for 5 minutes. Remove from the heat, cover and leave for 2 hours, then strain.

Drain the eggs and peel them, taking care to remove the membrane between the white and the shell. Sterilize two 250ml jars. Put the peeled eggs into the jars, topping up with the strained pickling mix. Screw on the lids tightly and place the jars in a cool, dark place. The eggs will be ready in 2 weeks, but will keep for at least 6 months (although once opened, they must be refrigerated and eaten within 1 week).

{yemen paste}

230g hot red chilli peppers, chopped
5 garlic cloves
¼ tablespoon black peppercorns
½ teaspoon coriander seeds

65g coriander leaves and stalks
½ teaspoon salt
150ml olive oil, plus extra for topping up

Liquidize all the ingredients together in a jug blender until they form a paste. Topped up with more oil to cover it completely, the paste will keep in the refrigerator for at least 1 month.

{lemony yemeni pickle}

3 lemons, peel and white pith removed, flesh cut into segments
100ml lemon
juice peel from 3 preserved lemons
150g caster sugar about
½ teaspoon Yemen Paste (see above)

Blend the lemon flesh, juice and peel together at high speed in a blender or food processor, then put this in a small pan with the sugar and heat gently, stirring to dissolve the sugar. Boil rapidly for 2 minutes. Now stir in the Yemen paste according to your taste (it's not for the faint hearted!). Leave to cool.

{sea salad tartare sauce}

1 nori sheet (dried seaweed)
40g parsley
100g capers, rinsed
100g gherkins, rinsed
100g Thai pink shallots
about 150ml Mayonnaise (see page 18)

Hold the nori sheet briefly over a flame to heat both sides, for no more than 2 seconds or it will burn. Finely chop the nori, parsley, capers, gherkins and shallots. Mix in enough mayonnaise to bind them all together, but not so much

(Continued on page 91)

Better Batter

(Continued from page 89)

that you can't see the lovely pink of the shallots. Keep the sauce refrigerated.

{vodka grape tomatoes}

400g grape tomatoes
1 star anise
¼ teaspoon caraway seeds
250ml white wine vinegar
40g caster sugar
250ml vodka

Prick each tomato twice with a cocktail stick. Put the spices, vinegar and sugar in a pan and simmer for 10 minutes, ensuring the sugar has dissolved. Pour this liquid over the tomatoes, add the vodka and stir well. Once cool, the vodka tomatoes can be stored in a covered container in the refrigerator for 2 weeks.

{chip shop batter}

150g plain flour
75g self raising flour
10ml white wine vinegar
240ml cold water
½ teaspoon baking powder
salt and freshly ground black pepper

Whisk all the ingredients together to create a batter with the consistency of double cream. Keep refrigerated until you are ready to coat and fry the halloumi.

{buttermilk soaked halloumi}

500g halloumi cheese (2 packs of 250g)
500ml buttermilk (or 250ml yogurt mixed
    with 250ml milk)
plain flour for coating
sunflower oil for deep frying

Carefully cut the halloumi into thin triangles (see picture). Submerge the cheese in the buttermilk and leave to soak in the refrigerator for several hours, preferably overnight. This really adds to the flavour and texture of the cheese.

Just before serving, drain the halloumi, dip in a little plain flour, then coat well in the batter. Heat the oil to 180°C in a deep fryer or deep pan (if you don't have a thermometer, drop a small piece of bread into the oil: if it turns golden brown within a minute, the oil is hot enough). Fry the battered halloumi, 2 pieces at a time, until crisp and golden brown. Drain on paper towels.

{minty mushy peas}

400g fresh or frozen peas
40g mint, leaves and stalks separated,
    leaves chopped
40g parsley, leaves and stalks separated,
    leaves chopped
50g unsalted butter
salt and freshly ground black pepper

In a pan of boiling salted water, cook the peas with the herb stalks until tender. Drain well, discarding the stalks. Blend the peas with the butter and herbs, then season to taste.

{to assemble}

1 lemon, peel and white pith removed,
    flesh cut into segments
2 tablespoons chopped mint
25g fresh pea shoots

Add the lemon segments and mint to the Yemeni pickle. Heat the mushy peas in a small pan. In another pan, gently warm the vodka tomatoes.

Now arrange the plates as artistically as you like. Divide the halloumi between the plates and add a spoonful of the pickle and a heap of the mushy peas, topped with a couple of vodka tomatoes. Finish with a dollop of sea salad tartare sauce, and garnish with fresh pea shoots and a quail's egg or two.

No Cocky Big Leeky

leek, sage, caerphilly and wensleydale sausages with celeriac and potato mash, cinnamon merlot onions, celeriac straw and rich gravy

This is a great dish, beautiful big bangers and mash; hearty, happy food that, as with all great traditions, warms the soul and satisfies the carnivore or campfire mentality in us all (or maybe the camp carnivore?). Crunchy coated sizzling sausages are the starting point – loaded with leeks, crumbly cheese and mustardy mouthfuls of garden fresh parsley and sage. We match them with plush potato and celeriac mash, heaps of soft, cinnamon-sweet onions lush with red wine, crunchy celeriac straws bundled on top and robust gravy with real depth of flavour. It's almost enough to make me get the tent out of the attic and build a campfire in the garden….

With their mild, oniony flavour and great texture, leeks are a perfect filler for sausages. Given their Welsh connections, it seems entirely appropriate that they should be mixed with Caerphilly, a hard, white Welsh cheese that combines well with English Wensleydale – originally made by French monks who settled in north Yorkshire. We use white Wensleydale here, but the blue variety would work just as well. And, yes, the name of this dish is a play on a rather meaty Scottish soup: we've taken the leek element and added cheese sausages to make this wholly satisfying main course.

serves 6

{rich gravy}

1 litre Demi Glace Sauce (see page 18)
500ml ripe, fruity red wine (Merlot is ideal)
salt and freshly ground black pepper
2 teaspoons redcurrant jelly

Put the demi glace sauce and wine in a large pan, bring to a simmer and leave over a low heat until reduced in volume by a third. Taste and season with salt and pepper, then stir in the redcurrant jelly. Leave to cool, strain through a fine sieve and keep in the refrigerator until required.

{cinnamon merlot onions}

1 tablespoon olive oil
250g red onions, finely sliced
½ cinnamon stick (or a good pinch of ground cinnamon)
2 allspice berries, crushed
3 black peppercorns, crushed
1 bay leaf
150ml ripe, fruity red wine (again, Merlot is ideal)
75ml White Stock (see page 18) or water
½ teaspoon soft light brown sugar
2 tablespoons balsamic vinegar
salt

Heat the oil in a saucepan, add the onions, cinnamon, allspice, black pepper and bay leaf and fry lightly. Pour in the wine and stock or water, cover and cook over a medium heat for 35 minutes, stirring regularly so the mixture does not stick to the bottom of the pan.

Remove the lid and add the sugar, vinegar and salt to taste. Cook for a further 15 minutes, or until the onions are sweet, soft and sticky. Be careful not to overcook or they will become jammy. They will keep for 1 week in a sealed container in the refrigerator.

{leek, sage and two cheese sausages}

250g fresh white breadcrumbs
250g Caerphilly cheese, grated
250g Wensleydale cheese, grated
150g leeks (white part only), finely chopped
2 teaspoons finely chopped sage
20g curly leaf parsley, finely chopped
2 teaspoons finely chopped thyme
salt and freshly ground black pepper
2 eggs
2 tablespoons coarse grain mustard (or Dijon mustard)
sunflower oil for deep frying

for the coating
40g plain flour, seasoned
2 eggs, beaten
150g fresh white breadcrumbs, seasoned

Combine the breadcrumbs, cheeses, leeks, sage, parsley, thyme and plenty of salt and pepper. Beat the eggs with the mustard and add this to the cheese and breadcrumb mix. Bind together thoroughly. Divide the mixture into 6 balls and roll each into a sausage shape about 2.5cm thick. Chill for at least 1 hour for the mixture to firm up.

Put the flour into a shallow bowl, the beaten eggs into another, and the breadcrumbs into a third. One by one, coat each sausage evenly in the flour, then the egg and finally the breadcrumbs. Now return the sausages to the refrigerator for at least 30 minutes.

Just before you are ready to serve, pour sunflower oil about 4cm deep into a skillet or deep pan and place over a medium heat. Add the sausages and fry for about 5 minutes, turning, until brown and crisp all over.

{celeriac straw}

225g celeriac, peeled

85g plain flour, seasoned with salt and
    pepper
sunflower oil for deep frying

Slice the celeriac as finely as possible
and then cut into fine shreds like straws
(we use a mandolin in the restaurant but
a sharp knife and a steady hand will do).
Toss these in the flour, coating them well.
To get a really crisp result, they need to
be fried just before serving, so keep the
floured shreds in the refrigerator, covered,
until required.

Just before your are ready to eat, and
using the same pan and same depth of oil
as for the sausages, add the celeriac straw
in bundles and fry until golden brown and
crisp. Drain on paper towels.

{potato and celeriac mash}

500g floury potatoes (Maris Piper is
    ideal), peeled and chopped
500g celeriac, peeled and chopped
50g unsalted butter 50ml double cream
½ tablespoon lemon juice
salt and ground white pepper
a little freshly grated nutmeg

Place the potatoes and celeriac in separate
pans of cold salted water, cover and bring
to the boil. Reduce the heat and simmer
until tender, then drain thoroughly. Return
them to their pans and put back over a
very low heat to remove any excess
moisture.

Separately mash the potato and celeriac.
Heat the butter and cream in a large
saucepan and add the potato and celeriac.
Season with the lemon juice, salt, pepper
and nutmeg, and combine everything well.

{to assemble}

Gently reheat the gravy, onions and mash.
Give everyone a sausage, a heap of mash,
a little pile of the sticky onions, lashings
of rich, red gravy and a bundle of celeriac
straw. Desperate Dan would be happy to
tuck into this!

Eely Good

salsify goujons with aubergine jelly eels, miso mashed potatoes, parsley liquor and lemon sage salt

Not exactly Bow bells, more Brighton belles, and definitely no eels. Since creating this dish, we have found that salsify, sometimes known as oyster plant, is a controversial vegetable among chefs – or, at least, the ones we know. They love it or they hate it and some have banished it entirely from their kitchens. But we are big fans and adore its mild, nutty, almost oyster-like flavour. Given that tenuous taste connection to the marine world, and our overactive imaginations, we felt that an aquatic avenue was the right one to follow.

This is what we came up with: hot, crisp-coated, fleshy salsify goujons with lemony sage salt and toasted nori, accompanied by terrific tatties enriched with savoury miso, olive oil and Dijon mustard. Just the best (sea!) bed for deep, rich, convincingly maritime mouthfuls of slippery aubergines with a herby hit, and an abundance of fresh, verdant parsley sauce.

Our lovely picture shows that this dish can be dainty and delicate, but it's equally satisfying just piled on to plates. As with all food, it's really about flavours rather than finesse, so whether you have polite or plentiful portions, just dig in and enjoy.

Salsify is harvested from the long root of the purple salsify plant, also referred to as 'goat's beard'. It can be grated raw into salads but is generally cooked, and sometimes the young shoots and flowers are also eaten. It's fallen out of favour in recent years and is more often considered an invasive garden weed than a useful vegetable.

Wakame is a highly nutritious seaweed, rich in protein, calcium and iron. Traditionally produced in Japan and Korea, it is now farmed in Brittany too. Soaking it before use will remove much of the saltiness – but if it's a taste of the sea you're after, wakame is hard to beat.

serves 6

{aubergine eels}

5g wakame (dried seaweed), chopped or crumbled
½ teaspoon sea salt
¼ teaspoon freshly ground black pepper
2 tablespoons nori flakes (dried seaweed)
¼ teaspoon fennel seeds
¼ teaspoon coriander seeds
400g aubergine, cut into fine shoelace strips
100g white onions, sliced
2 tablespoons olive oil
1 teaspoon lemon juice
1 tablespoon chopped tarragon
1 tablespoon chopped dill or fennel fronds
2 tablespoons chopped curly leaf parsley

for the jelly stock
5g kombu (dried seaweed)
100ml dry white wine
500ml White Stock (see page 18) or water
100g white onions, finely chopped
1 bay leaf
2 tablespoons porridge oats
3 teaspoons mirin (sweet rice wine)
1 teaspoon brown rice vinegar
2 tablespoons agar agar

Roast the wakame in the oven at 180°C/Gas Mark 4 for about 10 minutes or until it feels brittle. In a food processor or pestle and mortar, grind it with the salt, pepper, nori, fennel and coriander seeds. Toss this mixture with the aubergine strips, onions and olive oil. Spread out evenly on a baking tray, cover with foil and bake at 180°C/Gas Mark 4 for 40 minutes or until the aubergine is soft. Remove from the oven and leave to cool. Add the lemon juice and herbs, then set aside.

To make the jelly stock, soak the kombu in 100ml cool water for 15 minutes, until soft. Remove it from the bowl, chop roughly, then return it to the water.

Put the wine, stock or water, onions and bay leaf in a pan, add the kombu and its soaking water and bring to the boil. Simmer for 20 minutes, then strain the liquid into a clean pan, but keep the seaweed and onion mix to one side to reintroduce later. Add the oats to the strained liquid, bring slowly to a simmer and let it bubble for 5 minutes or until the liquid begins to thicken. Strain again, discarding the oats. Return the seaweed and onion mix to the thickened liquid and leave to cool, then add the mirin and rice vinegar and check the seasoning. Sprinkle the agar agar evenly over the top, bring to a simmer and cook for 5 minutes, stirring occasionally.

Line 6 dariole moulds with clingfilm and loosely fill them with a layer of the cooked aubergine. Top up with the warm seaweed and onion mix and put aside to set. These 'jellied eels' can be kept in the refrigerator, but bring them back to room temperature before serving.

{lemon sage salt}

4 tablespoons finely chopped sage
30g sea salt
1 tablespoon chopped lemon zest

Combine the sage, salt and lemon zest by bashing them in a pestle and mortar or in a sturdy bowl with a rolling pin – or, if you're feeling genteel, use a blender. If you prefer a dryer salt, first spread the mixture evenly on a baking tray and dry it overnight in an oven set on the lowest heat, then grind as above.

(Continued on page 96)

Eely Good

(Continued from page 94)

This makes far more than you need for this recipe, so keep it in an airtightcontainer and use it to liven up a multitude of dishes.

{parsley liquor}

100ml olive oil
700g white onions, finely chopped
30g garlic, finely chopped
500ml dry white wine
500ml White Stock (see page 18) or water
2 bay leaves
600g curly leaf parsley
salt and ground white pepper
50ml soya cream

Heat the olive oil in a heavy based pan, add the onions and garlic and cook slowly until they are opaque and sweet tasting. Add the wine, stock or water, bay leaves and 300g of the parsley. Bring to the boil and simmer until the liquid has reduced by a third. Put the mixture into a blender and blend on high speed for 5 minutes or until the sauce is smooth and creamy. Strain through a fine sieve, carefully pushing on the vegetables and herbs to extract all the flavour, then set aside.

Blanch 150g of the remaining parsley in a large pan of boiling salted water for 2 minutes, then drain, refresh in ice cold water and drain again. Squeeze out the excess water in paper towels or a clean cloth. Purée the parsley in a blender or food processor and set aside.

Finish the sauce shortly before serving: reheat it without letting it boil, then stir in the soya cream, followed by the parsley purée. Finely chop the remaining parsley, load it into the pan and stir well.

{salsify goujons}

5 large salsify (about 300g)
3 tablespoons lemon juice
250g silken tofu
a little soya milk (optional)
130g panko (Japanese dry breadcrumbs) – or use any fine dry white breadcrumbs
2 tablespoons nori flakes (dried seaweed)
1 teaspoon Lemon Sage Salt (see page 94)
35g rice flour
sunflower oil for deep frying

Peel the salsify, slice it widthways into barrels 5–6 cm long, then cut these in half lengthways. Blanch in boiling, salted water with the lemon juice to keep them white. Stop cooking the salsify before it gets too soft and lift it out to cool and dry on paper towels.

Purée the tofu in a blender or food processor until smooth, adding a little soya milk if it is too thick. Mix the panko crumbs with the nori and the lemon sage salt and place in a tray. Put the tofu in a second tray and the rice flour in a third. Now coat the salsify sticks by dipping and rolling them in the rice flour, then the tofu and finally the panko, making sure they are well covered at each stage. Place these goujons on a lined baking tray and keep in the refrigerator until you are ready to fry them.

Shortly before you are ready to eat, heat the oil to 170°C in a deep fryer or deep pan (if you don't have a thermometer, drop a small piece of bread into the oil; if it goes golden brown within a minute, the oil is hot enough). Lower the goujons into the oil and cook, turning once or twice, for about 3 minutes, until crisp and golden. Drain on paper towels.

{miso mashed potatoes}

1kg potatoes (preferably Maris Piper), peeled and chopped
25ml olive oil
2 tablespoons white miso (soy paste)
100ml soya cream
a good pinch of ground mace
2 teaspoons Dijon mustard
salt and freshly ground black pepper

Put the potatoes in a large pan of cold salted water and bring to the boil. Simmer until soft, then drain. They need to be completely dry, so either leave them to stand in the colander for a while or put them back into the pan to dry out over a low heat. In a separate pan, warm the olive oil, miso, soya cream, mace and mustard. Mash the potatoes, then add the warm cream mix. Combine well and season to taste.

{to assemble}

6 sprigs of curly leaf parsley
2 lemons, sliced into generous wedges

Gently reheat the miso mash if necessary. If the jellied eels have been in the refrigerator, you may want to steam them for just 1 minute to take off the chill.

Heap the miso mash on to 6 warmed plates and turn out a jellied eel pot on top of each mound. Flood the plates with the emerald sauce and rest the goujons on the potato, garnishing finally with a lemon wedge and a very English sprig of parsley. Jellied eels, but not as you know them!

Black Bean Cellophane Frisbee

rice pancakes filled with miso potato dauphinoise, served with tempura beansprout fritters, stir fried pak choi and fino chantilly, finished with shredded red peppers and tamari and lime glazed black beans

{WHEAT FREE}

There is real strength of flavour running through this dish, so if you feel like eating something potent and perky, this little pile is the one for you. Over the years we've called this dish 'the boomerang', for its tendency to keep returning to the menu by popular demand. If we can tempt you to make it, we're sure you'll understand why.

Plush layers of savoury, creamy miso potatoes wrapped in crisp cellophane rice papers are the main event, served with swiftly stir fried pak choi, lush and leafy, with the fresh taste of lemon and the prickly heat of ginger to give it a zap. What an ideal match for tempura beansprout fritters, a tasty tangle of bites zipping between tingling warm Szechuan pepper. These are delicious on their own, but heap them up with bright, piquant pepper slivers, faintly boozy fluffy cream, and a drizzle of the darkly delicious and potent tamari and lime glazed black beans and you will find that all together they elevate the dish to another flavour level.

Here we use both mirin and shao hsing rice wine. Mirin, a Japanese rice wine, characteristically contains very little alcohol but up to 50 per cent sugar, and therefore adds a mild, sweet taste to food. Shao hsing rice wine is most often used for seasoning and flavouring Chinese dishes and is often referred to as Chinese rice wine. Both are used sparingly but frequently in their national dishes, and you can find them here, together with preserved black beans, in Asian food stores.

serves 6

{miso dauphinoise}

1.5kg medium sized potatoes (preferably Maris Piper), peeled and sliced into 1–2mm thickness
450ml double cream
75g white miso (soy paste)
salt and freshly ground black pepper

Line a deep (6cm) baking tray with baking parchment and layer the potato slices in it. Now mix together the cream and miso paste, add seasoning to taste, and pour this over the potatoes. Press down on the potatoes with a heavy tray to make sure the miso cream is evenly distributed and to compress the layers. Leave to rest for 10 minutes and then press down again.

Cover the tray with foil and bake in the oven at 180°C/Gas Mark 4 for about 45 minutes, or until the potatoes are soft. Remove the foil and cook for a further 10 minutes, until the top is golden. Once the potatoes have cooled down, refrigerate before using to make the Cellophane Frisbees (see below).

{shredded red peppers}

100ml shao hsing rice wine (or other good quality rice wine)
1 tablespoon caster sugar
10 coriander seeds, cracked
1 small dried chilli pepper
200g red peppers, deseeded and cut into strips

Put the rice wine, sugar, coriander seeds and whole chilli in a stainless steel pan and bring to the boil. Remove from the heat and pour over the pepper strips. Allow them to cool in the liquid and drain them just before use, removing the chilli.

{tamari and lime glazed black beans}

100ml tamari (gluten free soy sauce)
2 tablespoons caster sugar
juice of 2 limes
30 preserved black beans

Place the tamari, sugar and lime juice in a pan and bring to the boil. Simmer until reduced by about half, forming a light syrup (it should be thick enough to coat the back of a spoon). Now add the black beans, combine well with the glaze, remove from the heat and allow to cool. The beans should be served at room temperature.

{fino chantilly}

75ml double cream
1 tablespoon medium dry sherry
1 teaspoon mirin (sweet rice wine)
a pinch of salt

Whisk the cream with all the remaining ingredients until it forms soft peaks. Refrigerate until required.

{cellophane frisbees}

12 round rice paper pancakes or spring roll wrappers (about 15cm diameter)
Miso Dauphinoise (see above)
a little cornflour mixed to a thin paste with water (optional)
about 500ml White Stock (see page 18) or water

Cut 6 rounds out of the chilled miso dauphinoise with an 8cm round biscuit cutter. Dip a pancake into a bowl of hot water until it is semi soft, then gently drain it and lay it out flat. Place a round of the dauphinoise in the middle of the

(Continued on page 99)

Black Bean Cellophane Frisbee

(Continued from page 97)

pancake. Then soak a second pancake, drain it and place it over the top. Now take a slightly larger cutter, turn it over and use the blunt edge to press down on the frisbee, sealing the 2 pancakes together. Make sure you don't cut right through, just seal the edges together and, if they seem reluctant, brush the inside edges with a little cornflour mixed with water to help them join. Repeat with the remaining pancakes and dauphinoise.

Shortly before serving, pour a shallow layer of stock or water into a baking tray and lay the frisbees in it. Only their bases should be moist: their tops must remain dry, so they can brown and crisp slightly. Cook in the oven at 180°C/Gas Mark 4 for 10–12 minutes.

{tempura beansprout fritters}

75g rice flour
25g cornflour
1 teaspoon gluten free baking powder
120ml iced sparkling water
salt and freshly ground black pepper
150g beansprouts
15g shiso shoots
15g daikon shoots
25g coriander, roughly chopped
30 preserved black beans
7 Szechuan peppercorns, cracked
sunflower oil for deep frying

Mix together the rice flour, cornflour, baking powder and water until smooth and creamy. Season with a good pinch of salt and pepper. Add all the remaining ingredients to the batter and combine well. You are now ready to start frying. Heat the oil to 175°C in a deep fryer or deep pan (if you don't have a thermometer, drop a small piece of bread into the oil; if it goes golden brown within a minute, the oil is hot enough). Carefully place dessertspoons of the batter into the oil and cook for 4–5 minutes, until crisp. To get them really crisp, it is important the fritters are not too large or thick. Drain on paper towels and serve immediately.

{stir fried pak choi}

1 tablespoon sunflower oil
25g fresh root ginger, finely chopped
500g oriental leaves (preferably baby pak choi or tot soi), cut into quarters lengthways
juice of 1 lemon
1 teaspoon toasted sesame oil

Heat the sunflower oil in a frying pan or wok and throw in the ginger, closely followed by the leaves. Cook for no longer than 1 minute. Add the lemon juice, cover for about 20 seconds, then pour over the sesame oil and it's ready to serve.

{to assemble}

2 tablespoons shiso shoots

Lay the warm pak choi on each plate, then top with a frisbee and garnish with a few strips of red pepper and some shiso shoots. Add a beansprout fritter, a spoonful of the chilled fino chantilly and a drizzle of the glazed black beans.

Potstickers

{VEGAN}

potstickers in chilli frilly skirts with purple sprouting szechuan stir fry, edamame pesto and dipping sauce

Never mind the 'dim sum', these pot stickers really 'go sum'! And believe me, they go down an absolute storm. Once you've mastered the art, you will be hounded to make them often. Our version is absolutely delicious: crisp on one side, mallowy soft on the other, and stuffed full of gingery, savoury tastes, meaty with mushroom and sticky with squash, all surrounded by doughy chilli frilly skirts and deliciously rich, dark dipping sauce. What's more, they have the ideal accompaniment of succulent spears of broccoli, fragrant with Chinese chives and Szechuan spice, all perfect for smudging into a smooth edamame pesto with a zingy nip.

Potstickers have been around for many hundreds of years. They are savoury dumplings with a crimped edge that are fried on one side and steamed on the other, then served with a dipping sauce. We have enjoyed a little 'primping up' of ours, with the addition of a delightful frilly skirt, some beautiful marigolds and a surprise hit of chilli. Purple sprouting broccoli is such a simple and colourful vegetable to serve. Quick to stir fry, steam or boil, it was originally cultivated by the Romans and is packed with many health-giving benefits, including high levels of vitamin C and calcium.

serves 6

{edamame pesto}

200g edamame beans, peeled (soya mangetout) - frozen are fine
40g cashew nuts
20g basil leaves
150ml grapeseed oil
1 teaspoon wasabi paste (Japanese horseradish)
100ml warm water
I tablespoon yuzu juice (Japanese citrus fruit) – or use lime juice
salt

Put all the ingredients in a food processor or blender and blitz to a smooth, bright green pesto. Cover and store in the refrigerator, where it will keep for few days.

{dipping sauce}

75ml Chinese black rice vinegar (or other good quality rice vinegar)
50ml shoyu (or other good quality soy sauce)
1 teaspoon toasted sesame oil (or 1 teaspoon hot chilli oil, if preferred)
1 tablespoon mirin (sweet rice wine)
1 tablespoon water

Mix all the ingredients together. Serve in small, shallow dipping bowls.

{potsticker filling}

2 large cabbage leaves, stalks removed, diced
¼ teaspoon salt
2 tablespoons sunflower oil
1 garlic clove, chopped
4 tablespoons grated fresh root ginger
75g butternut squash, peeled and grated
50g shiitake mushrooms, finely diced
50g oyster mushrooms, finely diced
75g smoked tofu, grated
50g spring onions, chopped

Sprinkle the cabbage with the salt and leave to drain in a colander for 30 minutes.

Heat the oil in a pan, add the garlic and ginger and fry until they start to colour. Add the butternut squash and cook for 3 minutes, then stir in the mushrooms and cook for 3 minutes longer.

Toss in the tofu, cook for 3 minutes, then stir in the spring onions and remove from the heat. Tip the mixture into a bowl to cool. After 20 minutes, stir in the cabbage and mix well. Cover and refrigerate until required.

{potstickers in chilly frilly skirts}

300g dumpling flour (or '00' pasta flour)
½ teaspoon salt
200ml warm water Potsticker Filling (see above)
sunflower oil

for frying for the frilly skirts
50g dumpling flour (or '00' pasta flour)
150ml water
8 chives or fennel fronds, finely chopped
1 small red chilli pepper, deseeded and finely chopped
petals of 2 marigolds
salt

Sift the flour and salt into a bowl, add the water and work the mixture to a smooth dough. Leave to rest for 30 minutes, then roll out to 2mm thick. Using a 10cm biscuit cutter, cut out 12 rounds. Place a tablespoon of the filling in the centre of 6 rounds, taking care not to overload them. Wet the edges with cold water and place the remaining rounds of dough on top. Wet your fingers and press down to crimp the edges and make a good seal. Place the potstickers on a clean tea towel to await cooking.

For the frilly skirts, whisk the flour and water together to make a smooth paste, then mix in all the other ingredients.

To cook the potstickers and their skirts, heat a little sunflower oil over a medium heat in an 18cm non-stick frying pan that has a tight fitting lid. Place a potsticker in the pan and fry until it starts to brown underneath. Turn the heat to low, add 50ml water to the pan, cover with the lid and let it steam for about 6 minutes, until all the water has gone.

Remove the lid and add 2 tablespoons of the frilly skirt mix. Tilt the pan so the mixture forms a very thin skirt around the dumpling, then turn the heat back up to medium and cook until it has formed a crisp, lace-like skirt. Transfer the potsticker to a baking sheet, cover with foil and keep warm in a low oven while you cook the rest in the same way.

{purple sprouting szechuan stir fry}

250g edamame beans (soya mangetout) – frozen are fine
2 tablespoons sunflower oil
1 garlic clove, crushed
2 teaspoons sesame seeds
1 teaspoon Szechuan peppercorns, cracked
800g purple sprouting broccoli
4 tablespoons water
4 tablespoons light shoyu (or other good quality light soy sauce)
petals of 2 marigolds
10 chives (ideally Chinese chives), finely chopped

Boil the edamame beans in salted water for 10 minutes, then drain and refresh under cold running water. Squeeze them from their pods. This can be done in advance, but the stir fry needs to be cooked just before serving.

Heat the oil in a large wok, add the garlic and sesame seeds and stir fry over a high heat until they start to colour. Stir in the Szechuan pepper, throw in the broccoli and keep stirring for 5–8 minutes, until the broccoli is just tender. Add the edamame beans and the water and cook

until the water has evaporated. Now add the shoyu, marigold petals and chives and stir well.

{to assemble}

a few marigold petals
1 teaspoon chopped chives

Put a potsticker on each plate, crisp side up, and sprinkle it with a few marigold petals and chopped chives. Spread a little edamame pesto on to each plate and heap some of the steaming stir fry next to it, with a saucer of dipping sauce on the side.

Bengal Babs

tandoori tikka halloumi kebabs with smoked almond custard, saffron and cardamom
{WHEAT FREE}   risotto, podi spice tomatoes, crazy onion salad and tamarind glaze

Scotch Eggs

sage and chive scotch eggs with piccalilli potato salad and watercress and parsley tangle

A cracking classic, but without the crackling, this is a tasty twist on a big British favourite. Zingy mustard and parsley, chives and sage lend the sizzling, light crust a super-savoury edge – a familiar flavour that is a little like a traditional stuffing. The eggs within are most deliciously soft and hot, but hard boil them for authenticity if you prefer.

Scotch eggs summon up memories of country pubs or dodgy service stations. We prefer to settle on the pub option because along with it come ploughman's lunches, pickles and beer gardens. This brings us neatly to the next scrumptious bit of the dish: potato salad, piquant with piccalilli and lush with crème fraîche. Along with heaps of robust, peppery watercress, it all makes a mighty pretty, pukka plateful. Now, who's for a game of darts?

Although traditionally served with ploughman's lunches, piccalilli is a versatile relish that will add a zip to all sorts of simple fare. There are regional variations but it is always bright yellow from the mustard and turmeric seasoning it contains, with a tangy, mildly sweet flavour that offsets savoury dishes well.

serves 6

{piccalilli}

125g butternut squash, peeled
125g button onions, peeled
400g cauliflower
125g carrots, peeled
75g French beans
200g sea salt
150ml cider vinegar
20g caster sugar
2 bay leaves
50g rice flour
1 tablespoon mustard powder
1 teaspoon curry powder
½ teaspoon ground turmeric
50ml water
1 teaspoon coriander seeds, cracked
1 teaspoon mustard seeds, cracked
25ml sunflower oil
2 teaspoons grated fresh root ginger
1 teaspoon crushed garlic
25g coriander, leaves and stalks chopped
    separately
12 small gherkins, rinsed and halved
salt and freshly ground black pepper

Have ready two 500g jars. Cut all the vegetables into uniform 2cm pieces. Place them in a colander over a large bowl or the sink, sprinkle over the sea salt and leave overnight. The next day, rinse and drain the vegetables.

Put the vinegar and sugar in a saucepan with the bay leaves and bring to the boil. Sift the rice flour with the mustard and curry powders and the turmeric, add the water and mix to a smooth paste. Whisk this into the boiling vinegar mixture and return to the boil. Reduce the heat and simmer for 20 minutes, stirring occasionally.

Fry the coriander and mustard seeds in a large, dry pan until they release their aroma, then add the sunflower oil, followed by the ginger, garlic and chopped coriander stalks. Add the salted vegetables and cook, stirring gently, for 5–10 minutes, until they have cooked through but still have a nice crunch. Pour the pickling liquid over the vegetables, bring back to the boil, then remove from the heat and add the chopped coriander leaves and the gherkins. Taste and season, spoon into warm sterilized jars while still hot, and seal. This piquant mixture is best left to mature for a few weeks before use.

{sage and chive scotch eggs}

6 eggs, at room temperature
salt and freshly ground black pepper
75g panko (Japanese dry breadcrumbs) –
    or use any fine dry white breadcrumbs
1½ tablespoons finely chopped sage
2 tablespoons finely chopped curly leaf
    parsley
1½ tablespoons finely chopped chives
50g Parmesan, freshly
grated grated zest of 1 lemon
1 tablespoon mustard powder
50g rice flour
150g silken tofu
sunflower oil for deep frying

Place the eggs in a pan of cold water and bring to the boil. Boil for 3 minutes, then remove from the heat and cool under cold running water. Peel and season with salt and pepper.

Mix the panko crumbs with the herbs, Parmesan, lemon zest, half the mustard powder and some seasoning. Mix the rice flour with the remaining mustard powder and season with salt and pepper. Blend the tofu until smooth, pour into a bowl and season well.

(Continued on page 106)

Scotch Eggs

(Continued from page 105)

Roll the eggs one at a time in the seasoned rice flour, then in the tofu and finally the panko mix, cupping the eggs firmly and patting the crumbs on securely. Chill until ready to cook them.

Shortly before serving, heat the oil to 180°C in a deep fryer or deep pan (if you don't have a thermometer, drop a small piece of bread into the oil; if it goes golden brown within a minute, the oil is hot enough). Fry the eggs for about 2 minutes until nut brown and crisp, then drain on paper towels.

{pickled lily pots salad}

1kg salad potatoes (ideally Pink Fir Apple)
500g fresh or frozen peas
500g Piccalilli (see page 105) – or use
  shop-bought (not nearly as delicious)
20ml water
50ml grapeseed oil
50ml crème fraîche
1 tablespoon chopped curly leaf parsley
1 tablespoon finely chopped chives
salt and freshly ground black pepper

Cook the potatoes in boiling water, or steam, until tender. Skin them while still warm, if you want to, then cut into bite-sized pieces. Cook the peas in a separate pan of boiling water, then drain.

Tip the piccalilli into a coarse sieve or a steamer basket set over a bowl and pour the water over it, stirring gently so the liquid drains off into the bowl. Whisk the oil and crème fraîche into this lovely juice, then add the potatoes, peas, the piccalilli vegetables and the fresh herbs. Combine thoroughly and season to taste. This is most delicious served at room temperature and makes more than enough for 6.

{to assemble}

2 lemons, cut into large wedges
150g watercress, trimmed
20g flat leaf parsley, stems removed

This dish is great for communal eating so get 3 big platters, one loaded with the pickled lily pots salad, one piled high with sizzling Scotch eggs and wedges of fresh lemon, and another full of the tangle of fresh green watercress and parsley.

Elephant and Rocket Oil Twice Baked Soufflé

twice baked jerusalem artichoke soufflés wrapped in hazelnut and rosemary parchment pastry, with elephant garlic velouté and rocket oil

There are a number of reasons to wrap the soufflés in pastry and all involve indulgence. The first reason is chiefly to do with how much sauce you can get into the collar to ensure maximum ooze on first cutting through the crispy pastry (don't hold back). The second reason is that you get bonus mouthfuls of crunchy filo sheets, smothered with aromatic rosemary butter and toasty hazelnuts, enveloping the rich, earthy soufflé. All in all, quite justifiable reasons, we think!

The hazelnut is a fantastic choice of nut, both for flavour and health reasons. With a combination of oil, proteins and essential minerals and vitamins (E and B in particular), it makes a lot of sense to get your daily fix. Hazelnuts are particularly delicious toasted or roasted and make a great accompaniment to chocolate, toffee, cakes and meringues – although if you're not a fan of sweet things, you could sprinkle them over soups, salads and your five a day.

A word about elephant garlic: it is not a true garlic as it belongs to the onion family, but it has a pleasant mild, nutty flavour, with salad onion and garlic backgrounds, and we rather like the description of it as an over-extended leek with garlic tendencies! It's a great co-star for the rocket, as it will not overwhelm the rocket's rich peppery taste. Again, use extra virgin olive oil for an authentic flavour.

serves 6

{rocket oil}

200g rocket
150ml grapeseed oil
100ml olive oil

This is best made at least 24 hours in advance and will keep for 1 week in a refrigerator. Blanch the rocket in a large pan of boiling salted water for 2 seconds, then drain and plunge into iced water for 10 seconds. Drain again and thoroughly wring out all the moisture in a clean, dry cloth or paper towels. Using a jug blender, blend the rocket and oils together at high speed for 30 seconds, until smooth, then transfer to an airtight container. Leave to infuse overnight.

Strain the oil through a muslin lined sieve set over a deep bowl; the base of the sieve must not touch the bottom of bowl or the mixture will not drip through. Leave it to drain for as long as it takes and then transfer to an airtight container.

{elephant garlic velouté}

125g white onions, finely chopped
125g whole garlic cloves (preferably big, fleshy elephant garlic or new season garlic)
125ml dry white wine
200ml White Stock (see page 18) or water
2 bay leaves
salt and ground white pepper
2 egg yolks
100ml double cream

Place the onions, garlic, wine, stock or water, and bay leaves in a roasting pan with a lid (or cover with foil) and bake at 180°C/Gas Mark 4 for 45 minutes or until the onions and garlic are soft. Season to taste with salt and pepper. Blend on a high speed in a blender or food processor until the mixture is thick and creamy, then strain through a sieve. This can now be refrigerated if you are making it in advance.

Just before serving, beat the egg yolks and cream together. Now, in a stainless steel pan, bring the garlic mixture to a simmer, then remove from the heat and stir in the beaten eggs and cream. Heat gently and, if the sauce is too thick, add a little water or stock. Finally, taste and check the seasoning.

{rosemary butter}

100g soft unsalted butter
1 teaspoon finely chopped rosemary

Cream the butter and rosemary together. This can be wrapped in clingfilm and stored in the refrigerator or frozen. What you do not need for this recipe can be used later, in sautés or as a garnish.

{jerusalem artichoke soufflés}

250g Jerusalem artichokes
350ml White Stock (see page 18) or water
juice of 1 lemon
35g Rosemary Butter (see above)
250ml whole milk
2 tablespoons chopped white onion
2 cloves
1 bay leaf
3 black peppercorns
a little freshly grated nutmeg
salt and freshly ground black pepper

(Continued on page 110)

Elephant and Rocket Oil Twice Baked Soufflé

(Continued from page 108)

30g unsalted butter
35g plain flour, plus extra for dusting
1 teaspoon chopped thyme
1 teaspoon chopped parsley
90g Parmesan cheese, freshly grated
3 egg yolks, beaten
4 egg whites

Peel and chop 100g of the artichokes. Put them in a small pan with the stock or water, bring to the boil and cook until soft, then mash to break down to a purée. Set aside.

Peel and grate the remaining artichokes and toss them in the lemon juice. Gently melt 15g of the rosemary butter in a frying pan and lightly sauté the artichokes until tender. Set aside.

Put the milk, onion, cloves, bay leaf, peppercorns and nutmeg in a pan, season to taste with salt, and heat gently for 10 minutes without letting the mixture simmer. Remove from the heat, cover and leave to infuse for 5 minutes. Strain into a jug or bowl, pressing down into what remains in the sieve to extract all the flavour.

Melt the butter in a clean pan and add the flour. Stir continually over a low heat until the mixture begins to look a little paler. Remove from the heat and gradually add all the warm milk, beating with a balloon whisk to make a smooth, thick, glossy sauce. Return to a low heat and cook for 5 minutes.

Prepare six 100ml ramekins by coating with the remaining 20g of rosemary butter and dusting with plain flour. In a large bowl, stir the artichoke purée into the warm sauce, then add the sautéed artichokes, thyme, parsley, Parmesan and egg yolks. Mix well.

In a dry grease-free bowl, beat the egg whites until stiff, and carefully fold them into the artichoke mixture. Season to taste with freshly ground black pepper. Divide the soufflé mixture between the prepared ramekins, stopping a little short of the top. Place these in a roasting pan filled with enough boiling water to reach half way up the side of the dishes. Bake at 180°C/Gas Mark 4 for 20–30 minutes or until risen (the soufflés should feel firm on top but still have a slight wobble).

Remove from the oven and, when cool enough to handle, gently ease the soufflés out of the ramekins and place upside down on a baking tray lined with silicone paper. Allow them to cool and then refrigerate. This can be done up to 24 hours before wrapping them.

{wrapped soufflés}

12 medium sized filo pastry sheets (or 6 large sheets)
65g Rosemary Butter, melted (see page 108)
30g ground hazelnuts
6 Jerusalem Artichoke Soufflés (see page 108)

Working swiftly to prevent the pastry sheets from drying out, place a sheet of filo on a clean, dry surface, brush lightly with melted rosemary butter and sprinkle with hazelnuts. Place a second sheet directly on top and again brush with butter. Flip the pastry sandwich over so it is buttered-side down, then fold the top edge down just past the middle of the sheets and fold the bottom edge up to overlap slightly. (If using large sheets, now cut the pastry in half vertically, so each half will wrap around one soufflé.)

Place a soufflé on the bottom edge of the wrapper and gently roll up, sealing the join with a little of the melted butter and some gentle persuasion. Repeat with the remaining soufflés and filo. Stand the wrapped soufflés upright on a baking sheet and chill them for at least 1 hour. This is vital, as it ensures that the pastry collar remains upright during cooking.

Just before serving, take the wrapped soufflés out of the refrigerator, brush with melted rosemary butter and sprinkle with the remaining hazelnuts. Bake in the oven at 180°C/Gas Mark 4 for 15 minutes, until the pastry is brown and the soufflés are hot and slightly risen.

{to assemble}

60g rocket
1 tablespoon Rocket Oil (see page 108), plus extra for splashing
½ teaspoon lemon juice
pinch of salt

Place a hot soufflé in the centre of each warmed plate and spoon some of the velouté inside the protruding filo collars. Now spoon more of the sauce around the plate and splash it with rocket oil. Mix the fresh rocket with 1 tablespoon rocket oil and the lemon juice, season with salt, and place a handful on top of each soufflé. Serve immediately.

Himmel und Erde

apple and cheddar potato latkes, baked beets with dill and caraway oil, spring slaw and iced horseradish cream

How we love these little beauties and, luckily for us, latkes are not just for Hanukkah. We have tinkered with culinary tradition by adding a few sound and synched ingredients, namely earthy beetroot and sweet apples, and we hope you enjoy this festival of flavours as much as our customers have done over the years. In the restaurant, we sometimes roll the latkes in flour and then egg and breadcrumbs for a crisper version. Scrumptious, sizzling latkes loaded with apple, cheese, sage and onion, are just perfect alongside baked beetroot and aromatic dill and caraway. We've added some crunchy, revitalizing slaw and then – our favourite part – melting, frozen horseradish cream, with just the right amounts of heat and chill.

Latkes are indeed usually served during the Jewish festival of Hanukkah, where traditional foods are fried to symbolize the miracle of the oil in the Temple, but they are also cooked throughout the year and are often tweaked according to seasonal produce. 'Himmel und Erde' means 'heaven and earth' and usually refers to a popular German winter dish of mashed apples and potatoes. It seemed too perfect a name not to borrow.

serves 6

{dill and caraway oil}

75g dill
1 teaspoon caraway seeds, toasted
200ml grapeseed or sunflower oil

Blanch the dill in boiling water for 2 minutes only, then drain and plunge it immediately into iced water. Drain again and then wring out the moisture in a clean cloth until the dill is completely dry.

Blend all the ingredients together on high speed in a jug blender. Transfer to a bowl, cover and leave to steep for 24 hours. Strain the oil through a muslin-lined sieve placed over a bowl. If you want a brilliant, clear, emerald colour, then strain very slowly, letting it drip through at its own speed without any forcing. If you do not have the time to do this, it is equally delicious but has a less dramatic colour. The oil will keep in an airtight container for up to 1 week.

{iced horseradish cream}

140ml soured cream
1 teaspoon freshly grated horseradish
1 teaspoon glucose (optional)
1 teaspoon lemon juice
salt and freshly ground black pepper

Mix all the ingredients together, including glucose if you want a smoother mix, and churn in an ice cream maker according to the manufacturer's instructions. Remove from the freezer 10 minutes before you want to serve it.

{baked crimson and golden beetroot}

180g crimson beetroot, peeled and cut into chunks
180g golden beetroot, peeled and cut into chunks
1 tablespoon olive oil
1 tablespoon water
salt and freshly ground black pepper

Keeping the 2 colours separate, put the beetroot chunks on 2 large pieces of foil in a roasting tin, pour ½ tablespoon oil and ½ tablespoon water over each colour group, and season with salt and pepper. Wrap the pieces of foil around the beetroot chunks and bake at 180°C/Gas Mark 4 for 30 minutes or until tender.

{crimson and golden beetroot dressings}

50g Baked Crimson Beetroot (see above)
50g Baked Golden Beetroot (see above)
100ml grapeseed oil
2 teaspoons balsamic vinegar
salt and freshly ground black pepper

Make the 2 dressings separately.

First make the Crimson Beetroot Dressing. In a jug blender on a high speed, blend the baked crimson beetroot, 50ml grapeseed oil and 1 teaspoon balsamic vinegar until they have emulsified. Season to taste with salt and pepper.

Make the Golden Beetroot Dressing in exactly the same way, using the baked golden beetroot, 50ml grapeseed oil, 1 teaspoon balsamic vinegar and seasoning.

{spring slaw}

35g spring onions, trimmed
65g celery, thinly sliced
35g apple, thinly sliced
1 tablespoon Dill and Caraway Oil (see above)
1 teaspoon lemon juice
salt and freshly ground black pepper

Gently mix all the ingredients together. Cover and keep in the refrigerator until required.

(Continued on page 113)

(Continued from page 111)

{apple and cheddar potato latkes}

400g potatoes (Desiree, Wilja or Maris
Piper are ideal)
100g mature Cheddar cheese, grated
2 tablespoons finely chopped parsley
1 tablespoon finely chopped sage
100g onions, finely chopped
100g dried apples, finely chopped
1 tablespoon mustard powder
2 eggs, beaten
100g cornmeal, quick cook polenta or
    potato flour
salt and freshly ground black pepper
sunflower oil for frying

In a large pan of salted water, parboil
the potatoes with their skins on for about
5 minutes. They must stay firm, so be
careful not to overcook them. Drain and
leave to cool. Peel and grate the potatoes,
then combine well with all the other
ingredients except the oil. Season to taste
and chill thoroughly.

Shape the chilled potato mix into
12 patties. Place them on a baking tray
lined with greaseproof paper and chill
again.

Shortly before serving, heat some
sunflower oil in a wide, non-stick frying
pan. Add the latkes and fry until crisp and
golden on both sides, then drain on paper
towels.

{to assemble}

Place a pile of baked beetroot, one
crimson and one golden, on each plate.
Top with the hot latkes, followed by a
spoonful of iced horseradish. Heap a good
bundle of the colourful slaw to one side
and smudge the plate with the crimson
and golden dressings, allowing the
contrasting colours to show. Finally,
drizzle the bright green oil around.

All you have to do now is tuck in,
although it's a shame to destroy
something so beautiful!

Lettuce and Lovage

pea and parsley pikelets with st germain sauce and a salad of seared lettuce, shallots and baby potatoes, finished with lovage salt and mint oil

{VEGAN} {WHEAT FREE}

This lovely dish screams out summer. A wonderfully fresh combination of elements, so vibrantly coloured you can almost see the vitamin content. It is loosely based on the delicate French classic, 'potage St Germain', a soupy homage to the perfect pea. The parsley packed pikelets, zesty with lemon, are perched on seared baby gem lettuce laced with the savoury taste of lovage and loaded with parsley pea mouthfuls of shallots and potatoes, then surrounded by rich, velvety, savoury St Germain sauce. It's a vivid, verdant display, finished with bright mint oil and sweet, snappy pea tendrils … full of straight-from-the-garden flavours.

Peas are spherical gems packed full of vitamins and protein, and what a colour! And lovage is such a beautiful, sculptural herb, often found at the back of herbaceous borders. Flowering at the height of summer, it can be used for culinary or medicinal purposes, particularly as an aid to digestion.

serves 6

{lovage salt}

2 tablespoons finely chopped lovage
30g sea salt

Crush the lovage and salt together in a pestle and mortar, or blender, or in a sturdy bowl with a rolling pin. If you would like finer, drier salt, set the oven to the lowest heat, evenly spread the lovage and salt on a baking tray and leave in the oven overnight before crushing it.

{mint oil}

200g mint leaves
150ml grapeseed or sunflower oil
100ml olive oil

Bring a large pan of salted water to the boil. Plunge the mint leaves into the boiling water for a few seconds, then instantly remove them and plunge them into iced water. Drain and wring out the moisture in a clean cloth until completely dry. Blend all the ingredients together in a jug blender on high speed. Transfer to an airtight container and leave in the refrigerator to steep for 12 hours, preferably overnight.

Strain the oil through a muslin-lined sieve suspended over a bowl, making sure the sieve is not touching the bottom of the bowl. To get a clear, bright oil. let it drip through at its own speed without forcing it through. This is not absolutely necessary but is well worth it if you want to retain the beautiful, verdant green of the mint.

{parsley purée}

200g parsley leaves
150ml cold water

Bring a large pan of salted water to the boil, add the parsley and blanch for 1 minute. Quickly remove and plunge into iced water until it has cooled down. Now squeeze out as much moisture as you can and place the parsley in a blender with the measured water. Blend at high speed until the purée is extremely smooth, stopping a few times to scrape down the sides of the blender. Covered, this will keep in the refrigerator for 2 or 3 days.

This process can be used with most leafy herbs. It adds a lovely fresh taste and colour to a dish. If you have a stock on the go, you could always add the remaining blanching water to it for extra flavour.

{pea and parsley pikelets}

100g dried split green peas
500g fresh or frozen peas
olive oil for frying
150g white onions, finely chopped
100ml dry white wine
1 bay leaf
20g gram flour
1 teaspoon lemon juice
4 tablespoons finely chopped parsley
    (stalks reserved)
3 tablespoons finely chopped mint leaves
    (stalks reserved)
50ml soya cream
salt and freshly ground black pepper
caster sugar

First make some green pea flour. Blitz the dried split green peas in a food processor, and then sieve. This should yield about 50g flour and 50g thicker particles (remaining in sieve). Reserve the thicker particles to use as ground split peas in the St Germain sauce.

Blanch the fresh or frozen peas in boiling salted water for 2 minutes, then drain (if using frozen peas, it is important to wring them dry in a tea towel afterwards to remove extra moisture). Heat 1 tablespoon olive oil in a large pan, add the onions and cook gently until they are soft but not brown. Add the wine and bay leaf and simmer until the wine has evaporated. Remove from the heat and leave to cool.

In a food processor, purée half the peas with the cooled onion mix, then scrape out with a spatula and set aside in a bowl. Again using the food processor, pulse the remaining half of the peas (for a chunkier texture). Add to the pea and onion purée and combine well.

Add the green pea flour, gram flour, lemon juice, herbs and soya cream to the pea and onion mix and stir thoroughly. Season with salt, pepper and sugar to taste. Divide the mixture into 12 patties and chill until ready to use.

Just before serving, heat some olive oil in a large frying pan and fry the pikelets for about 3 minutes on each side, until they are lightly coloured but still a fresh, bright green in the centre. Drain on paper towels.

{st germain sauce}

2.5 litres White Stock (see page 18) or
    water
400g baby potatoes
300g tiny shallots
250ml dry white wine
1 teaspoon salt
1 bay leaf, parsley and mint stalks (see Pea
    and Parsley Pikelets, page opposite)
15g mint leaves
2 tablespoons Mint Oil (see above)
200g frozen peas
200g onions, chopped
50g ground split peas (see Pea and Parsley
    Pikelets, page opposite)
3 tablespoons Parsley Purée (see page
    opposite)

Put the stock or water, potatoes, shallots, wine, salt, bay leaf and herb stalks in a large pan and bring to the boil. Simmer for about 15 minutes, until the potatoes and shallots are tender, then drain and place in a flat dish, reserving the cooking liquid. Remove the herb stalks. Scatter the mint leaves over the potatoes and shallots, pour over the mint oil and set aside to cool. This leftover mix becomes the core of Lettuce and Lovage (see below).

Now cook the frozen peas in boiling salted water until tender, then drain and purée in a food processor. Put the reserved potato cooking liquid in a pan, add the chopped onions and ground split peas and simmer until the pea particles are soft and the liquid has reduced by one third. Transfer to a food processor, add the puréed frozen peas and the parsley purée and blend until smooth. Pass through a fine sieve and check the seasoning. Set aside until required.

{lettuce and lovage}

200g fresh or frozen peas
3 baby gem lettuces, trimmed and halved
reserved cooked potatoes and shallots (see
    St Germain Sauce, above)
salt and freshly ground black pepper
1 tablespoon lemon juice
1 tablespoon roughly torn lovage
1 tablespoon roughly torn flat leaf parsley

Blanch the peas in boiling salted water for 2 minutes, then drain. Heat a non-stick frying pan and briefly sear the lettuce halves, just so they colour, then remove from the pan. Put the oily baby potatoes and shallots in the pan, add the peas, and warm through. Now return the lettuce halves to the pan and season with salt and pepper. Just before serving, add the lemon juice and torn herbs.

{to assemble}

25g pea shoots

Arrange the warm lettuce and lovage combination on serving plates and lay 2 pikelets on top. Splash a little of the vivid mint oil around and dust with lovage salt. Garnish with a sprinkling of pea shoots and pour the warm St Germain sauce all around.

Kibbi Our Soles

halloumi and almond kibbi wrapped in aubergine soles and chermoula spice seasoning, with 'kitchen sink pickles', big bean tagine, and olive, sultana and bulgur wheat salad

If you have a house full, this is great to whack on the table for a dig-in dinner. The big, bold, beautiful flavours make for easy eating and, as all the elements can be made in advance, stress levels will be low. Incidentally, all the elements are independently delicious, and versatile enough to be served separately or as accompaniments to other dishes (the kitchen sink pickles can lift any dish needing a bit of oomph.)

These stumpy, savoury little kibbi are quite a crowd pleaser: aromatic, almond and cheese- laden lovelies wrapped in succulent aubergine soles and rolled in chermoula seasoning. Kibbi are traditionally made with bulgur wheat and are popular throughout the Middle East and North Africa. Here we've used an authentic spice mix to create something rather different. Fragrant, fruity and just fabulous. (And we didn't forget the bulgur: it's there in the salad.)

The decision to marry all the elements of this dish together and serve them on a single platter came not only as the result of our absolute gluttony (and we are proud to be leading experts in this field) but for three equally compelling reasons. One being that the beautifully juicy big bean tagine, full of fleshy beans and robust, cinnamon and saffron-scented tomato sauce, loaded with peppers and coriander, is a must for 'saucing up' the kibbi. Two, the bulgur wheat salad is lemon-fresh and leafy, crammed with olives and pine nuts, and absolutely perfect for soaking up those lovely juices. And three, the 'kitchen sink pickles' are guilty of being positively perky and rammed full of 'everything but'…! They are crunchy and soft, spicy and sharp, with a citrus lift, and with nutty argan oil as a leveller. Well, we think these are reasons enough to have the full Monty, so we rest our case!

serves 6

{chermoula spice seasoning}

50g coriander seeds
2 tablespoons fennel seeds
2 tablespoons cumin seeds
2 tablespoons sumac
¼ teaspoon salt

Toast all the seeds, grind them in a pestle and mortar and then mix them with the sumac and salt. Store in an airtight container.

{halloumi and almond kibbi}

100ml orange juice
2 star anise
1 cinnamon stick
15 fennel seeds
250g halloumi cheese, washed and finely grated
200g cream cheese
200g pressed tofu (drained, put in paper towels and weighted down to squeeze out excess liquid)
400g ground almonds
100g gram flour
2 tablespoons cumin seeds, toasted and cracked
4 tablespoons coriander seeds, toasted and cracked
75g preserved lemon peel, finely chopped
grated zest of 2 oranges
grated zest of 2 lemons
70g flat leaf parsley, chopped
50g coriander, chopped
salt and freshly ground black pepper
450g aubergines, cut into lengths 5mm thick (like the sole of a shoe)
2 tablespoons whole milk
4 tablespoons rice flour
olive oil for brushing
Chermoula Spice Seasoning (see above)
sunflower oil for frying

Bring the orange juice to the boil in a small pan with the star anise, cinnamon and fennel seeds. Remove from the heat and leave to infuse.

Put the halloumi, cream cheese, tofu, ground almonds, gram flour, ground cumin and coriander seeds, preserved lemon, orange and lemon zest, parsley, coriander and seasoning in a large bowl. Mix well, adding 4 tablespoons of the infused orange juice (reserve the remaining juice for the Kitchen Sink Pickles, below). Refrigerate for at least 2 hours, then mould into 6 conical shapes. These are your kibbi.

Dip the aubergine slices in the milk, then in the rice flour, dusting off any excess. Now wrap them around the kibbi, securing the overlapping edges with a couple of cocktail sticks or skewers. Refrigerate for 1 hour.

Shortly before serving, brush the wrapped kibbi with olive oil, then roll them in the chermoula spice seasoning. Fry them gently in a little sunflower oil for about 2 minutes, until browned all over, then place them on a non-stick baking tray and bake at 180°C/Gas Mark 4 for 15–20 minutes.

{kitchen sink pickles}

200g cucumber
180g carrots
200g red onions
1 red pepper, deseeded
120g white cabbage, shredded
100g stoned green olives
250ml argan oil or olive oil
125ml white wine vinegar
3 tablespoons chopped thyme
3 tablespoons chopped oregano

(Continued on page 118)

(Continued from page 116)

1 tablespoon cumin seeds, toasted and
   cracked
1 tablespoon coriander seeds, toasted and
   cracked
a pinch of saffron strands
infused orange juice (reserved from
   Halloumi and Almond Kibbi, see page 116)
salt and freshly ground black pepper

Cut the cucumber in half lengthways,
remove the seeds and cut into 3mm thick
slices. Cut the carrots in half lengthways
and then into 3mm thick slices. Cut the
onions into quarters, remove the cores,
then cut each quarter in half and chop
into smaller pieces. Cut the red pepper
into 1.5cm dice. Mix together all the
ingredients and allow to stand at room
temperature for 2-3 hours, then refrigerate
until required.

{big bean tagine}

200g giant butter beans, soaked overnight
   in cold water
4 tablespoons olive oil
200g shallots
200g red peppers, deseeded and chopped
1 onion, chopped
25g garlic, chopped
½ teaspoon ground cinnamon
½ teaspoon finely chopped fresh root ginger
½ teaspoon saffron strands
½ teaspoon ground black pepper
grated zest of 1 orange
1 tablespoon diced preserved lemon peel
500g ripe tomatoes, chopped
100ml White Stock (see page 18) or water
3 tablespoons orange juice
1 tablespoon lemon juice
salt
1 tablespoon argan oil
2 tablespoons torn coriander

Cook the butter beans according to packet
instructions. Heat the olive oil in a casserole
dish with a tight fitting lid. Add the shallots,
peppers, onion and garlic and fry lightly
over a medium heat for 5 minutes. Add
the cinnamon, ginger, saffron and black
pepper and cook for 5 minutes longer. Stir
in all the remaining ingredients except the
argan oil and coriander, cover the casserole
and bake in the oven at 150°C/Gas Mark 2
for 1½ hours. Just before serving, sprinkle
on the argan oil and coriander.

{olive, sultana and bulgur wheat salad}

300ml White Stock (see page 18) or water
60g sultanas
200g bulgur wheat
2 tablespoons olive oil
100g onions, sliced
20g preserved lemon peel, diced
¼ teaspoon ground cinnamon
80g stoned green olives
200g curly leaf parsley, finely chopped
100g mint leaves
200g pine nuts, toasted
2 teaspoons Chermoula Spice Seasoning
   (see 116)
1 tablespoon lemon juice
salt and freshly ground black pepper

Bring the stock or water to the boil in a
small pan, add the sultanas and leave until
swollen. Put the bulgur wheat in a bowl
and pour over the sultanas and their
liquid. Cover and leave until the wheat
has absorbed all the liquid, then fluff up
with a fork and leave to cool. Heat the oil
in a frying pan, add the onions and fry
lightly until soft and sweet. Add the
preserved lemon peel, cinnamon and
olives, then turn out into the bowl of
bulgur wheat and mix thoroughly.
Shortly before serving, add the parsley,
mint, pine nuts, chermoula spice mix and
lemon juice and check the seasoning.

{to assemble}

2 lemons, cut into chunks

We think this works best as a 'dig in, grab
what you can' dish, so place the kibbi on
a warm serving dish with chunks of fresh
lemon. Serve the steaming tagine in its
cooking pot, and have the bulgur wheat
and the pickles in big glass bowls, to show
them in all their glory.

Send My Regards to Broadway

lemon pickle, broad bean and mint mille feuille, served with asparagus, broad bean and fennel salad, and seared cherry vine tomatoes

Celebrate the end of winter with this well stacked collection of spring's fresh and perky offerings – a gorgeous looking dish, and even lovelier to eat. Simple but scrumptious, it's great to serve whole, for guests to grab their own slice of the action. Luscious layers of dense, aromatic, broad bean mousse are sandwiched between puff pastry leaves, packed with heaps of refreshing mint and tangy lemon pickle, and topped with seared cherry vine tomatoes and their oily, peppery juices. Alongside, you have a fresh and leafy asparagus, broad bean and fennel salad – a clean, light collection of spring ingredients. And – not that you need convincing – it will also do you good.

Broad beans are one of the oldest cultivated crops in the world, dating back to the Stone Age, and there is much fascinating folklore surrounding them (give them as a wedding gift to ensure a baby boy!). They are a useful crop to grow, as they fix nitrogen in the soil and, yes, they are rich in protein and vitamins, particularly A and C. As an early crop, they are great to pair with asparagus, which can be harvested in the UK from mid-April.

Asparagus is full of antioxidants and even higher in vitamin C than the beans. For a long time it was considered a delicacy, hard to obtain and tricky to cook, but with some of the myths surrounding it gone, it's been much in demand in recent years and easier to find in the shops. Good thing too!

serves 6

{seared cherry vine tomatoes}

1 tablespoon olive oil
12 cherry vine tomatoes
salt and freshly ground black pepper

Heat the olive oil in a frying pan until it is smoking. Add the tomatoes and sear them in the hot oil, turning them around so they cook all over. This should only take about 1 minute. Season with salt and plenty of pepper, remove from the pan and leave to cool.

{broad bean mousse}

400g fresh (shelled) or frozen broad beans
400ml whole milk
60g onion, sliced
1 bay leaf
2 cloves
a few parsley stalks
a little freshly grated nutmeg
70g unsalted butter
70g plain flour
salt and freshly ground black pepper
2 eggs, whites and yolks separated, yolks
   beaten

If using fresh broad beans, blanch them in boiling salted water for 2 minutes, then drain. Peel the skins off the fresh or frozen beans.

Next, make a béchamel sauce. Put the milk into a pan with the onion, bay leaf, cloves, parsley stalks and nutmeg and bring to a simmer. Remove from the heat, strain the milk and discard the flavourings.

Melt the butter in a pan, add the flour and stir well to make a paste. Cook this roux over a low heat for 2 minutes, stirring constantly. Remove from the heat and beat in a ladleful of the hot milk. Return the pan to the heat and continue adding the milk, over a medium heat, a ladleful at a time. When all the milk has been

incorporated, simmer the sauce for 5 minutes, still stirring so that it does not catch on the bottom. Season generously with salt and pepper and pour into a bowl to cool down.

Put the skinned broad beans in a food processor and blend to a smooth, thick purée. Pass the purée through a fine sieve and then fold it into the cool béchamel, together with the beaten egg yolks. In a separate bowl, whisk the egg whites to soft peaks. Fold them into the broad bean béchamel. You need only a little lightness, so you do not have to be as gentle as you would with a soufflé. Season to taste.

Take a shallow baking tin or ovenproof dish, roughly 30 x 20cm, and line it with baking parchment. Pour in the broad bean mousse and gently spread it around the tin. Bake at 150°C/Gas Mark 2 for 30–40 minutes, until the mixture has risen slightly and a knife inserted in the centre comes out clean. Leave to cool, then store in the refrigerator until you are ready to assemble the mille feuille.

{lemon pickle, broad bean and mint mille feuille}

1 quantity Puff Pastry (see page 20) – or
   use any good quality puff pastry
1 egg yolk, beaten with 1 tablespoon milk
Broad Bean Mousse (see above)
2 tablespoons Lemony Yemeni Pickle (see
   Better Batter, page 89)
2 tablespoons chopped mint

On a lightly floured surface, roll out the puff pastry into a 32cm square and cut it into 3 equal strips. Put the strips on a lined baking tray and refrigerate for 1 hour. Remove the pastry from the refrigerator, prick 2 of the rectangles with a fork and make a criss-cross pattern on

(Continued on page 121)

(Continued from page 119)

the remaining one with the blunt side of a knife, taking care not to cut through the pastry. This piece will become the top layer.

Brush the pastry with the beaten egg yolk and bake at 180°C/Gas Mark 4 for 15–20 minutes, until nicely browned and cooked through. Remove from the oven and place a sheet of baking parchment and a baking tray on top of the pastry, to level the pieces out. Leave to cool.

Cut the broad bean mousse into 2 slices that will fit snugly between the pastry layers. Spread a tablespoon of the lemony yemeni pickle over the bottom layer of pastry and sprinkle half the chopped mint over it. Place one of the layers of mousse on this and then top with the second layer of pastry. Now repeat the layering: some pickle, a sprinkling of mint and the broad bean mousse. Place the third piece of pastry on top and the constructing is over.

Using a serrated knife, carefully cut the mille feuille into 6 slices. Take your time, don't apply too much pressure and, if you use a sawing action, it should cut cleanly.

{asparagus, broad bean and fennel salad}

24 asparagus spears, trimmed
100g fresh (shelled) broad beans
20g fennel fronds, roughly chopped
200g mixed salad leaves
20g mint, chopped
1 teaspoon chopped lemon thyme
2 tablespoons olive oil
juice of ½ lemon
salt and freshly ground black pepper

Blanch the asparagus spears in boiling salted water for 2 minutes, then drain. Blanch and drain the broad beans in the same way, then peel off the skins. Reserve 6 of the asparagus spears for garnishing the mille feuille. Cut the remaining asparagus to 7cm lengths and mix with all the remaining ingredients. Set aside.

Just before serving, dress the salad with the oil and lemon juice and season with salt and pepper.

{to assemble}

olive oil for brushing
6 asparagus spears (see Asparagus, Broad Bean and Fennel Salad, above)
6 sprigs of mint
6 sprigs of parsley nasturtium leaves and flowers (optional)
125ml crème fraîche

Brush the top of the mille feuille with a little olive oil and place all 6 slices on a large serving platter. Garnish with the seared cherry tomatoes, reserved asparagus spears and the mint and parsley sprigs. Add a few nasturtium leaves and flowers, if you like. Serve the salad and crème fraîche separately.

Uttapam and Dudhi

tamil red onion and chilli crumpets topped with coriander seed butter,
served with dudhi gourd crammed with mangosteen dhal,
cardamom and red pepper sauce and mango salad

{VEGAN} {WHEAT FREE}

What could be nicer than hot, aromatic crumpets drenched in melting butter? Well, we reckon a good helping of all the above extras as well, so go on, don't hold back…. These soft, colourful little beauties, loaded with melting butter and peppered with coriander seeds, are a treat on their own at any time but are also ideal for scooping up the dark, rich, tangy mangosteen masoor dhal, loaded with spice and textured bites of slightly bitter dudhi gourd. They're perfect, too, for soaking up the fabulously fresh-tasting cardamom and red pepper sauce and offsetting the sweet heat of the mango and chilli salad, crunchy with poppy seeds.

This is a curry to savour, so take time to appreciate its wonderful layering and surprising flavour matchmaking. There are a few interesting ingredients here. Kokum, or 'false mangosteen', is the sticky, dried fruit of a tropical evergreen tree. It has a slightly sour taste and is sometimes used as a substitute for tamarind. The dudhi gourd is one of the bottle gourds, so called for their ability to hold water once dried. Asafoetida has a pungent, rather unpleasant smell when raw (the name means 'stinking resin') but, once cooked, is reminiscent of garlic or onions: it is widely used in southern Indian dhals and vegetable dishes. You should be able to find all the ingredients called for in this recipe, in Middle Eastern and Indian stores.

serves 4-6

{tamil tiffin crumpets}

for the batter
300g easy cook basmati rice
100g urad dhal (black lentils) – or use
   moong dhal (split green lentils)
1 teaspoon fenugreek seeds
70ml water
½ teaspoon salt
90ml plain yogurt or soya yoghurt
½ teaspoon asafoetida powder

for the chilli mix
2 long red chilli peppers, finely sliced
1 red onion, finely sliced
10 curry leaves
100g coriander, chopped
1 teaspoon mustard seeds

To make the batter, put the rice, dhal and fenugreek seeds in a bowl, cover with cold water and leave to soak for 6–8 hours. Drain in a fine sieve and rinse well, then put in a food processor with 70ml water and the salt, and blend to a smooth batter. Transfer to a large bowl, cover with a clean tea towel and set aside at room temperature for at least 12 hours, until the batter ferments and increases in size and small bubbles appear. Stir in the yogurt and asafoetida to give a thick pouring consistency, adding more water if needed.

To cook the crumpets, you will need 3–4 muffin rings, 7.5cm in diameter, and a heavy based frying pan. There should be enough batter for about 8 crumpets. That's 2 crumpets each to serve 4, or 1 crumpet each to serve 6 (with 2 to spare). To make more, just increase the batter quantities.

Mix together the sliced chillies, onion, curry leaves, coriander and mustard seeds. Lightly oil the rings and the pan, then place the rings in the pan and let them heat up. Half fill each ring with batter and sprinkle a spoonful of the chilli mix over

each one. Cook for about 5 minutes, until the crumpets are golden underneath. Remove the rings, carefully turn the crumpets over and cook on the other side, then remove them from the pan and keep warm. Repeat until all the batter has been used.

{coriander seed butter}

1½ teaspoons coriander seeds
125g soft unsalted butter or vegan spread
½ teaspoon grated lime zest

Toast the coriander seeds in a heavy based pan until they release their aroma, then crush in a pestle and mortar. Beat the butter with the coriander and lime zest until well combined. Place the spiced butter on a piece of clingfilm and roll it up to form a cylinder 4cm in diameter. Place in the freezer to harden.

{mangotango salad}

1 green mango, peeled
1 ripe but firm yellow Alphonso mango,
   peeled
1 tablespoon coconut oil
1 teaspoon mustard seeds
½ teaspoon poppy seeds
a pinch of ground turmeric
a pinch of chilli powder
4 tablespoons lime juice
2 tablespoons white wine vinegar
a pinch of salt

Slice the green mango thinly (about 4mm) and the yellow one slightly thicker. Heat the oil in a heavy based pan and add the mustard and poppy seeds. When they pop, add the turmeric, chilli, lime juice, vinegar, salt and green mango. Cook gently until the mango is just tender, then remove from the heat and carefully stir in the yellow mango, making sure it is well incorporated.

Transfer the salad to a serving dish and leave to cool, then cover and refrigerate.

{dudhi gourd with mangosteen masoor dhal}

200g masoor dhal (brown lentils)
2 pieces of kokum, each about 5cm long
1 teaspoon cumin seeds
1 teaspoon coriander seeds
1 tablespoon sunflower oil
1 teaspoon black mustard seeds
125g onions, chopped
2 garlic cloves, finely chopped
1 teaspoon finely chopped green chilli pepper
1 teaspoon finely chopped red chilli pepper
8 curry leaves
¼ teaspoon turmeric powder
½ cinnamon stick
200g tomatoes, skinned, deseeded and chopped (canned are fine)
15g palm sugar, chopped (or dark muscovado sugar)
salt
3 tablespoons chopped coriander
1 large dudhi or bottle gourd (about 500g)

Soak the lentils in cold water for 1 hour, then drain and rinse well. Rinse the kokum, chop it into small pieces and soak them in 500ml cold water for 5 minutes. Put the lentils, kokum and kokum soaking water into a large pan and bring slowly to the boil. Simmer for about 30 minutes, until the lentils are soft.

Dry roast the cumin and coriander seeds in a heavy based frying pan until they release their aroma, then tip them into a spice grinder or pestle and mortar and grind to a powder. Heat the oil in another pan, add the mustard seeds and cook over a low heat until they pop. Add the onions and garlic and fry until they start to colour. Now stir in the chillies, curry leaves, turmeric and cinnamon stick and cook for 2 minutes.

Add the tomatoes and cooked lentils and cook for a further 10 minutes. Add the palm sugar and stir until dissolved. Tip the cumin and coriander spice mix into the simmering lentils, and cook for a further 10 minutes, then season with salt and stir in the chopped coriander. Keep warm.

Peel the skin from the dudhi gourd as thinly as possible to retain some of its colour. Cut the gourd across in 5cm slices. Scoop out some of the centre with a teaspoon and discard the seeds, then plunge the slices into boiling salted water and cook for 5 minutes, until they start to soften. Lift them out, drain and allow to cool. Set aside until you are ready to assemble the dish.

{cardamom and red pepper sauce}

3 black cardamom pods
3 green cardamom pods
2 tablespoons cumin seeds
2 teaspoons olive oil
300g red peppers, deseeded and roughly chopped
100g onion, roughly chopped
1 litre White Stock (see page 18) or water
15g palm sugar, chopped (or dark muscovado sugar) salt and freshly ground black pepper

Crack open the cardamom pods, then toast the seeds in a heavy based pan with the cumin seeds until they release their aroma. Add the oil, red peppers and onion and cook gently, uncovered, until the vegetables begin to soften. Add the stock or water and the palm sugar, bring to the boil and simmer gently for 10 minutes. Remove from the heat.

Transfer the mixture to a food processor or liquidizer and blend until smooth. Pass through a fine sieve, season to taste and keep warm.

{to assemble}

a little butter or oil, for brushing

Brush the dudhi gourd slices with butter or oil and reheat them either in the oven at 150°C/Gas Mark 2 for 10 minutes or under a medium grill for 8 minutes. Gently reheat the mangosteen dhal.

Put 1 or 2 crumpets per person on to warmed plates and top with a splodge of coriander butter. Put the warm gourd slices on the plates and fill the hollows with the dhal, then spoon on some of the cardamom and red pepper sauce. Serve with the mangotango salad in its separate dish, to share.

Sodden Socca

chickpea pancakes with warm caponata, marmara tapenade
and orange, thyme and saffron dressing

{VEGAN} {WHEAT FREE}

A 'sock it to me' dish for those who like a hearty plate of Mediterranean delights, rich with the scents, colours and tastes of that sun-baked region. Traditionally thin, Provençal chickpea pancakes have been chubbied up here, making them a little more substantial, and a lot more sodden with the deliciously rich juices surrounding them.

Bright, bold and beautiful, this is the absolutely perfect pile of pancakes to plunge into: sumptuous and colourful caponata, similar to ratatouille but lush with little juicy bursts of sweet and sour sultanas, black olives and salty capers, balanced by the tapenade, packed full of garlic, chilli, peppers and almonds. The whole rich feast is dressed with a fresh orange and saffron sauce. Can there ever be too much of a good thing?

Caponata is a Sicilian dish based on aubergine and tomato, but there are many similar dishes around the world, including the classic Provençal ratatouille and the Catalan samfaina, all with their own regional fine tunings.

serves 6

{marmara tapenade}

40g shallots, chopped
150g red peppers, deseeded and chopped
1 tablespoon chopped red chilli pepper
2 tablespoons olive oil
½ teaspoon cumin seeds
1 teaspoon chopped rosemary
2 tablespoons chopped garlic
salt
½ teaspoon freshly ground black pepper
½ teaspoon ground coriander seeds, toasted
1 tablespoon puréed garlic
½ lemon, peeled and chopped
4 tablespoons chopped coriander
75g ground almonds, toasted

Put the shallots, red peppers, chilli, olive oil, cumin, rosemary and chopped garlic in a baking tin, season with salt and bake at 180°C/Gas Mark 4 until the shallots and red peppers are soft. Transfer to a food processor and blend until smooth, then leave to cool. Add all the remaining

ingredients and mix well. Store in the refrigerator in an airtight container.

{orange, thyme and saffron dressing}

4 tablespoons olive oil 5
0g shallots, diced
1 bay leaf
¼ teaspoon saffron strands
¼ teaspoon chopped thyme
2 oranges, peeled and chopped
1 teaspoon orange juice
1 teaspoon lemon juice
salt and freshly ground black pepper

Heat the olive oil in a stainless steel pan, add the shallots and cook until tender. Add the bay leaf, saffron, thyme and oranges, cover and simmer for 5 minutes. Remove the bay leaf, blend until smooth, then strain through a fine sieve and leave to cool.

Add the orange and lemon juices and season to taste. Keep the dressing refrigerated until required.

{chickpea socca}

250g cooked chickpeas (canned are fine)
25g basil, chopped
2 tablespoons chopped mint
2 tablespoons chopped curly leaf parsley
1 tablespoon chopped garlic
60g onion, finely chopped
20g gram flour, plus extra for dusting
2 teaspoons lemon juice
salt and freshly ground black pepper
sunflower oil for frying

Put all the ingredients except the sunflower oil into a food processor and blend until they bind together. Check the seasoning, turn out into a bowl, then cover and chill for 1 hour. Shape into patties (there is enough mixture for about 12) and dust lightly with gram flour. Refrigerate again, as they cook better when chilled.

Just before serving, heat some sunflower oil in a non-stick frying pan, add the socca and fry for 3 minutes on each side, until golden brown. Drain on paper towels.

{caponata}

4 tablespoons olive oil
125g red onions, diced
125g aubergine, diced
125g red pepper, diced
75g courgette, diced
25g capers, rinsed
25g sultanas
75g stoned black olives, roughly chopped
1 teaspoon chopped oregano
1 bay leaf
25g basil leaves, chopped
25g celery leaves, chopped
250g ripe tomatoes, chopped
1 tablespoon sun dried tomato paste or ordinary tomato paste
1 tablespoon balsamic vinegar
50ml red wine
salt and freshly ground black pepper

Heat the olive oil in a stainless steel saucepan, add the onions and cook until tender. Add the aubergine and cook until it has absorbed most of the oil and is starting to feel soft. Add the red pepper and courgette and fry lightly. Stir in all the remaining ingredients. Cover and simmer gently for 30 minutes, then check the seasoning. Serve the caponata warm.

{to assemble}

torn basil leaves

Divide the warm caponata between the plates, along with the tapenade, and place a hot socca to the side. Drizzle the dressing around and garnish with torn basil leaves. Alternatively, this dish is equally at home served in big bowls and platters so that guests can help themselves. Either way, generous amounts of fresh basil are essential.

Poke Mole

coconut, coriander and sweet potato beignets topped with poke mole, served with {VEGAN} {WHEAT FREE} fresh tomato chilli gazpacho, and avocado lime mayonnaise

This is a chirpy little dish, stacked with nifty flavours and cheerful colours, with a sting in its tail. It leaves you wanting it all over again, and again…. Sweet potato fritters, full of coconut, spicy ginger and lime, are set against a good whack of nippy gazpacho, and a cool, creamy avocado mayonnaise. Then there's the 'poke' bit (pronounced pokay) – a heavenly, aromatic blend of sweet-sharp guindilla chilli, fresh red chilli, pumpkin seeds, heady spices and the rich taste of dark chocolate. The mother of all 'moles'.

Moles (not the furry kind) are thick, spicy Mexican sauces that usually contain many ingredients and are laborious to prepare. There are many myths about how they originated (my favourite involves nuns, an archbishop and an old turkey) but they are indisputably one of the best known and most loved elements of Mexican cuisine, and are now served with many adaptations all over the world. Here we use guindilla chilli, which is medium hot with a sweetish flavour and tart edge, and mix it with ordinary red chillies, but some moles are made with a combination of up to 10 named chillies. The traditional inclusion of chocolate adds to the marvellously complex layering of flavours.

serves 6

{poke mole}

220g yellow peppers
40g guindilla chillies, deseeded and chopped
1 teaspoon cumin seeds
1 teaspoon coriander seeds
1 clove
1 allspice berry
5 black peppercorns
1 teaspoon sesame seeds
1 teaspoon raw pumpkin seeds
4 teaspoons chopped red chilli pepper
1 teaspoon chopped garlic
¼ teaspoon ground cinnamon
40g dark chocolate (70 per cent cocoa solids), melted

Blister the skins of the yellow peppers under the grill or in the oven at 200°C/Gas Mark 6 until they are charred and the flesh softens. Put them into a container, cover tightly and leave to steam for 10 minutes (this makes it much easier to remove the skins). Peel off the skins and deseed the peppers.

Fry the guindilla chillies, cumin, coriander, clove, allspice, peppercorns, sesame seeds and pumpkin seeds in a dry frying pan until they release their aroma. Grind in a pestle and mortar, coffee grinder or food processor. Put the roasted yellow peppers, chopped red chilli and garlic in a food processor with the ground spice mixture and process until smooth. Add the cinnamon and melted chocolate and refrigerate for 3–4 hours, until set.

{tomato chilli gazpacho}

60g red onion, finely diced
70g cucumber, finely diced
1 teaspoon finely diced red chilli pepper
100g yellow pepper, deseeded and finely diced
280g tomatoes, skinned and diced
250ml tomato juice (about 7 fresh tomatoes blitzed in a blender)
2½ tablespoons lime juice
3 tablespoons chopped coriander
1 tablespoon olive oil
salt and freshly ground black pepper

Put all the ingredients in a bowl, stir well and season to taste. Cover and keep refrigerated until required.

{avocado lime mayonnaise}

300g ripe avocados, peeled, stoned, chopped
2 teaspoons lime juice
grated zest of 1 lime
25ml avocado oil or olive oil
1 teaspoon chopped garlic
1 tablespoon chopped coriander
1 teaspoon salt

Put all the ingredients in a blender or food processor and blitz on high speed until smooth. Season to taste and chill before serving.

{coconut, coriander and sweet potato beignets}

1kg sweet potatoes
1 tablespoon finely grated fresh root ginger
1 teaspoon crushed garlic
3 tablespoons coriander seeds, toasted and cracked
1 teaspoon finely chopped red chilli pepper
50g coconut powder
grated zest and juice of 2 limes
100g white maize meal (or quick cook polenta)
sunflower oil for deep frying

Put the sweet potatoes on a baking tray and bake at 200°C/Gas Mark 6 until soft. Remove the skins, put the flesh in a bowl and mash well. Add all the other ingredients except the oil and mix until smooth. Refrigerate for at least 30 minutes, then shape the mixture into 12 quenelles (small ovals) or any other shape, as long as they are equal in size. These are your beignets (staying with the French!) ready for frying. Refrigerate until needed.

Shortly before you want to serve, heat the oil to 170°C in a deep fryer or deep pan (if you don't have a thermometer, drop a small piece of bread into the oil; if it goes golden brown within a minute, the oil is hot enough). Fry the beignets, 2 or 3 at a time, for 3–4 minutes, until golden and crisp. Drain on paper towels.

{to assemble}

Place the hot sweet potato beignets on 6 plates and top them with a little of the mole. Spoon a generous amount of gazpacho on one side and a good smudge of avocado mayonnaise on the other.

Miso Pretty

reverse rolled ginger sushi in szechuan dust, served with cashew and coriander salad, roast yellow pepper and miso dressing, tamari and lime glaze, and hot and sour tea

{VEGAN} {WHEAT FREE}

Uramaki sushi or, to you and me, inside-out rolls. Not only is this dish beautiful in a less-is-more way but it tastes sensational – in a more-is-more way! There is certainly some dexterity required when making sushi, and a little more required to roll it inside out, but it is one of those things that really does get easier with practice. To the soft sushi with crisp middles, rolled in punchy miso with tangy Szechuan heat, we've added refreshing bites of creamy cashews with zesty leaves, the chilli heat of hot and sour tea, an intense dark and salty lime reduction, and a fruity mellow yellow dressing. It sounds a lot of tastes at once, but they intertwine to produce unforgettable Eastern fireworks.

A thick paste used to flavour sauces and soups or as a pickling agent or spread, miso has been an integral element in the Japanese diet since the 6th century. Most commonly produced by the fermentation of rice, barley and soya beans, it can be white, black or red, although there are many other types, made from a wide range of ingredients. It is rich in vitamins and minerals and we use it frequently, taking advantage of the depth of flavour it imparts to savoury dishes. You can find it in Asian supermarkets, alongside many of the other ingredients used here. For more on tamarind paste, see page 152.

serves 6

{szechuan dust}

1 teaspoon white miso (soy paste)
¼ teaspoon Szechuan peppercorns
¼ teaspoon chopped dried chilli pepper

Preheat the oven to 180°C/Gas Mark 4. Spread out the miso evenly on a piece of baking parchment laid on a baking tray, then place in the oven. Immediately turn off the heat and leave the miso in the warm oven for 2 hours. When the miso has cooled down, grind it with the other ingredients. Store the dust in an airtight container.

{roast yellow pepper and miso dressing}

160g yellow peppers
20g white miso
a pinch of salt

Blister the skins of the peppers under the grill or in the oven at 200°C/Gas Mark 6 until they are charred and the flesh softens. Put them into a container, cover tightly and leave to steam for 10 minutes (this makes it much easier to remove the skins). Peel off the skins and deseed the peppers. With a hand blender, purée the peppers with the miso and salt until smooth.

{tamari and lime glaze}

100ml tamari (gluten free soy sauce)
60g caster sugar
2 tablespoons lime juice

Put all the ingredients in a small stainless steel pan, bring slowly to the boil and simmer over a very low heat, stirring, until the mixture takes on the consistency of treacle. This needs to be done as gently as possible and the mixture will need skimming a few times to remove the skin that forms on the surface. Leave to cool and store in an airtight container until required.

{hot and sour tea}

2 tablespoons toasted sesame oil
300g onions, chopped
5 large garlic cloves, chopped
4 tablespoons roughly chopped coriander
40g red chilli peppers, chopped (or more if you like it really hot)
25g fresh root ginger, chopped
½ teaspoon ground Szechuan pepper
1 star anise
2 litres White Stock (see page 18) or water
50ml tamari (gluten free soy sauce)
2 tablespoons mirin (sweet rice wine)
2 tablespoons rice vinegar
10g kombu (dried seaweed)
50g tamarind paste
30g dried shiitake mushrooms
10g dried porcini mushrooms

Heat the oil in a large saucepan, add the onions, garlic, coriander, chilli and ginger and fry until the onions are soft. Add all the remaining ingredients, bring to the boil and simmer for 30 minutes, or until the volume has reduced by at least a third. You could strain it and use straight away, but it's best to leave it unstrained – in which case allow it to cool, then refrigerate overnight to marinate, and strain just before use.

{reverse rolled sushi}

100g cucumber, peeled, deseeded and cut into long, thin batons
1 yellow pepper, deseeded and cut into long, thin strips
salt
250g sushi rice

(Continued on page 128)

(Continued from page 127)

450ml water
100ml sushi vinegar
3 nori sheets (dried seaweed)
¼ teaspoon wasabi paste
30g best quality sushi ginger (pickled
   ginger), shredded
3 teaspoons shredded coriander

A sushi rolling mat (30 x 27cm) is vital for this recipe. Start by sprinkling the cucumber and pepper with salt, leave them to drain for 30 minutes, then pat dry with a clean tea towel or paper towels.

Put the rice in a fine sieve, rinse under cold running water until the water runs clear, then leave to drain for 10 minutes. Put the rice in a pan with the measured water, bring to the boil, stir and cover tightly with a lid. If the lid does not fit tightly, put a layer of foil under it, as it is crucial that all the heat and steam are contained (this is one of the secrets of perfect sushi rice). Immediately turn down the heat to very low and leave for 10–12 minutes, until the rice has absorbed all the water. Remove the pan from the heat and leave to steam with the lid on for a further 10–12 minutes. Immediately spread the rice on to a tray, pour over the vinegar and season with salt, gently mixing it in with a fork. Leave to cool completely.

You will find it easier to roll the sushi if you have damp hands. You are making 3 long sushi rolls, so divide the mixture accordingly.

Cover the sushi mat with a layer of clingfilm and spread a layer of rice on top of this to cover the mat entirely. Lay a sheet of nori in the centre of the rice so there is a clear border of rice around the edges, then spread the wasabi thinly over the nori. Now very gently place the vegetable strips, ginger and coriander on the nori along the edge that is closest to you. You can layer them slightly so that, when sliced, they look pretty in a cross section.

Now start rolling the sushi. Pull it slightly towards you while rolling away and applying a little pressure to the mat. Continue rolling it over and tightening it up (keeping the mat and clingfilm out of the roll) and suddenly you have a finished sushi roll. It takes a little practice to get the tension right but, once you do, it is quite compulsive! Wrap the sushi rolls tightly in the clingfilm (you will remove this after slicing).

These are best sliced and served immediately; if making them in advance, keep the long rolls refrigerated.

{cashew and coriander salad}

20g cashew nuts, finely chopped
50g red onion, finely chopped
1 small red chilli pepper, finely chopped
100g cucumber, deseeded and finely diced
1 tablespoon finely shredded mint
1 tablespoon finely shredded coriander
1 tablespoon lime juice
1 tablespoon wasabi paste (Japanese
   horseradish)

Mix together the cashews, red onion, chilli, cucumber and herbs and refrigerate until required. Beat together the lime juice and wasabi paste and toss with the salad just before serving.

{to assemble}

2 tablespoons lime juice
1 tablespoon finely chopped chives
   (ideally Chinese chives)

Heat the hot and sour tea. Meanwhile, cut each sushi roll into 6 slices, first of all slicing off and discarding the ends of the rolls. It is important to use a very sharp knife to cut the sushi and to wipe the knife with a damp cloth after each cut.

Divide the cashew salad between 6 plates. Add the lime juice and chives to the hot and sour tea and pour it straight into the most delicate bowls you possess!

Gently unwrap the sushi from the clingfilm and roll in a little of the Szechuan dust (not too much, as it has quite a kick). Arrange 3 slices of sushi with great precision on each plate, add a little pool of yellow pepper dressing for dipping, a tiny heap of Szechuan dust and a button of the tamari glaze. Serve with the hot and sour tea and, hopefully, you will not be too shattered to enjoy the fruits of your labours!

Coca Salad

potato, onion and thyme flat bread with rocket pesto, feta and gremolata,
served with horiatiki salad with lemon oil, fresh oregano, mint and parsley,
kalamata tapenade and cucumber tzatziki

Coca is a fabulous, flattish, super-savoury bread. We have added a little potato and polenta to make it sturdier and topped it with oily rosemary onions. We could leave it at that – warm, just-torn chunks eaten dipped into oil – but why leave the party early? So we've turned it into a gorgeous, fit-for-a-gourmand Greek feast. Mamma Mia or Zorba the Greek? You know how old you are…

Hot, springy slabs of savoury bread piled with emerald-green peppery rocket pesto and topped with rich, salty feta, then sprinkled with gremolata, zesty with fresh citrus and garlic flavours. (And you thought you were getting cheese on toast.) These are combined with colourful heaps of leafy, lemon dressed horiatiki salad, full of tomatoes and oregano, a sticky, dark Kalamata tapenade and a refreshingly cool tzatziki.

Oregano grows wild in many Mediterranean countries, hence its frequent use in regional cooking, particularly on pizzas. It can be cultivated here in Britain without too much difficulty and is one of the few herbs that has a stronger flavour when dried than fresh – although for the horiatiki salad, a traditionally rustic Greek country dish, fresh leaves are an absolute must. And only Kalamata olives will do for the tapenade. With a meaty texture, glorious aubergine colour and sweet, rich, fruity flavour, they are considered the finest of all olives for the table. A key element in Greek salad, they are a natural accompaniment for the feta – a tangy, salty sheep's milk cheese that often includes a proportion of goat's and even cow's milk. Finally, this is one ensemble where extra virgin olive oil is essential, so it's best to use it throughout.

serves 6

{coca bread}

90g floury potato, peeled
90ml warm water
1 teaspoon dried yeast
200g plain flour
50g quick cook polenta
1 teaspoon caster sugar
½ teaspoon salt
1 tablespoon chopped thyme
2 tablespoons olive oil

for the topping
100g red onions, finely sliced
2 teaspoons chopped rosemary
2 tablespoons olive oil
salt and freshly ground black pepper

Cook the potato in boiling salted water until tender, then drain well. Crush the potato, add the warm water and stir in the yeast. Stand this mixture in a warm place for about 20 minutes until it has a thick, yeasty foam on top.

Mix together the flour, polenta, sugar, salt and thyme. Stir in the potato yeast mixture and then add the olive oil. Knead the dough on a floured surface for 20 minutes, then put it in a bowl and cover with a cloth. Leave in a warm place until doubled in size. Knock back the dough, turn out and knead for 10 minutes. Roll out to a thickness of about 2cm and place on an oiled baking sheet.

To prepare the topping, mix together the onions, rosemary and olive oil and scatter them on top of the dough, gently pressing them in. Leave in a warm place to prove for 20 minutes and then sprinkle with salt and pepper. Bake in the oven at 180°C/Gas Mark 4 for 20 minutes.

{rocket pesto}

200g rocket
1 small garlic clove, peeled
100ml olive oil
100g Parmesan cheese, freshly grated
80g pine nuts, toasted
2 tablespoons lemon juice
salt and freshly ground black pepper

Blitz all the ingredients together in a food processor. Store in an airtight container in the refrigerator until needed.

{gremolata}

1 tablespoon finely grated lemon zest
1 teaspoon finely chopped garlic
1 tablespoon finely chopped parsley
1 tablespoon olive oil
salt and freshly ground black pepper

Mix all the ingredients, then cover and refrigerate until needed.

{kalamata tapenade}

160g Kalamata olives, stoned
3 tablespoons finely chopped mint
1 teaspoon garlic purée
1 tablespoon olive oil
2 teaspoons lemon juice
1 tablespoon capers, rinsed

Blend all the ingredients in a food processor until smooth (watch out for any sneaky olive stones). Cover and refrigerate until needed.

{cucumber tzatziki}

250g cucumber, deseeded
1 teaspoon salt
2 tablespoons chopped mint
2 tablespoons chopped parsley
1 tablespoon crushed garlic
1 tablespoon olive oil
250ml Greek yogurt
freshly ground black pepper

Grate the cucumber and place it in a colander over a dish. Sprinkle with the salt and leave to drain for 30 minutes. Squeeze the remaining moisture from the salted cucumber by gently wringing it in a clean tea towel. Transfer to a bowl, add all the other ingredients and mix well.

{lemon oil}

25ml olive oil
2 teaspoons lemon juice
salt and freshly ground black pepper

Put all the ingredients in a small jar, cover and give it a good shake.

{horiatiki salad}

24 cherry tomatoes, halved
500g cucumber, peeled and diced
150g red onions, finely sliced
25g flat leaf parsley, mint and oregano,
    mixed together
100g rocket

Combine all the ingredients in a bowl. The salad will be dressed and seasoned just before serving.

{to assemble}

210g feta cheese, crumbled

Heat the grill. Slice the bread, cover it with the rocket pesto and divide the feta evenly between each piece. Place on a baking tray and set aside.

Divide the tapenade and tzatziki between 6 serving plates. Toss the salad with the lemon oil and check the seasoning. Grill the cheese and coca bread until the bread begins to crisp and the cheese is warmed through. Heap bundles of salad on to each serving plate and prop the cheesy toasted bread to one side. Finally, sprinkle the plates generously with the gremolata.

Alternatively, each of the components can be served on separate dishes and your guests can help themselves.

Skinny Melinky

{VEGAN}

linseed flatbreads topped with butter bean crush, rocket with lemon herb mayonnaise, and potager pickles

Perfect for a party and prettier than a pitta, this is always one of the first treats to be eaten at a celebration. Fabulous, snappy little flatbreads, nutty with linseeds, are loaded with mashed butter beans, creamy with garlic and lemon, then a layer of lush leaves and, on top of that, a hotchpotch of perky pickled pieces. You can swap the collection of vegetables around in the pickle mix, depending on your preference and the season. But, whatever your choice, the finishing touch of mayonnaise, laced with linseed and flush with fragrant herbs, is the extra mile we decided to go.

'Potager' is the French word for kitchen garden, but we use it over here too. More carefully laid out and ornamental than a humble vegetable patch, it's a place where speciality varieties (such as baby vegetables) and herbs may be grown.

Golden linseeds, otherwise known as flaxseeds, are pretty high in the nutrition stakes. The richest plant source of omega 3, which is so good for us, they are also a fantastic way to get fibre (just sprinkle some of them, crushed, on your cereal in the morning) and are particularly beneficial for women's health. With their subtle, nutty flavour, we think they make a great topping for these breads.

serves 6

{potager pickles}

500ml water
600ml cider vinegar
2 tablespoons salt
5 tablespoons demerara sugar
2 bay leaves
10 black peppercorns
15 coriander seeds
15 fennel seeds
1 red pepper, cut into strips
1 yellow pepper, cut into strips
12 spring onions, trimmed
2 baby cauliflowers, divided into florets
6–8 baby carrots, trimmed
150g baby courgettes
2 baby cucumbers, each cut into
6 strips
40g parsley, roughly chopped
25g mint leaves, chopped

50ml olive oil
juice of ½ lemon

This pickle is best made 1 or 2 days in advance. Put the water, vinegar, salt, sugar, bay leaves, peppercorns, coriander and fennel seeds into a stainless steel pan and bring to the boil. Add all the vegetables except the cucumber strips and simmer for 2 minutes. Remove from the heat, leave to cool, then add the cucumber. Cover and refrigerate. Shortly before serving, drain the pickle, leaving the liquid in the bowl to be used again (for pickling more vegetables). Stir the parsley, mint, olive oil and lemon juice into the vegetables.

{butter bean crush}

450g cooked butter beans (canned are fine)
50ml soya cream
2 garlic cloves, finely chopped
grated zest and juice of 1 lemon
100ml olive oil
salt and freshly ground black pepper

Blend all the ingredients together with a hand blender until you get a nice, thick consistency. Refrigerate until required.

{lemon herb mayonnaise}

200ml soya cream
grated zest and juice of 1 lemon
100ml linseed oil
130ml olive oil
4 tablespoons chopped flat leaf parsley
4 tablespoons chopped basil
2 tablespoons chopped oregano
2 tablespoons chopped lemon thyme
salt and freshly ground black pepper

Pour the soya cream and lemon juice into a jug and blitz with a hand blender until the mixture starts to thicken (this will take only a few seconds). Slowly drizzle in the oils, while still mixing. Add the lemon zest and herbs and blitz until the mayonnaise is smooth and evenly green (there will still be some flecks of herbs). Season with salt and pepper, then stir in more soya cream if the mayonnaise is too thick or keep blending if it is too thin. Store in the refrigerator.

{linseed flatbreads}

175g plain flour
½ teaspoon caster sugar
1 teaspoon salt
2 teaspoons dried yeast
90ml warm water
50ml olive oil, plus extra for brushing
30g linseeds

Sift the flour, sugar and salt into a bowl. Stir the yeast into the warm water until dissolved, then add the olive oil. Make a well in the centre of the flour and pour in the yeast mixture. Mix to a dough, using a fork at first, then kneading to a smooth elastic consistency with your hands (this will take about 5 minutes). Place in a small bowl, cover with clingfilm or a damp cloth, and leave in a warm place until doubled in size.

Knock the dough back to release any air bubbles. Divide into 6 and shape into balls. Roll out thinly into a surfboard shape, about 5mm thick, and place on a baking sheet lined with baking parchment. Brush with olive oil and press the linseeds into the surface. Leave to rest for 5–10 minutes.

Cover the flatbreads with baking parchment, place another tray on top to weight them down, and bake at 190°C/Gas Mark 5 for 15–20 minutes, until golden brown. Remove from the oven and allow to cool on a wire rack.

{to assemble}

a few rocket (or torn lettuce) leaves

Put a flatbread on each serving plate and spread with a generous amount of the butter bean crush. Arrange a scattering of rocket or lettuce leaves on top, then dot with a few teaspoons of the herb mayonnaise. Spoon the pickled vegetables precariously on top of the leaves. Any remaining dressing from the vegetables can be drizzled over the top.

Sweetcorn Stingo

sweetcorn fritters with pickle pepper stingo and chipotle ancho refry

{VEGAN}

Sweetcorn fritters are hard to beat – fun, filling and fiery, and always welcome at a party. These are sizzling golden gems, loaded with sweet bursts of corn kernels, savoury chunks of sun dried tomatoes and fresh accents of coriander and spring onion. And they come with some of the best refried beans this side of Mexico City. Honest!

Pinto beans are a good source of protein, two important B vitamins, and all essential minerals. They are perfect for picking up the sweet, smoky punch of chipotle and ancho chillies – and when you add crushed cumin too, you're on the way to a memorable refry. Next up is a feisty stingo, its catch-you-in-the-throat sharpness offset by the deep aromas of allspice and soft charred peppers, with a zing of sherry, a touch of dry chilli heat, and the added sweetness of fresh tomatoes. Time to cool down the action with a good heap of refreshing soured cream, so crack open some icy beers and it's a private carnival you're having. Or you're starting your own Mexican wave!

The chipotle chilli is a ripe jalapeño that's been smoked until it dries out. This gives a smoky, sharp edge to its spicy heat. It's often mixed with ancho chillies, which are dried poblanos. These are fairly sweet and fruity, and generally quite mild, although every now and then there's one that packs a real punch.

serves 6

{chipotle ancho refry}

5g dried chipotle chilli
5g dried ancho chilli
200g dried pinto beans, soaked overnight in cold water
2 bay leaves
1½ teaspoons cumin seeds, cracked
2 tablespoons sunflower oil, plus extra for frying the patties
100g onion, chopped
2 garlic cloves, crushed
¼ teaspoon salt
4 tablespoons finely chopped oregano
freshly ground black pepper

Pour boiling water on to the dried chillies and leave to soak for 20 minutes, then drain, deseed and finely chop. Rinse the pinto beans, cover with fresh cold water and bring to the boil. Allow to boil rapidly for 10 minutes, skimming off any foam. Then add the bay leaves, cover and simmer for 1–1½ hours, until the beans are soft and tender but still retain their shape. The cooking time will vary depending on the age and size of the beans. Do not add salt before the beans are cooked, as this will toughen their skins and make them less tender. Always ensure there is enough water to cover the beans throughout the soaking and cooking process, otherwise they will cook unevenly.

Toast the cumin seeds in a wide, heavy based pan until they release their aroma, then add the oil, drained chillies, onion, garlic and salt. Cook until soft, then add the drained pinto beans and cook, stirring and crushing the beans as you go. The beans will start to catch on the bottom of the pan; this is a good thing and adds to the flavour. Keep stirring the beans and scraping the bottom of the pan until the beans have broken down almost to a paste but still retain some texture. Stir in the oregano and season to taste.

Let the mixture cool, then shape it into small patties, about 8cm in diameter and 2cm thick. When you are ready to serve, fry the patties in a little oil for about 2 minutes on each side, until crisp.

{pickle pepper stingo}

2 red peppers
2 yellow peppers
200ml fino sherry
1 large red chilli pepper, deseeded and finely sliced
1 allspice berry, cracked
100ml apple balsamic vinegar
200g tomatoes, skinned, deseeded and diced
1 tablespoon olive oil
1 tablespoon agave syrup
2 teaspoons finely chopped chives

Blister the skins of the red and yellow peppers under the grill or in the oven at 200°C/Gas Mark 6 until they are charred and the flesh softens. Put them into a container, cover tightly and leave to steam for 10 minutes (this makes it much easier to remove the skin). Peel off the skins, deseed the peppers and slice them finely.

Put the sherry, chilli and allspice into a stainless steel pan and bring to the boil. Simmer until reduced by half, then add the vinegar and bring back to the boil. Remove from the heat and add the tomatoes, olive oil and agave syrup. Tip into a food processor or liquidizer and blitz until smooth.

Pour this sauce over the peppers, stir gently, cover and leave to infuse for at least 30 minutes. Serve at room temperature, adding the chopped chives at the last minute.

{sweetcorn fritters}

200g cooked sweetcorn (canned is fine)
100g plain flour
2 teaspoons baking powder
80g fine cornmeal (or semolina)
2 eggs (or 3 teaspoons egg replacer)
100ml whole milk (or 200ml soya milk)
30g spring onions, finely sliced
3 tablespoons chopped coriander
½ teaspoon salt
½ teaspoon freshly ground black pepper
grated zest and juice of 1 lime
50g sun dried tomatoes, chopped

Blitz 50g of the sweetcorn in a blender or food processor, then set aside. Mix the flour, baking powder and cornmeal together. Whisk the eggs (or egg replacer) and milk together, then slowly add them to the flour mixture, stirring until you have a smooth batter. Add all the other ingredients, including the whole and crushed sweetcorn, and combine well.

Lightly oil a griddle pan or a heavy based frying pan and place over a medium heat. When it is hot, pour on 1 tablespoon of the mixture for each fritter and cook for 3–4 minutes on each side, until they are a lovely light golden colour. Serve the fritters hot, straight from the pan.

{to assemble}

3 tablespoons chopped coriander
2 limes, cut into chunks
250ml soured cream (or Lemon Herb
    Mayonnaise – see page 132)
Avocado Lime Salsa (see page 28)
Tequila Lime Ice (see page 176)

This is very easy. You can be as 'restauranty' as you wish in your presentation but we prefer this dish 'family style'. Heap the stingo into a lovely bowl and pile the refried beans and fritters on to a big serving platter. Liberally scatter the whole lot with fresh coriander and chunks of lime. Serve with soured cream or lemon herb mayonnaise for scooping, a bowl of avocado lime salsa and, just for good measure, ice cold glasses full of tequila lime ice. Enjoy!

Squish Squash

butternut and pernod terrine with green olive and tarragon hash, ricotta dumplings and lentil, oregano and clove milk

Earthy, intense flavours mark out this dish. It's both robust and refined, and good looking too. Pressed squash, layered with Pernod, buttery soft onions and aromatic sweet fennel, makes for a novel flavour combination. You could serve this lovely terrine only with the olive hash, as a starter, or you can build them both into something bigger, adding one or two extras. We do just that, and it doesn't disappoint. The little dumplings are simple and straightforward. Filled with soft herbs and lightly browned all over, they lend a creamy richness to the dish, but the real linchpin is the much maligned butt of many veggie jokes, the humble red lentil. Effortlessly delicious, with earthy tastes, but perfumed with oregano and lemon thyme and lightened with a little cream, it is transformed into a delicious 'milk' that draws all the many elements of the dish together. Just perfect!

Beautiful butternut squash has a sweet, nutty flavour and bright orange flesh, which not surprisingly has high levels of vitamins A and C. The elongated shape makes it ideal for the long, thin strips needed to make a terrine. The inclusion of lentils in this recipe is a way of showing that, far from being a boring, tired, 'vegetarian' foodstuff, they are a marvellously adaptable and delicious ingredient, with a lovely, savoury flavour that's a useful addition to many dishes. Their nutritional content is also important, as they are a great source of iron and protein. It is easy to see why lentils are a staple in so many cultures.

serves 6

{green olive hash}

280g stoned green olives, finely chopped
4 tablespoons chopped flat leaf parsley
2 tablespoons capers, rinsed and chopped
1 tablespoon chopped tarragon
grated zest and juice of 1 lemon
20ml olive oil
freshly ground black pepper

Mix all the ingredients together in a bowl and refrigerate until required.

{butternut and pernod terrine}

400g butternut squash
55g unsalted butter
250g onions, finely sliced
200g fennel, finely sliced
1 teaspoon finely chopped rosemary
5 tablespoons Pernod
salt and freshly ground black pepper

Cut the long, narrow end from the butternut squash. Peel the squash and slice lengthways as thinly as possible, using a mandolin or a knife.

Melt 40g of the butter in a pan, add the onions, fennel, rosemary and Pernod and cook until the vegetables are soft and almost sweet in flavour.

Line a terrine or ovenproof mould with baking parchment, letting it overhang the long sides, and start to layer the filling in it: butternut squash first, then seasoning, and finally onion and fennel mix. Repeat until the mould is full, finishing with a layer of squash and dotting the remaining butter over the top. Cover the top with the overlap of parchment, folding the edges together to make it secure, and place the terrine in a roasting tin. Pour enough boiling water into the tin to come three quarters of the way up the sides of the terrine, then bake at 160°C/Gas Mark 3 for 60–70 minutes. Remove from the oven.

Take a large sheet of foil, fold it over at least 4 times and place it over the terrine. Now it needs to be weighted down; a couple of cans of food work well, but make sure the surface of the terrine remains flat. Leave to cool, then refrigerate while still weighted down, preferably overnight. The terrine should emerge well set and easy to slice with a serrated knife.

{ricotta dumplings}

500g ricotta cheese, drained
60g Parmesan cheese, freshly grated
30g maize flour or quick cook polenta
finely grated zest of 1 lemon
2 tablespoons chopped parsley
1 tablespoon chopped marjoram
1 tablespoon chopped oregano
2 eggs, whites and yolks separated, yolks beaten
salt and freshly ground black pepper
150g fine semolina
olive oil and butter for frying

Put the ricotta in a mixing bowl and break it up with a spoon or spatula. Add the Parmesan, maize flour, lemon zest and herbs and mix well. Beat in the egg yolks and season with salt and pepper.

In a large bowl, whisk the egg whites until they form firm peaks, then carefully fold them into the ricotta mixture in 2 batches. Using your hands, shape the mixture into 12 dumplings. Put the semolina into a tray and add the dumplings. Shake the tray gently to make sure the dumplings are well coated, then transfer them to a tray lined with clingfilm. They can be stored in the refrigerator until you are ready to cook them.

(Continued on page 138)

(Continued from page 136)

Just before serving, gently fry the dumplings in a little olive oil for about 3 minutes until light brown, then add a small knob of butter and allow them to crisp up.

{lentil and oregano milk}

4 tablespoons oregano
4 tablespoons lemon thyme
100g red lentils
100g onions, chopped
2 garlic cloves, chopped
40g celery, chopped
1 small bay leaf
3 cloves 600ml White Stock (see page 18) or water
salt and freshly ground black pepper
1 tablespoon double cream

Tie the oregano and lemon thyme in a piece of muslin. Put the lentils in a pan with the muslin wrapped herbs and all the other ingredients except the seasoning and cream. Bring to the boil, cover and simmer for 30–40 minutes, until the lentils and vegetables are tender. Take the pan off the heat and remove the herb bundle (squeezing out any herby liquid), the bay leaf and cloves. Pour the cooked mixture into a jug blender and blend until really smooth, then pass through a fine sieve. Return the lentil milk to a clean pan and set aside.

Just before serving, reheat the lentil milk, season to taste and stir in the double cream.

{to assemble}

The terrine can be served hot or cold. Turn it out of the mould and cut into slices. If you want to reheat it, put the slices on a lined baking tray and place in the oven at 160°C/Gas Mark 3 for about 10 minutes.

Arrange the slices on 6 serving plates, with the dumplings on one side and a little heap of green olive hash on the other. Finally, divide the lentil and oregano milk between the plates.

Steaming Kraut

mushroom ragout steamed puddings with broccoli and hazelnut confetti, spiced
{VEGAN}   cranberries and two cabbages – one mulled, the other practically pickled

A warming, savoury, hearty feast for a cold winter's day, or maybe just for when you feel in need of some serious sustenance. A plentiful plateful with full-on flavours, textures and Christmas colours, a cracking combination and all guaranteed to recharge your batteries. Individual steamed puddings always feel like such a treat, and these steamy suets are stuffed to the gunnels with beautifully rich and boozy mushroom ragout and fresh herbs. They're delicious served with mulled mouthfuls of spice-rich, sticky red cabbage and the feisty, fresh taste of practically pickled red kraut. We've also brought in little bursts of tart ruby cranberries, plus sautéed broccoli and hazelnut confetti – all combining to fill your plate to epic proportions. Hot, cold, savoury, sweet, spicy, pickled, red, green… you can't have one without the other!

Whether or not cranberries turn out to have 'super' status in terms of health benefits, we love them for their brilliant colour and wonderfully sharp yet sweet taste. They are forever linked to Christmas and Thanksgiving, so are a fitting ingredient here for a warming, hearty, end-of-year meal.

Speciality mushrooms, although limited to specific periods of harvesting in the wild, are now cultivated artificially and are therefore available pretty much throughout the year. They are often known by their French names. Girolle (or chanterelle) has the colour and aroma of apricots and can be picked in the UK from July to November. Pied bleu (or wood blewit) has a robust texture and rich, distinctive flavour, and is ready from October to December. Any combination of mushrooms will do, however. Mix and match, and try to use whatever is fresh and in season. But remember not to eat the pied bleu raw, as this can be poisonous. Always take specialist advice

if you are on a fungi foray and are not sure what you have found.

serves 6

{red kraut}

300ml red wine vinegar
50g caster sugar
2 teaspoons dill seeds
1 bay leaf
250g red cabbage, finely sliced
125g red onions, finely sliced
salt and freshly ground black pepper

Put the vinegar, sugar, dill and bay leaf in a large pan and bring to the boil. Add the cabbage and onions, cover and simmer for 10 minutes. Remove from the heat, season to taste and leave to cool. This is best made 24 hours before it is needed.

{spiced cranberries}

60ml cider vinegar
45g caster sugar
½ cinnamon stick
1 star anise
100g fresh or frozen cranberries

Put the vinegar and sugar in a small pan with the spices and bring to the boil, stirring to dissolve the sugar. Simmer until the mixture is syrupy and has reduced by about two thirds. Put the cranberries in a heatproof bowl, pour the spiced vinegar over them, then cover with clingfilm and leave to cool. They can be kept in the refrigerator until required.

{mulled cabbage}

550g red cabbage, finely sliced
50g red onion, finely sliced
grated zest and juice of ¼ orange
½ teaspoon lemon juice
1 teaspoon sherry vinegar
65ml red wine

65ml ruby port
1 bay leaf
1 teaspoon chopped rosemary
1 teaspoon chopped thyme
2 cloves, crushed
2 juniper berries, crushed
2 allspice berries, cracked
40g soft dark brown sugar
salt and freshly ground black pepper

Place all the ingredients apart from the sugar, salt and pepper in a large, stainless steel pan. Bring slowly to the boil and cook over a low to medium heat for about 5 minutes, until the cabbage is tender. Reduce the heat to low and continue to cook until the liquid has almost evaporated. Add the sugar and cook until the cabbage is lightly caramelized. Season to taste and leave to cool. Set aside until required.

{mushroom ragout}

20g dried porcini mushrooms
250ml hot water
50ml olive oil
150g white onions, finely chopped
1 garlic clove, chopped
70g carrot, finely chopped
50g celery, finely chopped
200g mixed mushrooms, sliced (girolle, pied bleu and shiitake are ideal)
2 bay leaves
½ teaspoon chopped rosemary
1 tablespoon chopped curly leaf parsley
½ teaspoon chopped thyme
100g sun dried tomato paste
50ml tamari (gluten free soy sauce)
300ml red wine
100ml ruby port
salt and freshly ground black pepper

Soak the porcini mushrooms in the hot water for 30 minutes, then strain off and reserve the soaking liquid. Squeeze the

(Continued on page 141)

TERRE À TERRE

(Continued from page 139)

porcini dry in paper towels and chop them finely. Heat the olive oil in a deep pan, add the onions and cook over a medium heat until they start to colour. Add the garlic, carrot and celery and cook for 5 minutes. Then add the porcini, all the other mushrooms, the bay leaves, rosemary, parsley and thyme, and cook until the mushrooms begin to soften. Finally, add the sun dried tomato paste, porcini soaking liquid, tamari, wine and port. Bring to the boil and simmer for 35 minutes. Taste and season.

Leave to cool, then cover and refrigerate until needed. This will make enough to fill the puddings and leave you plenty to use as a garnish.

{mushroom ragout puddings}

Mushroom Ragout (see page 139)
soya margarine for coating
plain flour to dust

for the suet crust pastry
300g self raising flour
150g vegetable suet
40g curly leaf parsley, chopped
4 tablespoons chopped sage
2 tablespoons chopped chives
½ teaspoon salt
½ teaspoon freshly ground black pepper
    about 160ml White Stock (see page 18)
    or water

First make the suet crust pastry. Mix the self raising flour, suet, herbs and seasoning in a large bowl, then stir in the stock or water a little at a time until you have a malleable dough. Wrap in clingfilm and chill until you are ready to make the puddings.

Grease and flour six 100ml dariole moulds. On a lightly floured surface, roll out the pastry to about 5mm thick, then cut out 18cm rounds to line the moulds and 7.5cm rounds for the tops. Carefully line the moulds with the larger pastry rounds, squeezing out all the air bubbles and leaving a slight overhang. Fill with the cooled ragout, moisten the pastry overhang with water and cover the filling with the smaller pastry rounds, pinching slightly to seal the edges and trimming the pastry if necessary.

Place the puddings in a deep roasting tin. Pour enough boiling water into the tin to reach half way up the sides of the moulds, then cover the whole roasting tin with foil and cook in the oven at 180°C/Gas Mark 4 for 30 minutes. They can also be cooked on the hob, in a steamer, for 30 minutes.

Allow to cool slightly before gently easing the puddings from the moulds. They are best served immediately, although it is possible to make them 24 hours in advance and reheat them. This mix could be used to make one big pudding in a 1 litre basin, which would need to be steamed for 1 hour.

{broccoli and hazelnut confetti}

25g unsalted butter, optional, or 1 tablespoon
    olive oil to replace butter as a vegan option
2 teaspoons olive oil
70g hazelnuts, cut into slivers and roasted
500g broccoli florets and trimmed stalks,
    finely sliced
2 tablespoons toasted hazelnut oil
salt and freshly ground black pepper
40g curly leaf parsley, chopped
40g chives, chopped

Make the confetti just before serving. Heat the butter and oil in a large frying pan until bubbling, then add the roasted hazelnut slivers and the broccoli. Fry over a high heat for 2 minutes, until the broccoli has softened slightly and has a nutty colour on some of the florets. Stir in the hazelnut oil, seasoning and herbs.

{to assemble}

Miso Mashed Potatoes (see page 96) or
    Creamy Mashed Potatoes – a non-vegan
    option – (see page 20)

The puddings are best when freshly cooked but, if you made them in advance, wrap them in foil and warm in the oven at 150°C/Gas Mark 2 for about 15 minutes. Heat up the mulled cabbage and the remaining mushroom ragout. Place a pudding on each serving plate, with spoonfuls of the mulled cabbage and the broccoli. Spoon the piping-hot ragout over the puddings, and top the hot mulled cabbage with some cold kraut and a sprinkling of cranberries. This dish goes well with a giant bowl of steaming mash.

Yuba Juba Beefy Tea

yuba rolls filled with assam noodles, served with stuffed steamed buns,
mushroom beefy tea, pickled aubergines, soya bean pesto and
shimeji tat soi dry spice stir fry

{VEGAN}

Beefy flavour and no bull! This is a fabulous collection of the most delicious flavours and textures, and it's good looking too. Big, bold, beefy gulps of soup, packed full of meaty mushroom flavour and 'must-have-more-of' soya and seaweed – deep, rich and salty. Perfect with the fluffy buns, with their super-savoury centres, plump to dunk. The buns are delicious on their own but splendid to smudge into the creamy soya bean and cashew pesto, zingy with wasabi heat. Then there's a sweet and sour pickled baby aubergine, a steaming yuba roll – bursting with delicately perfumed Assam cellophane bean noodles – and a heap of shimeji mushroom stir fry, punchy with pepper and ginger.

Not quite your regular tea and bun teatime treat but equally (or possibly more) satisfying in a savoury and ceremonial way. Stand on ceremony and serve the beefy tea in a pot and the buns in a steamer – or let it all hang out, as we've done in Lisa's lovely picture, opposite.

Yuba sheets are bean curd sheets made from the skin that forms on soya milk when it's heated. As for the soy sauces, if you can't find tamari or ketjap manis, just use the very best quality available.

serves 6

{beefy tea}

1.75 litres water
50ml mirin (sweet rice wine)
2 tablespoons tamari (gluten free soy sauce)
1 tablespoon ketjap manis (Indonesian sweet soy sauce)
grated zest and juice of 2 limes
50g wakame or kombu (dried seaweed)
25g fresh root ginger, finely chopped
25g fresh galangal, finely chopped
2 dried chilli peppers
1 teaspoon coriander seeds, toasted and cracked
3 star anise
3 small garlic cloves, crushed

for the garnish
1 tablespoon toasted sesame oil
1 tablespoon chilli oil
1 tablespoon finely chopped chives
2 tablespoons shredded pak choi

This is best made a day in advance to allow the flavours to infuse. Put all the ingredients in a large pan, bring to the boil, cover and simmer for 15 minutes. Leave to cool, then store in the refrigerator for 24 hours, if possible, to infuse.

Shortly before serving, strain the tea (discarding what remains in the sieve), ready for reheating. Combine all the garnish ingredients and set aside.

{pickled baby aubergines}

1 teaspoon coriander seeds, toasted and cracked
2 star anise
700ml water
100ml sushi vinegar
juice of 1 lemon
2 tablespoons caster sugar
6 baby aubergines

Put all the ingredients except the aubergines in a pan and bring to the boil. Meanwhile, prepare the aubergines. With a sharp knife, make 2 or 3 cuts in each one, from the base up to the stalk, leaving them still whole, and looking rather like castanets!

Place the aubergines in the boiling pickling liquid and simmer for 5 minutes or until tender. Remove the pan from the heat and leave to cool. The aubergines can be refrigerated for up to 2 days and warmed through when you are ready to serve them.

{soya bean pesto}

200g edamame beans, peeled (soya mangetout) – frozen are fine
40g cashew nuts
20g basil
150ml grapeseed oil
1 teaspoon wasabi paste (Japanese horseradish)
100ml warm water
1 tablespoon yuzu juice (Japanese citrus fruit) – or use lime juice
salt

Put all the ingredients in a food processor or liquidizer and blend until they become a smooth, bright green pesto. Stored in the refrigerator in a sealed container, the pesto will keep for few days.

{duxelles bun filling}

2 tablespoons sunflower oil
45g onion, finely chopped
30g fresh root ginger, finely chopped
150g mixed mushrooms
grates zest and juice of 1 lemon
12 preserved black beans
1 teaspoon ketjap manis
1 teaspoon mirin (sweet rice wine)
1 spring onion, finely shredded
1 tablespoon toasted sesame oil

Heat the sunflower oil in a pan, add the onion and ginger and cook gently until soft. Blitz the mushrooms in a food processor, add them to the pan and cook for about 10 minutes, until there is hardly any liquid remaining. Now add the lemon zest and juice, black beans, ketjap manis and mirin. Carry on cooking until the mixture loses all its liquid and starts to stick to the bottom of the pan. Remove from the heat, add the spring onion and sesame oil, and leave to cool.

{stuffed steamed buns}

1 teaspoon dried yeast
1 teaspoon caster sugar
125ml warm water
1 teaspoon toasted sesame oil
200g plain flour
½ teaspoon baking powder
1 teaspoon salt Duxelles Bun Filling (see above)

Dissolve the yeast and sugar in the warm water and leave for about 10 minutes, until the mixture starts to froth. Brush a mixing bowl with the sesame oil, tip in the flour, baking powder and salt and add the yeasty liquid. Mix to a dough. Knead gently for 5 minutes, then cover with clingfilm and leave in a warm place for 15–20 minutes, until doubled in size. Knead again for 30 seconds, then cut the dough into 6 pieces and roll them into balls.

Roll each ball out into a round. Put a heaped teaspoonful of the duxelles filling in the centre of each one, lightly wet the edges, then pull them up over the filling

(Continued on page 144)

(Continued from page 143)

and roll them in your hands so the filling is sealed in the centre of the dough ball. Place the balls on individual squares of greaseproof paper and put these on a lightly floured tray. The paper is important, as the buns are tricky to handle when hot, so it needs to be large enough for you to hold the edges when you are moving the balls about. Now cover the balls with a cloth and leave in a warm place until doubled in size.

Cook the buns shortly before serving. Place them in a steamer, still on their squares of greaseproof paper, and steam for about 17 minutes.

{yuba rolls}

2 Assam tea bags
a pinch of salt
2 litres water
100g cellophane bean noodles
1 tablespoon sunflower oil
100g onions, thinly sliced
20g fresh root ginger, finely chopped
2 tablespoons finely chopped garlic
100g red pepper, shredded
100g carrot, cut into thin strips
15 preserved black beans
1 tablespoon tamari
2½ tablespoons ketjap manis
juice of 2 limes
150g beansprouts
150g pak choi, shredded
2 teaspoons finely diced red chilli pepper
1 teaspoon toasted sesame oil
50g coriander, roughly chopped
yuba sheets (bean curd sheets) – enough
    for 6 pieces, each about 22cm square

for cooking the rolls
50ml White Stock (see page 18) or water
1 teaspoon ketjap manis (see above)
2 teaspoons sunflower oil
1 tablespoon dry sherry (optional)

Put the teabags, salt and water into a pan and bring to the boil. Remove the teabags and add the noodles to the pan. Cook for 3 minutes, then drain and leave to cool.

Heat the sunflower oil in a large wok, add the onions, ginger, garlic, red pepper, carrot and black beans and stir fry for 1½ minutes. Add the tamari, ketjap manis and lime juice, cook for 30 seconds, then add the beansprouts, pak choi, noodles, chilli, sesame oil and coriander. Toss them together and spread the mixture out on a tray to cool.

Cut the yuba sheets into 6 pieces, each about 22cm square. Bring a large pan of water to the boil and, using long-handled tongs, dip each square into the water for 30 seconds, then lay on a tray to cool.

This is how we suggest you make the rolls, but you can also make them to your own design. Just make sure the parcels are sealed and the contents don't spill out. Take one square of yuba and spoon one sixth of the filling parallel to the side nearest you, 2–3cm away from the edge. Lift up the yuba and fold it away from you over the mixture, then slightly tuck it under the filling. Fold in the right and left sides to seal the ends, then carry on rolling away from you to make a fat cigar shape. Slightly moisten the last flap so that it sticks down and seals well. The rolls can now be covered with a damp cloth or a sheet of damp greaseproof paper and refrigerated until you are ready to cook them.

Cook the rolls shortly before serving. Put them on a baking tray, mix together the stock or water, ketjap manis and oil, and sherry if you like, and pour this mixture over the rolls. Place in the oven at 180°C/ Gas Mark 4 for about 10 minutes, until they are thoroughly heated through.

{shimeji tat soi dry spice stir fry}

1 tablespoon sunflower oil
300g shimeji mushrooms, clumps broken
    into individual mushrooms
1 tablespoon finely chopped fresh root
    ginger
3 tat soi heads (Asian greens) – or 1 large
    pak choi, cut into 4
juice of 2 limes
1 tablespoon tamari
2 tablespoons ketjap manis
1 teaspoon toasted sesame oil
2 teaspoons coriander seeds, toasted and
    cracked
5 Szechuan peppercorns, cracked 5 black
    peppercorns, cracked
¼ teaspoon salt
1 teaspoon sesame seeds, toasted
4 tablespoons roughly chopped coriander

Heat the sunflower oil in a large wok and flash fry the mushrooms for 1 minute. Add the ginger and tot soi and fry for 1 minute longer. Now add the lime juice, tamari, ketjap manis and sesame oil. Fry for 1 minute more or until the vegetables start to look glazed, then add the remaining ingredients, stir well and serve instantly.

{to assemble}

Divide the leafy stir fry between 6 serving plates and place the yuba rolls on top. Put a warmed pickled aubergine next to each roll and smudge the pesto liberally on to each plate.

Reheat the beefy tea. Serve either in traditional lidded Chinese cups, with a good spoonful of garnish and the steaming buns sitting on top – or in small coffee cups, but well garnished, with a saucer on top to hold the buns. Put the cups to one side of the plates, for polite slurping, mopping and dunking!

Between the Sheets

lasagne with a filling of creamy goat's cheese, zesty salsa verde and seared cherry tomatoes, served with courgette noodle tangle and cheese fritters

There is a real vibrancy to this pasta dish and it's ever so easy to assemble. We love the hot and cold combination, and the simple freshness that this quick but delicious tomato sauce brings to the plate; a tried and well tested partner for thin pasta sheets concealing just-melting, nutty goat's cheese, juicy seared cherry tomatoes and zesty mouthfuls of salsa verde. We've added little textured bundles of black rice noodles, twisted with threads of tender courgette and scented with lemony basil. And, to complete this fabulous collection of tastes and flavours, we just had to include crispy, sizzling, smoky, melt-in-the-middle fritters.

The black rice noodles bring a wonderful, almost gelatinous texture to any dish, and also a rather bold, nutty flavour – unlike most noodles, which just carry the taste of the sauce they're in.

serves 6

{salsa verde}

25g flat leaf parsley
25g chervil
40g capers, rinsed
3 garlic cloves, crushed
grated zest and juice of 1 lemon
50ml olive oil
salt and freshly ground black pepper

Roughly chop the herbs and capers, then mix with all the other ingredients. Refrigerate the salsa until required. It should be served at room temperature.

{courgette noodle tangle}

125g black rice noodles
25ml olive oil, plus extra to drizzle
140g green courgettes
140g yellow courgettes
15g torn basil leaves
juice of 1 lemon
salt and freshly ground black pepper

In a large pan of boiling salted water, cook the noodles according to packet instructions. Drain immediately and plunge straight into cold water. Once cold, drain again, drizzle with olive oil and place in the refrigerator.

Now cut the courgettes into long, thin strands. The easiest way to do this is with a mandolin, but if you don't have one, cut them lengthways into thin strips, as finely as possible. You are looking for spaghetti thinness, but if you manage only tagliatelli, all well and good!

Mix the noodles, courgette strands, torn basil leaves, 25ml olive oil, lemon juice and seasoning. Twist the strips well to make sure the colourful ingredients are distributed evenly throughout. Serve cold.

{fresh tomato sauce}

600g ripe vine tomatoes
3 garlic cloves
1 tablespoon olive oil
salt and freshly ground black pepper
a pinch of caster sugar (optional)

Put the tomatoes and garlic in a blender, then blitz together until smooth. Push this purée through a fine sieve into a bowl, to remove any lumps.

Add the olive oil and seasoning, and sugar if needed (depending on the sweetness of the tomatoes). Refrigerate until required.

{cheese fritters}

100g plain flour
a pinch of salt
2 teaspoons baking powder
1 egg
85ml whole milk
40g smoked sun dried tomatoes, chopped
50g mature Cheddar cheese, grated
50g Parmesan cheese, freshly grated
freshly ground black pepper
sunflower oil for deep frying

Sift the flour, salt and baking powder into a large bowl. Lightly beat the egg and milk together and mix this into the flour to make a thick, sticky batter. Add the tomatoes, cheeses and pepper. The batter can now be refrigerated until required, but it must be brought back to room temperature before it is used.

Heat oil in a deep fryer or deep pan to 170°C (if you don't have a thermometer, drop a small piece of bread into the oil; if it goes golden brown within a minute, the oil is hot enough). Gently lower half tablespoons of batter into the hot oil, turning them once or twice until they are golden brown but

(Continued on page 147)

(Continued from page 145)

still soft in the middle. This will take no more than 2 minutes. Drain on paper towels.

{to assemble}

18 lasagne sheets
olive oil for frying, plus extra to sprinkle
400g soft goat's cheese
grated zest of $1/2$ lemon
freshly ground black pepper
12 cherry tomatoes
Salsa Verde (see page 145)

Cook the lasagne sheets according to packet instructions. (If using fresh, home-made lasagne, plunge the sheets into boiling salted water for 1 minute only.) Drain well and sprinkle with a little olive oil to prevent the sheets from sticking together. Mix the goat's cheese with the lemon zest and pepper. Heat a very little olive oil in a frying pan and quickly sear the tomatoes.

Now construct the lasagne stacks. Put a sheet of lasagne on the bottom, a splodge of goat's cheese, a heap of salsa and a tomato, then a sheet of lasagne topped with a final splodge of cheese, some salsa and a tomato, then a final sheet to go over the top.

Gently heat the tomato sauce. Place a tangle of courgette noodles next to the lasagne stack, put a fritter on the noodle heap and pour the bright tomato sauce between the stacks.

Dhal Vada

masala vada kebabs with moroccan stick salad marinated in argan oil and preserved lemon, with purple flowering chive basmati, mint oil and pickled chillies

{VEGAN} {WHEAT FREE}

This is a pretty snazzy street food that, with a few additions, becomes a whole load more than a snack. A sort of delicious savoury doughnut, perfect for piling up for a party, or equally stunning arranged on individual plates. It's a spectacle of vibrant colours and snappy textures, although the wonderfully strong flavours should be approached with caution by the faint hearted!

We start with fabulous soft silky vada, chilli-hot, pungent with fenugreek seeds and asafoetida, and drenched in spice-fuelled yogurt. (For more on asafoetida, see page 122.) Next up are mouthfuls of pillowy basmati, peppered with purple flowers and faint onion tastes, splashed with bright cooling mint oil and served with salty, citrus, snappy stick salad and refreshing, pucker-up, pickled chillies.

Vada is a traditional southern Indian food, often eaten with 'sambar' (stewed vegetables) and coconut chutney. It's also a popular snack, sold by street vendors, particularly at breakfast. Sorry we don't open until noon...

serves 4–6

{pickled chillies}

100g long red chilli peppers
100g long yellow chilli peppers
600ml cider vinegar
1 teaspoon ground allspice
1 teaspoon coriander seeds
1 cinnamon stick
4 bay leaves
1 small dried bird's eye chilli
100g caster sugar
2 sprigs of thyme

Put the chilli peppers (except the bird's eye) in a pan, cover with cold water and bring to the boil. Reduce the heat and simmer gently for 4 minutes, then drain and lay the chilli peppers on paper towels to dry.

In a stainless steel pan, bring the vinegar, spices, bay leaves and bird's eye chilli to a simmer, and stir in the sugar until it dissolves.

Pack the fresh chillies into a large, clean, dry jar, push in the thyme and bay leaves and then pour in the warm vinegar and spices to within 1cm or so of the top. Tap the jar to dispel any air bubbles beneath the surface, and put on a vinegar-proof lid.

Store the jar in a cool, dark cupboard for 2–3 weeks. Once opened, store in the refrigerator.

{purple flowering chive basmati}

200g basmati rice
300ml water
50ml olive oil
salt and freshly black pepper
10 purple flowering chives, finely chopped (flowers reserved to garnish)

Wash the rice in several changes of cold water, then leave to soak for about 30 minutes in fresh cold water.

Drain the rice and put it into a large pan. Add the 300ml water, bring to the boil, stir, then cover with a tightly fitting lid. Turn the heat to low and leave the rice to cook for 10 minutes before turning off the heat. Do not lift off the lid, but leave the rice to continue cooking in the pan for a further 5 minutes. By now the rice should have absorbed all the water.

Pour over the olive oil, add salt and pepper to taste, then add the chopped chives, fluffing up the rice with a fork. Press the rice into six 100ml dariole moulds, or small cups, and leave it to mould into shape.

{yogurt masala}

1 green chilli pepper, deseeded and
    chopped
200ml creamed coconut
3 tablespoons freshly grated coconut (or
    use dessicated coconut)
500ml yogurt (or soya yogurt)
1 tablespoon sunflower oil
1 teaspoon mustard seeds
1 teaspoon cumin seeds
1 teaspoon ground turmeric
$1/2$ teaspoon asafoetida powder
6 curry leaves
1 teaspoon finely chopped red chilli pepper
salt
120g coriander, leaves chopped (stalks and
    roots reserved for Vada, opposite page)

Blend the chilli pepper with the creamed coconut and grated coconut, then stir in the yogurt.

Heat the oil in a pan and throw in all the dry spices, the curry leaves and the red chilli pepper. When the seeds start to crack and splutter, tip them into the yogurt mix, add salt to taste and stir well.

Stir in the fresh coriander just before you are ready to use the marinade.

{vada}

175g urad dhal (black lentils) – or use
   moong dhal (split green lentils)
1 teaspoon fenugreek seeds
500ml cold water
4 green chilli peppers, deseeded and chopped
reserved coriander stalks and roots, chopped
   (see Yogurt Masala, opposite page)
1 tablespoon grated fresh root ginger
1 teaspoon asafoetida powder
1/2 teaspoon salt
Yogurt Masala (see opposite page)
sunflower oil for deep frying

Soak the dhal and fenugreek seeds in the
cold water for 2 hours, then drain in a fine
sieve. Place in a food processor with the
chillies, coriander stalks and roots, ginger,
asafoetida and salt. Process to a thick,
smooth batter.

Heat oil in a deep fryer or deep pan to
180°C (if you don't have a thermometer,
drop a small piece of bread into the oil; if
it goes golden brown within a minute, the
oil is hot enough). Wet your hands, take a
tablespoonful of the batter, roll and flatten
it slightly in the palm of your hand, then
make a hole in the centre. The vada you
are making should look like small
doughnuts. Slip them gently and carefully
into the oil, a few at a time, and fry for
about 5 minutes, turning once, until
golden brown.

Prepare a bowl of warm water, large
enough to take all 12–16 pieces. As the
vada come out of the fryer, drop them
straight into the water and leave to soak
for 10 minutes. Then lift them out, one at
a time, gently squeezing out any excess
water. Put them into the yogurt masala to
marinate for at least 30 minutes.

Remove from the vada from the marinade
when you are ready to reheat them.

{moroccan stick salad}

150g carrots, cut into matchsticks
100g celery, cut into matchsticks
150g kohlrabi, cut into matchsticks
100g spring onions, sliced
60g radishes, sliced
150g asparagus or sugar snap peas,
   thinly sliced
100g fenugreek leaves
for the dressing
50ml freshly squeezed orange juice
50ml argan oil
25ml preserved lemon liquor
peel from 3 preserved lemons, finely diced

First make the dressing. Whisk all the
liquids together, then add the finely diced
lemon peel.

Toss all the prepared vegetables together
(omitting the fenugreek leaves), and chill
the salad until 10 minutes before required.
At this point, remove from the refrigerator
and combine with the dressing to allow
the salad to marinate. Just before serving,
add the fenugreek leaves and mix in well.

{to assemble}

4–6 cinnamon sticks (optional)
a little mint oil (see Herbs Oils, page 20)
reserved chive flowers (see Purple Flowering
   Chive Basmati, page opposite)

Take 2 or 3 vada per person and push
them on to a cinnamon stick or just stack
them up in piles. Place them on a baking
tray and heat in the oven at 200°C/
Gas Mark 6 for 10 minutes.

Gently warm the yogurt masala, taking
care not to boil it. Pile the salad on to
serving plates and carefully turn out the
warm basmati rice from the moulds.

Nestle the vada beside the rice, coating
them with some warmed yogurt, then
splash a little mint oil over the rice.
Garnish with pickled chillies and chive
flowers.

HAPPY
EVER
AFTERS

Chai Chikki Fried Rice Puddings

{VEGAN} {WHEAT FREE}

coconut rice puddings stuffed with cardamom apricots,
served with tamarind toffee and chai spiced custard

The warm musky flavour of cardamom scented apricots, encased in a coconut creamy rice pudding, is a match made in heaven, with the addition of tangy tamarind toffee and aromatic custard, making the whole combination plate licking good! We have used dried apricots as they make a more robust filling and have the condensed flavour that we were after. All the components can be made well in advance.

Tamarind is a fabulous sweet but tart flavouring that comes from the fruit of the tamarind tree, which originated in Africa but is found all over Asia. The fruit is a small brown pod which, when ripe, contains a sweet pulp that is pressed into a small brick: chunks can then be broken off, soaked in boiling water and pressed through a sieve, to extract the paste for cooking. The name 'tamarind' means 'Indian date', and the texture is indeed soft and chewy like a date, although the flavour is decidedly less sweet and more sour. Tamarind is often added to preserves and puddings, as well as many Asian dishes. It is also a key ingredient in Worcestershire sauce – which not many people know! You can find it as a brick in Asian food stores, and process it yourself, or you can buy the ready-made paste.

Palm sugar or jaggery is a concentrated product made from cane juice, and features widely in sweet and savoury dishes across India and other parts of South East Asia.

serves 6-8

{coconut rice puddings with cardamom apricots}

800ml coconut milk
½ vanilla pod, split and scraped
2 tablespoons vegetable oil, plus extra for frying
250g Arborio rice
50g caster sugar

for the cardamom apricots
20 cardamom pods, crushed
300g dried apricots
300ml fresh orange juice

First prepare the cardamom apricots. Tie the crushed cardamom pods in a small square of muslin cloth and put this bundle with the dried apricots in a small pan and cover with the orange juice. Cook on a very low heat until the apricots are nice and plump. Remove from the heat and allow to cool thoroughly, then remove the muslin bag, squeezing out the juice, and chop each apricot into 3 or 4 strips and set to one side.

To prepare the rice, warm the coconut milk with the vanilla pod and scraped out seeds and set aside. Heat the oil in a heavy based pan and cook the rice for about 30 seconds, stirring constantly. Strain the coconut milk and add slowly to the rice, a small ladleful at a time, still stirring constantly. The rice should absorb all the liquid before the next addition. Cook until the rice is soft and creamy, then remove from the heat and stir in the sugar before allowing the mixture to cool.

To create the puddings, you will need 6-8 dariole moulds. Line them with clingfilm and press some of the cooled rice pudding mix into each mould, leaving a cavity in the middle. Spoon cardamom apricots into the cavity and cover over again with more rice pudding. Press down on the top, cover with clingfilm and refrigerate until ready to fry.

When you are ready to serve, turn the puddings out of the moulds. You can either shallow fry them in a little oil for 3-4 minutes, turning once, before putting them on to a lined baking tray and baking in the oven at 180°C/Gas Mark 4 for about 15 minutes. Or you can deep fry them for about 2 minutes until golden brown, then bake for 10 minutes.

{black jaggery tamarind toffee}

25g tamarind paste
75g palm sugar (or jaggery)
100g caster sugar
50ml water
250ml soya cream

Place the tamarind, palm sugar, caster sugar and water in a heavy based pan and bring to the boil. Once boiled, turn the heat down to a simmer and cook for 10 minutes until the mix is thick and bubbly. Add the cream and simmer for another 5 minutes. Take off the heat, strain and allow to cool.

{chai custard}

350ml coconut milk
250ml almond milk
2 chai tea bags
3 tablespoons cornflour
75ml water
50g caster sugar
50ml soya cream

Place 250ml coconut milk and the almond milk in a heavy based pan. Add the chai tea bags and infuse over a low heat for 10 minutes, then remove the bags. Meanwhile mix the cornflour with the water to make a smooth paste. Bring the milk mix to the boil and whisk in the cornflour paste to thicken. Add the sugar and simmer for 1 minute, whisking continuously, then take off the heat. Strain through a fine sieve and allow to cool, then mix in the remaining coconut milk and the soya cream. Refrigerate until you are ready to use it.

{to assemble}

Top each fried rice pudding with a blob of tamarind toffee, and serve with a jug of chai custard on the side. The cool toffee and custard go beautifully with the hot puddings, but can also be served warm if preferred.

Cigarillos Medjoolie

{VEGAN}

deep fried date, frangipane and pomegranate parchment wraps,
served with frozen mint tea

I love these scrumptious delights: the hot, crispy, golden leaved, paper thin pastry makes a perfect wrapping for the succulent, fleshy Medjool dates, paired with flowery almond paste, and peppered with juicy pink pomegranate seeds, bursting with sweet-sour squirts in every bite. To dream of pomegranates traditionally signifies good health and longevity, and the reality is that they are chock full of antioxidants, so the consumption of this pud should be encouraged on health grounds!

This dish has always been a firm favourite in the restaurant, and both components can be prepared well in advance. It is particularly refreshing teamed, as here, with a revitalizing chilly mint tea granita but if you fancy something a little more robust, good strong black cardamom coffee is a winning taste combination too.

serves 6

{cigarillos}

400g fresh Medjool dates, stoned
6 filo pastry sheets (but have more on
   standby as it is a temperamental
   product!)
75g pomegranate seeds
50g soya margarine, melted
oil for deep frying

for the frangipane
50g caster sugar
100ml water
1 tablespoon orange flower water
80g ground almonds

First make the frangipane. Bring the sugar, water and orange flower water to the boil in a small pan. Stir in the ground almonds, then cool and refrigerate.

Next, prepare the dates. Have a large sheet of greaseproof paper ready on a baking tray. Press the date halves on to the paper in the shape of a rectangle 8 x 25cm. Cover the dates with another sheet of greaseproof paper and, using a rolling pin, flatten the dates, enlarging the rectangle a little more. Refrigerate the tray for 1 hour.

You are now ready to make the cigarillos. Remove the tray of dates from the refrigerator. With the layers of paper still on, cut the date rectangle in half lengthways. Now remove the top layer of paper. Working one half at a time, spread a layer of frangipane in a central strip along the top, and on to this place a scattering of pomegranate seeds. Bring the 2 edges up together and seal to form a long 'sausage' (still keeping the paper on). Repeat this with the other half of the date rectangle. Refrigerate both sausages for 1 hour to firm them up.

Cut each sausage into 3 pieces. Lay a sheet of filo pastry on your worktop and brush it with melted soya margarine before folding in half. Place a sausage on the filo and roll up in the pastry to make a cigarillo. Leaving 1cm filo at each end to seal, trim off any excess. Now twist the ends to seal the cigarillos. Refrigerate until needed.

Just before you are ready to eat, preheat the oil to 180°C/Gas Mark 4 and deep fry the cigarillos for about 2 minutes until the pastry is golden brown and crispy. Drain on paper towels.

{mint tea granita}

50g1 litre water
100g caster sugar
25g mint leaves
6 peppermint tea bags

Put the water in a pan and bring to the boil. Stir in the sugar, half the mint leaves and the tea bags. Remove from the heat, cover and leave to infuse. Once cool, strain, discarding the mint leaves and tea bags. Finely chop the remaining fresh mint leaves and add to the mint tea. Now freeze the liquid, stirring every 30 minutes, until crystals are formed. Remove the granita from the freezer 10 minutes before serving, to thaw slightly. Fork through before spooning into frozen cups or glasses.

{to assemble}

pomegranate seeds to sprinkle

Serve the freshly fried cigarillos while still piping hot, with a generous sprinkling of fresh pomegranate seeds and a glass of mint tea granita. The icy mint tea adds a lovely freshness to the sweetness of the dates.

Two Fat Tarts

spiced roasted figs and plums on sheep's milk cheese cream and honeyed plums,
all crammed into almond pastry shells, drenched with a figgy sherry syrup and
served with basil and lemon ice cream

These filled to bursting tubby little tarts are ideal for a teatime treat: crispy almond pastry shells loaded with mild sweet sheep's milk cheese, layered with sticky pockets of runny plum compote and each one crowned with a whole plump plum or fig. Then, just for good measure, we've finished off with liberal amounts of silky sherry and fig syrup. (Dark, sweet and smooth, Ximénez is perfect for this.) Oh, and let's not forget the aromatic, crisp citrus ice cream (there's plenty here, so you'll have lots left over to use on other occasions).

We love Slipcote, our delicious Sussex sheep's milk cheese: the mild creamy taste is an ideal partner for the heady richness of ripe fruit, and here it's a perfect foil for the more powerful flavours of the velvety fig syrup. The cheese is organic and we use it in many dishes: it has a higher fat and protein content then cow's or goat's milk cheeses, giving it a naturally sweet taste (that, and the Sussex grass!).

serves 6

{whole roasted figs and plums}

6 figs
6 plums
50ml sherry
40g caster sugar
50ml water

Using a sharp knife, cut a cross in the tops of the figs, a little way into the flesh. Place in an ovenproof dish, splash with sherry and sprinkle with half the sugar. Score the top of the plums with a cross, place in another ovenproof dish, splash with water and sprinkle with the remaining sugar. Bake both dishes at 180°C/Gas Mark 4 for about 10 minutes until the fruits are soft. The skin of the plums should be starting to peel away.

{ximénez and fig syrup}

3 ripe figs, halved
250ml Ximénez sherry
100g caster sugar

Mix all the ingredients together in a heavy based pan and bring to the boil, stirring gently. Simmer until the liquid has reduced by half, then remove the figs and set them to one side, reserving the syrup.

{basil and lemon ice cream}

300ml double cream
300ml crème fraîche
200ml whole milk
20g basil leaves
grated zest of 1 lemon
9 egg yolks
175g caster sugar

In a small heavy based pan put the cream, crème fraîche, milk, basil leaves and lemon zest. Bring slowly to the boil, then quickly blend in a liquidizer (or with a small hand blender). Return to the pan over a low heat. In a large bowl whisk the egg yolks and sugar until they become light and creamy in texture. Bring the basil cream mix to the boil, pour one third of it on to the egg mixture, stir together thoroughly and return to the rest of the basil cream in the pan. Keep stirring this mixture over a medium heat until the custard thickens and coats the back of the spoon. Pour into a bowl to cool and then chill in the refrigerator for at least 2 hours before churning in an ice cream maker. Freeze ready for use.

{almond pastry cups}

150g plain flour
85g ground almonds
85g caster sugar
100g unsalted butter, diced
1 egg yolk

Grease and base-line the hollows of a non-stick muffin tin, using small rounds of greaseproof paper. You need to make 12 small tarts.

Place the flour, ground almonds, sugar and butter in a food processor and pulse them until they resemble breadcrumbs. Add the egg yolk and mix to form a soft dough. Wrap in clingfilm and chill for 1 hour.

Roll out the pastry and cut into discs just bigger than the hollows in the muffin tin. Lay the discs gently in the tin. Watch out as the pastry will break if rolled out too thinly. Chill in the freezer for 30 minutes, or in the refrigerator for 1 hour.

Now blind bake the pastry cups: line them with greaseproof paper, fill with baking beans and cook at 180°C/Gas Mark 4 for 15-20 minutes until the pastry is

(Continued on page 156)

Two Fat Tarts

(Continued from page 155)

colouring around the edges. Carefully remove the beans and paper and return the cups to the oven for 10 minutes until the pastry is golden brown and crispy.

Allow the cups to cool and keep them in the refrigerator until you are ready to fill them.

{plum compote}

500g slightly under-ripe plums
4 tablespoons runny honey
½ vanilla pod, split and scraped
1 star anise

Cut each plum into 8 pieces, removing the stones, and put in a heavy based pan with the honey, vanilla pod and seeds, and star anise. Cover and simmer gently for 10-15 minutes, stirring occasionally, until the plums start to break down and a nice syrup is forming. Remove from the heat and allow to cool, then remove the vanilla pod and star anise.

{to assemble}

200g soft sheep's milk cheese (Sussex
   Slipcote is ideal)
100ml crème fraîche
½ teaspoon vanilla extract
grated zest of ½ lemon
mint and basil leaves

Mix the cheese with the crème fraîche, vanilla extract and lemon zest until smooth.

Place a spoonful of plum compote in the empty pastry cups, followed by a spoonful of cheese mix and then a little more of the compote. Rest a fig or a plum on top of this and pour some of the Ximénez and fig syrup over the whole thing.

Put one fig and one plum tart on each plate and serve with a spoonful of the plum compote, a scoop of basil and lemon ice cream, one of the reserved fig halves, and a few fresh mint and basil leaves.

Rhubarb and Custard Bricks

deep fried custard filled pastry parcels served with baked early rhubarb
and a rhubarb and rosehip sorbet

Piping hot, mace laced little pastry parcels packed with a rich, velvety custard are a perfect match for a chilly sharp tasting rhubarb and rosehip sorbet, and sweet tender sticks of simple baked rhubarb. This combination is shockingly good with a shot of ginger wine and if you can get hold of some rosehip syrup, try a little poured over the sorbet. All these elements can be prepared in advance, with only the custard bricks left to deep fry at the last moment.

Rhubarb is enjoying a popular resurgence, which can only be good. It's technically a vegetable, although nearly always prepared as a fruit. Early or 'forced' rhubarb is pink or scarlet, and has lovely long, fleshy stems and a sweet fragrant taste. It's grown in sheds – hidden under chimney pots or wrapped in brown paper, to keep it warm and shield it from the light. But really it shouldn't be kept under wraps: we think it has been buried under crumble far too long! Pâte à brique is a north African pastry which resembles a fine crêpe. We love it, in the restaurant, as it produces an incredibly crisp crust (try saying that after a few ginger wines!).

serves 6

{baked rhubarb}

400g young rhubarb
150ml water
100g caster sugar

Cut the rhubarb into 4cm lengths and lay in a deep sided baking tray. Pour the water over the rhubarb and sprinkle with the sugar. Bake at 160°C/Gas Mark 3 for 10-15 minutes until the rhubarb is just cooked and soft to touch. Allow to cool, then chill.

{custard bricks}

6 pâte à brique sheets (or use filo pastry)
1 egg, beaten
oil for deep or shallow frying
½ teaspoon ground mace
2 tablespoons icing sugar

for the custard filling
500ml single cream
250ml whole milk
1 vanilla pod, split and scraped
grated zest of ½ lemon
40g cornflour
250g caster sugar
8 egg yolks

First prepare the custard filling. Place the cream, milk, vanilla pod and seeds, and lemon zest in a heavy based pan and cook over a low heat for 10 minutes without letting the mixture boil. Put the cornflour, sugar and egg yolks in a bowl and whisk together until combined. Pour one third of the warm infused cream mix on to the sugar and egg mixture. Quickly stir together and pour back into the rest of the cream mix in the pan. Cook over a low heat, whisking constantly with a small balloon whisk, until the mixture comes to the boil. Remove from the heat and pour into a cold bowl to cool down. Remove the vanilla pod, giving it a squeeze to extract all the flavour.

To make the bricks, cut the pastry rounds into thirds, as if you were cutting a pie into 3 pieces. Take each fan shaped piece of pastry and brush all around the edges with beaten egg. Place a spoonful of the custard in the centre of the pastry and fold up the pastry into a sealed brick shape. Here is how to do this: place the point of the fan shape towards you, bring the point up and over the filling, fold the sides in to overlap each other like an envelope and then bring the top down to seal the parcel. Place each parcel on to a lined baking tray, cover in clingfilm so they do not dry out and refrigerate until needed.

Just before you are ready to serve, heat oil in a deep fryer or deep pan to 180°C and fry the custard bricks for 1-2 minutes until golden brown and crispy. (They can also be shallow fried in hot oil, turning frequently.) Drain on kitchen paper to soak up any excess oil. Mix the mace with the icing sugar and sprinkle over the bricks.

{rhubarb and rosehip sorbet}

900g rhubarb
250ml water
175g caster sugar
2 rosehip tea bags
juice of 1 lemon

Wash the rhubarb and chop into small pieces. Put in a heavy based pan with the water, sugar and rosehip tea bags. Bring to the boil, then reduce the heat and simmer until the rhubarb is tender (about 5-6 minutes). Remove the tea bags and cool the mixture down. Purée in a food processor until smooth, then pass through a fine sieve. Add the lemon juice and a little more sugar if required. Churn the purée in an ice cream maker, then freeze until required. If you do not have an ice cream maker, place the purée in a container suitable for freezing and freeze until slushy. Remove the slushy ice mix from the freezer and whisk until the icy lumps are broken up and the mixture is smooth. Place back in the freezer and repeat this chilling and whisking process until the sorbet reaches the consistency required. Freeze until required.

{to assemble}

12-18 fresh raspberries 1 tablespoon
   rosehip syrup (optional)

Serve the fried custard bricks with a little stack of baked rhubarb and a scoop of rhubarb and rosehip sorbet. Spoon over a little of the baked rhubarb syrup and sprinkle on a few raspberries. If using rosehip syrup, pour a little over the sorbet.

Cherry Apple Eccles

warm eccles cakes served with cinnamon cherry apples and calvados ice cream

Here's our version of 'entente cordiale', a perfect Anglo-French collaboration, our crisp apples and their inimitable smooth tasting apple brandy. These little baked beauties are cracking served warm with a cuppa, but with a few simple additions they perk up into the perfect plush pudding. Juicy cinnamon scented cherry apples and generous amounts of velvety Calvados ice cream are the perfect match. We've made the Eccles cakes with Granny Smiths, but you could also use Discovery or Cox's Orange Pippin – in fact, any apple variety with a firm texture and acid sweetness.

serves 4-6

{eccles cakes}

500g Puff Pastry (see page 20)
50ml vegetable oil

for the apple filling
2 large Granny Smith apples, peeled and cored
350g currants
350g sultanas
zest and juice of 2 oranges
zest and juice of 1 lemon
175g muscovado sugar
1 teaspoon ground mixed spice
1 teaspoon ground cinnamon
50ml brandy or rum

First prepare the filling. Grate the apples and combine them with all the other ingredients. Leave in a sealed container in a cool dark place for at least 2 days. (This is best made a couple of days in advance to allow the juice and alcohol to soak into the fruit.)

Roll out the puff pastry to ½cm thick and cut into 15cm discs. Place a good heaped tablespoon of filling into the centre of each disc and flatten it out slightly. Fold the edges of the pastry disc into the centre of the circle, pinching together gently to seal the pastry. Flip the Eccles cakes over, score once in the middle of each cake and chill for 1 hour.

Heat the oil in a non-stick frying pan and fry the cakes for 1 minute on each side until golden brown. Transfer to a lined and lightly greased baking tray and bake at 160°C/Gas Mark 3 for about 15 minutes until the pastry is cooked through.

{calvados ice cream}

1 quantity Vanilla Ice Cream (see page 21)
about 50ml Calvados

Follow the recipe for vanilla ice cream, using 50g less sugar than stipulated. Churn the ice cream as usual and when it is three quarters churned, pour in Calvados to taste (about 50ml, or more if you dare!). Freeze in a sealed container.

{cinnamon cherry apples}

18 canned cherry apples, drained and juice reserved (or 2 large Granny Smith apples and 75ml apple juice)
100g caster sugar
½ teaspoon ground cinnamon
1 cinnamon stick

Cherry apples are tiny apples which you may be able to find online, canned. If not, just use regular apples, peeled and cut into wedges with the core trimmed out.

Heat a non-stick frying pan, dip your apples into the sugar and place quickly into the dry pan, shaking the apples around until a light caramel is formed. Lower the heat and add 75ml reserved juice from the can (or apple juice). Add the ground cinnamon and cinnamon stick and the remaining sugar and boil quickly for 1 minute. Remove from the heat, allow to cool, then remove the cinnamon stick.

{to assemble}

You can either serve the Eccles cakes straight from the oven, or cook them a few hours in advance and warm through at 160°C/Gas Mark 3 for about 10 minutes. Serve with a scoop of Calvados ice cream and the warm cinnamon cherry apples spooned over the top.

Nosey Parkin Pudding

hot stem ginger parkin pudding, with toasted oatmeal praline ice cream,
sticky ginger sauce, and spiced damson compote

Nothing could be more satisfying than mouthfuls of plush damsons with this date moist, ginger rich, hot pudding, soaked with a cheeky trickle of velvety muscovado ginger caramel…. Well, strictly speaking, that isn't true, because I strongly suggest the uplifting crunch of toasted oatmeal praline ice cream with it – a tad self indulgent, I know, but isn't life too short not to? (You don't need to eat all the parkin and ice cream at one sitting – there will be plenty of both to spare.)

September is the peak season for these little big fruits, with their powder like, dusky blue-black jackets. If you can't find damsons proper in your local greengrocers, ask why not. They deserve more recognition than they get these days, and it would be a crime for them to disappear completely from our shelves. Belonging to the plum family and with a natural pucker-up sourness, they need generous amounts of sugar to transform their taste to a voluptuous sweet mouthful. They also don't like giving up their stones easily, so these are best removed after cooking.

Damsons are endlessly adaptable: they're high in pectin so obvious candidates for making jams, jellies, cheeses and chutneys, and they add interesting possibilities to wines, spirits and beer as well as cordials, ice creams, sorbets and fools. Chuck a handful into pies, bread mixes and other baked goodies for their rich crimson colour and deep plummy flavour.

serves 4-6

{spiced damson compote}

500ml water
250g caster sugar
1 cinnamon stick
2 allspice berries
1 star anise
3 cloves
350g damsons, washed, stalks removed

Put the water in a pan with the sugar and spices. Bring to the boil, stirring, and cook for 1-2 minutes to make a syrup. Add the damsons and simmer gently until the fruit is tender but not broken. Remove the fruit from the syrup with a slotted spoon and continue to boil the syrup for 5 minutes. If you want to remove the stones from the fruit, now is the time to do it. Strain the syrup over the damsons and allow to cool.

{parkin pudding}

200g stoned dates
250ml water
½ teaspoon bicarbonate of soda
70g butter, softened
200g muscovado sugar
2 eggs, lightly beaten
1 teaspoon vanilla extract
140g self raising flour
½ teaspoon baking powder
70g medium oatmeal
2 pieces of stem ginger in syrup, finely chopped

Place the dates and water in a pan over a low heat and simmer gently, stirring frequently, until the dates have broken down and form a soft purée. Remove from the heat and stir in the bicarbonate of soda.

Cream the butter and sugar together until light and fluffy. Add the eggs a little at a time, beating well between each addition. Add the warm date purée and vanilla extract and mix in thoroughly. Fold in the sifted flour and baking powder, the oatmeal and the chopped stem ginger.

Pour the mixture into a lined and greased baking tray and bake at 160°C/Gas Mark 3 for 40 minutes. Be careful not to open the oven too soon as this would make the parkin sink in the middle. Once cooked, allow to cool in the tin.

{toasted oatmeal ice cream}

400ml whole milk
60g medium oatmeal, toasted
½ teaspoon ground cinnamon
½ teaspoon salt
3 egg yolks
140g soft light brown sugar
300ml double cream

for the praline
100g caster sugar
4 tablespoons water
50g medium oatmeal, toasted

First, make the praline. Have a baking tray ready, lined with greaseproof paper. Put the sugar and water in a small heavy based pan and bring to the boil. Boil rapidly until the sugar starts to change colour. When it has turned a light golden brown, remove from the heat and stir in the toasted oatmeal. Pour on to the baking tray, to cool and set. Do not get caramel on your skin as it will really burn! Once cool, bash with the end of a rolling pin until it is nicely crushed and crumbled.

Now for the ice cream. Put the milk, toasted oatmeal, cinnamon and salt in a small pan. Bring to the boil and simmer over a low heat for 10 minutes, stirring occasionally, then remove from the heat. Meanwhile, whisk together the egg yolks and sugar until light and fluffy. When the

(Continued on page 162)

Nosey Parkin Pudding

(Continued from page 161)

oatmeal mix is ready, pour on to the egg and sugar mix and stir well. Cool slightly. Lightly whip the cream, then fold into the custard. Chill in the refrigerator, then churn in an ice cream maker. Once churned, add some crushed oatmeal praline for a lovely crunchy texture, then freeze.

{sticky ginger sauce}

600ml whipping cream
40g muscovado sugar
60g demerara sugar
3 teaspoons ground ginger

Place all the ingredients in a heavy based pan and bring to the boil, stirring. Simmer for 7-8 minutes and serve immediately or cool down and reheat when required.

{to assemble}

30ml whisky (optional)

The parkin can be served straight from the oven but will be stickier and even more delicious if kept in an airtight container for a few days. When you are ready to serve it, cut into 8 portions and place the required number on a tray lined with greaseproof paper. Put another layer of greaseproof loosely on top, then a sheet of foil, and seal the edges around the tray. Place in the oven at 160°C/Gas Mark 3 for about 15 minutes. Meanwhile, gently heat up the sauce ready to coat the pudding. Once the pudding is hot, put the portions into serving bowls and coat with a generous amount of sauce. Spoon a smudge of damson compote alongside, topped by a scoop of oatmeal ice cream. Now add a splash of whisky if you dare!

A'right Treacle

treacle tart served with gooseberry compote, custard, and cinnamon crumble cheesecake ice cream

Quintessentially a British favourite, completely comforting, you can't beat a good and sinful treacly pudding. It is a perfect partner for the succulent, sharp tang of gooseberries, and a good thud of old-fashioned vanilla ice cream, peppered with crunchy little nuggets of cinnamon crumble. And, staying sinful, what could be more traditional than a dollop of creamy custard on the side?

Gooseberries can vary quite a bit in sourness so you might need to adjust the amount of sugar specified, depending on the variety you choose and your taste. Small green cooking gooseberries are available throughout June and July. Look for firm undamaged berries. Dessert gooseberries found later in the season are often red, yellow or golden; choose those with a chubby grape-like appearance. It's a nice idea to throw a few uncooked ones on to the compote just before serving, as their fresh tartness cuts through the sweetness of the compote and treacle.

In the Middle Ages, gooseberries were called feaberries or fever berries, referring to their medicinal ability to help bring down a fever. They are wonderfully high in vitamin C and A, and their tartness is a fabulous foil to oily or very sweet tastes.

serves 8

{cinnamon crumble cheesecake ice cream}

400g cream cheese
300ml Custard (see opposite page)
175g caster sugar
75ml water
2 egg whites

for the crumble mix
75g unsalted butter, softened
100g plain flour
50g demerara sugar
½ teaspoon ground cinnamon

First prepare the crumble mix. Rub the butter into the flour until it resembles breadcrumbs. Add the sugar and cinnamon and pour the mix on to a lined baking sheet. Put in the oven at 180°C/Gas Mark 4 and take it out to stir it every 10 minutes or so until the mix is golden brown and crunchy. Remove from the oven, stir again and leave to cool. Store in an airtight container. This is more than you need for this recipe so keep it to sprinkle on desserts.

To make the ice cream, mix together the cream cheese and custard until smooth. Put the sugar and water in a heavy based saucepan and bring to 121°C, using a sugar thermometer. Meanwhile whisk the egg whites to form stiff peaks. Pour the syrup into them, whisking continually until the mix has cooled down. This is much easier to do with an electric whisk. Fold the cream cheese mix into the meringue, together with a good sprinkle of crumble mix. Place in a plastic tub and freeze overnight.

{treacle tart}

225g plain flour
60g icing sugar, sifted
zest of ½ lemon
100g unsalted butter, cubed
1 egg and 1 yolk, lightly beaten

for the treacle filling
650g golden syrup
85g ground almonds
250ml double cream
2 eggs, beaten
175g fresh white breadcrumbs

First prepare the pastry. Sift the flour, icing sugar and lemon zest into a mixing bowl and rub in the butter until the mix resembles breadcrumbs. Bind together with the beaten eggs and knead to a smooth dough. The mix will feel quite sticky. Wrap in clingfilm and refrigerate, preferably overnight.

Line a 25cm loose based tart ring with a disc of greaseproof paper. Chop the refrigerated pastry and work it with your hands into a pliable dough. Roll out on to a floured surface to make a disc larger than your tart ring, then gather on a rolling pin and carefully lower on to the tart ring. Press the pastry into the corners and up the sides of the ring, leaving a slight overlap. Now chill for 1 hour in the refrigerator or 30 minutes in the freezer.

Line the cold tart shell with greaseproof paper and weigh down with baking beans. Place on a baking sheet and cook in the middle of the oven at 180°C/Gas Mark 4 for 15-20 minutes until the pastry is lightly coloured and cooked in the middle. Take the shell out of the oven and remove the baking beans and paper.

Mix all the treacle filling ingredients together and pour into the cooked pastry shell, as far to the top as possible. Return to the oven at 160°C/Gas Mark 3 for about 1 hour. When cooked the filling should be golden brown and set; it should have risen slightly and be not too wobbly. Remove from the oven, allow to cool, then chill.

{gooseberry compote}

300g fresh or frozen gooseberries
75g caster sugar
200ml water
grated zest and juice of 1 lemon
½ vanilla pod, split and scraped

Place all the ingredients in a stainless steel pan and bring to the boil. Simmer for 8-10 minutes or until the gooseberries start to soften. Cool and refrigerate until needed. Remove the vanilla pod before serving.

{custard}

600ml whole milk
400ml double cream
1 vanilla pod, split and scraped
6 egg yolks
140g caster sugar

In a heavy based pan, infuse the milk, cream, and vanilla pod and seeds, and bring to the boil slowly. Meanwhile in a large bowl whisk together the egg yolks and sugar until light in colour and creamy in texture. Pour half of the boiled milk and cream on to the yolks and whisk together thoroughly. Return the pan to a low heat, pour the yolk mix back into the milk mix and cook slowly, stirring constantly, until the custard has thickened and coats the back of a spoon. Remove from the heat and strain into a cold bowl to cool. Refrigerate the custard until needed. You will need 300ml to make the ice cream, and the rest will be served separately.

{to assemble}

50g fresh or frozen gooseberries (optional)

Cut the chilled treacle tart into portions of the size you require, then warm in the oven at 180°C/Gas Mark 4 for 5-10 minutes. Serve with some chilled custard and a scoop of cheesecake ice cream and spoon a little gooseberry compote over the top. Scatter over a few raw gooseberries, to add a sharper note, if you like. If refrigerated, the treacle tart will keep well for a few days.

Boiled Egg and Chubby Soldiers

{WHEAT FREE}

mango, crème diplomate and passion yolk,
topped with meringue, served with fat pineapple soldiers

The thickest, creamiest queen of creams, the sunniest mango and passion 'yolk', topped with a brittle sweet meringue, just crying out to be cracked open by a fat, zingy pineapple soldier, just doing his duty! The success of this is largely down to our lovely Jossy, a genius amongst pastry chefs, who for years has aided and abetted my sometimes whimsical but always edible fantasies (and had a fair few of her own).

We like the simplicity of this pudding's name, which belies its complex layering. The meringue 'dome' is in homage to the outrageously overblown Royal Pavilion, a stone's throw from the restaurant (well, you'd have to be a good shot) and as with much of Brighton, so it is with our menu, things are not always what they seem!

Serves 6

{crème diplomate}

1/2 vanilla pod, split and scraped
125ml whipping cream
15g cornflour
50g caster sugar
1 large egg
150ml double cream

Begin by making a crème pâtissière. Put the vanilla pod and seeds in a small pan with the milk and cream, and heat. Mix the cornflour, sugar and egg. When the vanilla mix has come to the boil, pour half of it on to the egg mix and whisk thoroughly. Return this to the pan, stirring constantly until it comes to the boil. Once boiled, remove the pan from the heat and cool the custard in a bowl, putting some greaseproof or parchment paper on top to prevent a skin forming. Refrigerate. The final stage is to turn your crème pâtissière into a crème diplomate. Just whisk the double cream until it forms soft peaks. Add the cold crème pâtissière to the cream, removing the vanilla pods. Whisk together to form firm peaks.

{meringue nests}

2 egg whites
125g caster sugar

Place a half filled pan of water on the stove to simmer. In a metal bowl whisk the egg whites and sugar together. Once combined, place the bowl over the saucepan and whisk by hand or with an electric whisk. Keep whisking constantly until the temperature reaches 63°C on a sugar thermometer. The mix should look white and foamy and near to the ribbon stage (when it leaves a track on the surface). Remove from the heat and carry on whisking until the mix has cooled down. This will take about 10 minutes.

Line a baking tray with baking parchment. Spoon some of the mix into a piping bag fitted with a large plain nozzle. Pipe meringue dome shapes on to the tray, the bases of which should be the size of the espresso cups you will be serving the dish in. Bake in a preheated oven at 90°C for about 11/2 hours until set.

This recipe will make about 12 meringues. You will need only 6 for the dish we are assembling here, but the remainder will keep in an airtight container in a cool place for a couple of weeks.

{mango purée}

1 ripe mango, peeled and stoned

Cut the mango into large chunks and purée with a hand blender, then pass through a fine sieve. You will need only 75g purée for this recipe, but the remainder can be frozen or used in smoothies or as a sauce for ice cream.

{passion fruit curd}

12 passion fruit
100g caster sugar
2 eggs
2 egg yolks
200g butter, cubed

Cut 10 passion fruit in half, then scoop out the pulp and seeds into a bowl. Add the sugar, eggs and egg yolks. Mix well and place the bowl over a pan of simmering water. Cook the passion fruit mix, stirring constantly, until it thickens and coats the back of a spoon. This will take about 10 minutes. Remove the bowl

from heat and stir in the butter until it is all combined. Strain the curd through a fine sieve. Halve the 2 remaining passion fruit, scoop out the pulp and seeds and stir into the curd. Refrigerate until needed.

{soldiers}

1 medium pineapple

for the lime leaf sugar
3 dried lime leaves
1 tablespoon caster sugar

Remove the leaves from the pineapple, reserving 2 per portion for the garnish. Cut the bottom and top off the pineapple and peel it with a sharp knife. Cut vertically into quarters. Cut out the woody middle section. Cut each quarter into 3 pieces to create 12 equal portions – these are your soldiers. Refrigerate until you are ready to use them.

To make the lime leaf sugar, blitz the lime leaves and sugar in a blender, or mash them until powdery with a pestle and mortar.

Remove the pineapple soldiers from the refrigerator and dust with the lime leaf sugar.

{to assemble}

Spoon some crème diplomate into a piping bag fitted with a medium plain nozzle. Put 2 teaspoons mango purée in the bottom of each espresso cup. Pipe the crème diplomate around the inside of the cups, leaving a cavity in the middle of each one. Spoon some passion fruit curd into another piping bag, pipe some into each cup, filling to the top, and refrigerate immediately. When ready to serve, place a meringue on top of each cup, stand 2 or 3 pineapple soldiers alongside them and garnish with the pineapple leaves.

Melon Marble Ab Dab

{VEGAN} {WHEAT FREE}

mixed melon sorbet marbles with strawberry sherbet dust and liquorice dipper, served with galia galliano smash

An artist's palette of perfectly scented, perfectly spherical icy melon balls – and, for the child in you, the sharp sweet sherbet dust to be dibbed up with a stick of liquorice and, for the adult in you, a frozen glass of melon Galliano smash, to be sipped ever so politely!

The Galia, Charentais and watermelon make a colourful trio: the Galia has yellowy green flesh, the Charentais has a glorious orange hue, and the watermelon is generally a bright pinky red. In this country we eat only the flesh of watermelon, but in some parts of the world, notably China and the southern states of the USA, the rind is treated as a vegetable and served fried, stewed and pickled. Although 92 per cent water, watermelon is high in vitamin C – which is great, as I've yet to meet a child who doesn't love it!

serves X

{galia galliano smash}

300g Galia melon
1 tablespoon icing sugar
about 25ml Galliano

Remove the skin and seeds from the melon, cut the flesh into pieces and crush down with a fork. Sprinkle on the icing sugar and Galliano according to taste and mix well. Chill the smash until you are ready to serve it in small chilled glasses.

{melon sorbet marbles}

450g Galia melon
450g Charentais melon
450g watermelon
450g caster sugar
400ml water
3 tablespoons lemon juice

Remove the skin and seeds from the Galia melon, cut the flesh into pieces and blitz in in a food processor. Pass the purée through a fine sieve and reserve. Repeat these steps with the other 2 melons, to make 3 separate purées. Bring the sugar and water to the boil, stirring, and simmer for 5 minutes. Remove from the heat and cool. This makes your syrup base. To each of the melon purées add 100ml syrup plus 1 tablespoon lemon juice. Churn each sorbet separately in an ice cream maker and freeze. Put a tray in the freezer lined with greaseproof paper or clingfilm.

Once the sorbets are frozen, dip a melon baller into boiling water and scoop out balls of each sorbet on to the frozen tray (1 or 2 of each sorbet per person – depending on the size of scoop you use). Freeze until you are ready to use them. It is best to do this in advance so the balls set nicely.

{strawberry sherbet dust}

150g strawberries
1 tablespoon icing sugar
25g caster sugar
10 pink peppercorns, crushed

Preheat the oven to 70°C/Gas Mark ¼. Slice the strawberries as thinly as possible, lay them on a lined baking sheet and sprinkle finely with icing sugar. Put in the preheated oven and leave for 2-3 hours (they need to dry out completely, so the thinner they are cut the better).

Remove the sliced strawberries from the oven and allow to cool down, then blend in a food processor with the caster sugar and crushed pink peppercorns. Store the 'dust' in an airtight container or cover with clingfilm until you are ready to use it.

{to assemble}

120g liquorice sticks, cut into shoelaces

We present this dish on frozen snail plates, but if you do not have any, frozen plates will do; they need to be frozen to prevent the sorbet balls from sliding around. Serve 1 large or 2 smaller scoops of each sorbet per person, with a chilled glass of the Galia Galliano smash, some liquorice strips and a little spoonful of strawberry sherbet dust to dip the liquorice into.

Bread of Heaven

sticky chocolate brioche pudding served with cobnut ice cream
and chunks of fresh, ripe pear

This sumptuous chocolate pudding will instantly transport you to culinary heaven. It's based on a classic brioche loaf recipe, a sweet butter enriched dough – to which we have added a little extra brute cocoa powder. If you aren't up for the baking challenge, it's not obligatory to make the brioche part, as it's pretty easy to find in shops and bakeries. Sliced, layered and loaded with chocolate custard, and baked until the meltingly hot middle and crunchy top are screaming to be eaten, it works a treat with a smidgen of hot dark chocolate sauce, mouthfuls of frosty cobnut ice cream and chunks of fresh, juicy pear.

Cobnuts are an ancient British treasure: a cultivated variety of hazelnuts grown in gardens and orchards since the 16th century. Their soft shells can easily be cracked between your teeth and there's nothing like an early autumn walk, snacking on cobnuts on the way. They are harvested from the beginning of September until the end of October, making them great to pair with the first of the season's apples and pears. Roasted and coarsely ground, they give a delicious, nutty tang to both sweet and savoury dishes.

serves 6-8

{cobnut ice cream}

100g caster sugar
4 egg yolks
280ml whole milk
175g cobnuts, roasted, peeled and
  chopped (or hazelnuts if cobnuts are
  unavailable)
280ml whipping cream

In a bowl whisk together the sugar and egg yolks until light and creamy. Gradually add the milk, mixing in thoroughly. Pour this mix into a small heavy based pan and cook on a medium heat, stirring constantly, until the custard thickens and coats the back of the spoon. Remove from the heat, tip into a bowl and add the chopped cobnuts. Leave to cool.

Refrigerate the custard and once it is cold, whip the cream to soft peaks and fold into the mix. Churn in an ice cream maker. Freeze until you are ready to use it.

{chocolate brioche}

350g strong flour
140g good quality cocoa powder
50g caster sugar
a pinch of salt
75ml whole milk
6g dried yeast
4 eggs, beaten
150g unsalted butter, softened

for the egg wash
1 egg yolk
2 tablespoons milk

This is best made with an electric mixer but is possible to do by hand. Sift the flour and cocoa into a mixing bowl and add the sugar and salt. Warm the milk, mix it with the yeast and eggs and add to the flour. With a dough hook mix these ingredients together to form a smooth dough. Knead in the machine for 5 minutes. Add the butter to the dough and mix again until all the butter is incorporated and the mix becomes smooth. If it is a bit too sticky (it should leave the sides of the bowl clean), add a small handful of flour.

Cover with clingfilm and leave to prove (double in size) for about 1 hour. Turn out on to a lightly floured surface, knock back and knead lightly. Divide into 8, knead each portion and roll to a smooth ball. Press the balls into a buttered 1.5kg loaf tin, 2 rows of 4 balls. Cover the tin and allow the dough to prove until it is nearly at the top of the tin. To make the egg wash, beat the egg yolk with the milk. Brush the dough gently with egg wash and bake at 180°C/Gas Mark 4 for 40 minutes.

If you are not sure if the brioche is ready, insert a skewer. If it comes out clean, the loaf is cooked. Run a knife around the edge and turn out on to a wire rack immediately.

{chocolate sauce}

300ml whipping cream
165g dark chocolate (70 per cent cocoa
solids)

Bring the cream to the boil in a small pan
and remove from the heat. Add the
chocolate, broken into pieces, and whisk
well to make a smooth sauce. Once cooled,
refrigerate until you are ready to use it.

{chocolate brioche pudding}

8 (5mm thick) slices Chocolate Brioche
(see separate recipe, or use shop-bought
brioche)
150g dark chocolate (70 per cent cocoa
solids)
550ml whipping cream
100g caster sugar
90g unsalted butter
3 eggs

Cut each slice of brioche into 4 triangles.
Put the chocolate, cream, sugar and butter
in a pan over a low heat and stir until the
chocolate and butter have melted and the
sugar has dissolved. Beat the eggs, then
pour the chocolate cream into them and
mix well.

Arrange half the brioche triangles in a
buttered ovenproof dish, then pour over
some of the chocolate custard, to coat
them. Arrange another neat layer on top
and cover with the rest of the chocolate
custard. Press down lightly with a fork
so that all of the brioche is covered.
Cover with clingfilm and leave at room
temperature for 2 hours, then refrigerate
– overnight if possible.

Remove the clingfilm and bake at
180°C/Gas Mark 4 for 30-40 minutes
until the top looks crunchy. The inside
will be moist and gooey. Stand for
10-15 minutes before serving.

{to assemble}

3 ripe pears, peeled and sliced

Serve the pudding while still warm or – if
you have made it in advance – just reheat
at 150°C/Gas Mark 2 for about 20
minutes, covered in foil to stop it drying
out. Warm the chocolate sauce without
boiling it, and spoon it generously over
each portion. Put a blob of cobnut ice
cream to one side and add a few slices of
fresh pear. Mmmm....

Big Lemon

sicilian lemon tart served with fresh raspberries, and gin and tonic sorbet

This is a damn good place to find yourself at the end of a meal. Simple to make and impressive to serve, this terrific tart is refreshingly full of flavour, with zingy wobble and melt in the mouth pastry – altogether the ultimate match for a slug of gin and tonic sorbet, slightly melting, and a handful of succulent berries … Guaranteed to hit the spot!

Big spoonfuls of thick cream may be gilding the lily, but still a great idea...and if you like a bitter kick, pour a little reduced tonic over the tart before piling on the cream. I suggest using raspberries because I have a personal weakness for them (no guessing why I suggest the gin and tonic sorbet then) but almost all berries and a wide variety of ripe fruits would make an excellent companion for the tart. If you can lay hands on Sicilian unwaxed lemons, that's great. If not, regular unwaxed lemons will do – or you could use lime juice. Ice and a slice, anyone?

serves 6

{gin and tonic sorbet}

350ml Sugar Syrup (see page 21)
250ml tonic water
75ml gin
juice of ½ lemon

Combine all the ingredients together and churn in an ice cream maker. Freeze the sorbet until you need it. If you do not have an ice cream maker, place the mixture in a container suitable for freezing and freeze until slushy. Remove the slushy ice mix from the freezer and whisk until the icy lumps are broken up and the texture is smooth. Place back into the freezer and repeat this chilling and whisking process until the sorbet reaches the consistency required. Freeze until ready to use.

{sicilian lemon tart}

250g plain flour
60g icing sugar, sifted
grated zest of ½ unwaxed lemon
100g unsalted butter, cubed
1 egg and 1 yolk, lightly beaten beaten egg
   to glaze

for the lemon filling
150g caster sugar
grated zest and juice of 6 unwaxed lemons
6 large eggs, beaten
600ml double cream

First prepare the pastry. Sift the flour, icing sugar and lemon zest into a mixing bowl and rub in the butter until the mix resembles breadcrumbs. Bind together with the beaten eggs and knead to a smooth dough. The mix will feel quite sticky. Wrap in clingfilm and refrigerate, preferably overnight.

Line a 30cm loose based tart ring with a disc of greaseproof paper. Chop the refrigerated pastry and work it with your hands into a pliable dough. Roll out on to a floured surface to make a disc larger than your tart ring, then gather on a rolling pin and carefully lower on to the tart ring. Press the pastry into the corners and up the sides of the ring, leaving a slight overlap. Now chill for 1 hour in the refrigerator or 30 minutes in the freezer.

Line the cold tart shell with greaseproof paper and weigh down with baking beans. Place on a baking sheet and cook in the middle of the oven at 180°C/Gas Mark 4 for 15-20 minutes until the pastry is lightly coloured and cooked in the middle. Take the shell out of the oven and remove the baking beans and paper. Brush the pastry with some beaten egg and return to the oven for 2 minutes only, to seal.

To make the lemon filling, place the sugar and lemon zest and juice in a stainless steel pan and bring to the boil, stirring. Remove from the heat and pour on to the beaten eggs, whisking continuously, then immediately add the cream. Strain the mixture through a fine sieve and pour into the pastry shell, filling it as high as you dare. Gently place in the oven at 130°C/ Gas Mark ½ and cook for 30-40 minutes. Allow to cool, then refrigerate. This tart is best eaten on the day it is baked but will be fine the next day.

{to assemble}

150ml tonic water (optional)
icing sugar to dust (optional)
whipped cream (optional)
125g raspberries

To add extra bitterness, make a reduction of tonic water: heat the tonic in a small pan until reduced by half, then allow to cool. Cut the chilled lemon tart into slices with a long thin bladed knife that has been dipped in very hot water. This gives a sharp clean edge. If you would like a thin crispy glaze, dust the tart with icing sugar and finish with a blow torch, but this is not essential. A drizzle of reduced tonic and big spoonfuls of thick cream are also optional. Serve with a scoop of gin and tonic sorbet and a scattering of fresh raspberries.

Mincing Quince Dosas

quince-filled tofu coated pancake rolls with agave coconut sorbet,
cider toddy and coriander seed crackle

{VEGAN} {WHEAT FREE}

Heaped full of heavenly aromatic quince and rolled in silky coconut tofu, these golden dosas are fried to crispy hot perfection. A sumptuous match for fruity warm spicy gulps of hot cider toddy, refreshing spoonfuls of coconut ice and – why stop there? – crackling crunches of caramel coriander.

Dosas are a Tamil speciality, and pretty much a staple food in southern India. We have taken a few liberties with the original form, by making it more of a sausage than a pancake and by giving it an extra layer of absolute deliciousness before it is fried. We hope you approve.

serves 6-8

{agave sorbet}

150ml agave syrup
150ml water
zest of 1 lime
juice of 2 limes
400ml coconut milk

Bring to the boil the agave syrup, water, and lime zest and juice. Remove from the heat and allow to cool, then add the coconut milk. Chill and then churn in an ice-cream maker. Put in the freezer until ready to use.

{coriander crackle}

100g granulated sugar
20ml water
1 teaspoon coriander seeds, toasted and crushed

Put the sugar and water in a small heavy based pan, taking great care not to get any sugar at all on the sides of the pan. Bring to the boil and cook, without stirring, just until golden. Immediately remove the pan from the heat, add the coriander seeds, and quickly place over iced water to stop the cooking process.

Dip a small, round, heat-resistant pastry brush into the caramel and carefully brush straight on to a non-stick heatproof mat in 13cm strips, which will set firm. (Alternatively use baking parchment laid on a heatproof surface, and carefully peel away the caramel strips when cold.) Store the strips on parchment in a sealed container until needed.

{hot toddy}

500ml medium cider
75ml sloe gin
½ lemon, sliced
3 cinnamon sticks
1 cardamom pod
2 allspice berries
1 star anise
4 coriander seeds

Combine all the ingredients and heat through without letting them boil. Remove from the heat and leave to infuse for 1 hour. Strain before using.

{quince dosas}

150g rice flour
100g gram flour
40g potato flour
335ml water
80ml soya yogurt
1 tablespoon grated lime zest
35g caster sugar
oil for shallow and deep frying
rice flour for coating

for the quince mince
2 large quinces, peeled, cored and cut into quarters
juice of 1 lemon
150g caster sugar
1 star anise
2 allspice berries
1 cinnamon stick
2 cloves

for the tofu batter
125g silken tofu
1 teaspoon egg replacer powder
85ml soya cream
1 tablespoon desiccated coconut
1 tablespoon caster sugar

To prepare the batter for the dosas (savoury pancakes), combine all the flours, then add the water, yogurt and lime zest and whisk until smooth. This mix is best made a day in advance, so leave it in the refrigerator overnight.

Next, prepare the quince mince. Put the quinces in a deep sided ovenproof dish and add the lemon juice, sugar and spices. Now pour on water, just enough to cover the tops of the fruit. Cover the dish with foil and bake at 180°C/Gas Mark 4 for 1-1½ hours until the quinces are soft and starting to change colour to a lovely orangey red. Allow them to cool, then remove the fruit from the syrup and chop into 1cm cubes.

To make the tofu batter, mix all of the ingredients with a whisk. The mixture will still look a bit lumpy – don't worry about that. Refrigerate until ready to use.

To cook the dosas, coat a 20cm non-stick frying pan with a very little oil, then place over the heat. Remove the dosa batter from the refrigerator and give it a good stir. Once the pan is really hot tip in 50ml batter and tilt the pan to coat the surface. Once the dosa starts to brown, flip it over and cook the other side. Remove it from the pan and repeat the process until you have enough dosas, stacking them meanwhile on sheets of greaseproof paper. (There is enough batter to make 8-10.)

To fill the dosas, place each one in turn on a piece of clingfilm. Put a spoonful of quince mince on to the dosa, in a line about one third of the way up, then fold the bottom edge of the dosa over the quince and roll up into a sausage shape. Wrap in the clingfilm and, once wrapped, hold the 2 ends of the clingfilm and carefully roll the sausage along the worktop to firm it up. Refrigerate for 1 hour before cooking.

When you are almost ready to eat, preheat oil in a deep fryer or deep pan to 180°C. Remove each filled dosa from the clingfilm, dip into rice flour, then roll each 'sausage' in some tofu batter (this will be messy!). Gently lower the sausages (only 1 or 2 at a time) into the hot oil and fry for 1-2 minutes until the batter is brown and crispy. Drain on paper towels.

{to assemble}

Serve one deep fried dosa for each person, with a glass of hot toddy, a scoop of coconut agave sorbet and half a coriander crackle.

Mellow Mallow

{WHEAT FREE}

toasted marshmallow skewers served with
passion shake and tequila lime ice

What could be more delicious than big mouthfuls of snow white gooey marshmallow, cold on the inside, but with hot charred sugary jackets? They're a wonderful contrast to the intensely scented sharp tasting passion pulp, and nicely rounded off with generous slurps of slushy tequila lime ice. Passion fruit are amazingly good for you: rich in vitamins A and C and high in potassium and iron. There is also much evidence that they can reduce anxiety and have a calming effect: every reason then to eat more than your fair share!

serves 4-6

{marshmallow}

3 egg whites
130ml water
1½ teaspoons agar agar
250g caster sugar
50g glucose syrup
½ vanilla pod, split and scraped

First line and lightly oil a deep sided baking tray. Next, put the egg whites into a large bowl, ready for whisking – preferably in a mixer with a whisk attachment. Warm 30ml of the water in a small saucepan and sprinkle the agar agar on top. Do not mix it in, just warm through.

In another small saucepan bring to the boil the sugar, glucose syrup and remaining water. Checking with a sugar thermometer, bring the mix to 140°C. Meanwhile, start whisking the egg whites until they make stiff peaks. Now gradually pour the boiling sugar into the beaten egg whites while mixing at high speed. Continue whisking until the mixture has cooled down (it does not have to be stone cold).

Now put the seeds from the vanilla pod into this meringue mix. (You will not need the pod itself, but it will come in handy for making vanilla sugar.) Bring the agar agar/water mix to the boil and cook for 1 minute, giving a quick whisk by hand to make sure the agar agar is incorporated into the water and not lumpy.

Pour this mix into the vanilla meringue and whisk quickly for only 30 seconds. Now fold through by hand, making sure it is well mixed, but without knocking out any air. Quickly spread on to the prepared baking tray and allow to cool. Place in the refrigerator to set, overnight if possible.

{passion shake}

8 passion fruits
1 ripe banana
400g pineapple, peeled and chopped
200ml coconut milk

Scoop out the flesh of the passion fruits and place in a jug blender with all the other ingredients. (You can also use a hand blender.) Blend for 1-2 minutes until the mixture is smooth. Strain through a fine sieve and chill in the refrigerator before using.

{tequila lime ice}

200g caster sugar
500ml water
finely grated zest of 2 limes
100ml lime juice
100ml gold tequila
salt to taste

Bring the sugar, water and lime zest to the boil and simmer for 2 minutes. Cool the mixture down, then add the lime juice, tequila and salt. Put in the freezer and fork through every half hour or so, to form tequila lime crystals.

{to assemble}

Cut the marshmallow into cubes and thread on to skewers (4 pieces per skewer, 2 skewers per person). Keep in the refrigerator until you are ready to use them. Just before serving, glaze the edges with a blow torch if you have one. Serve with a glass of passion shake and a scoop of tequila lime ice.

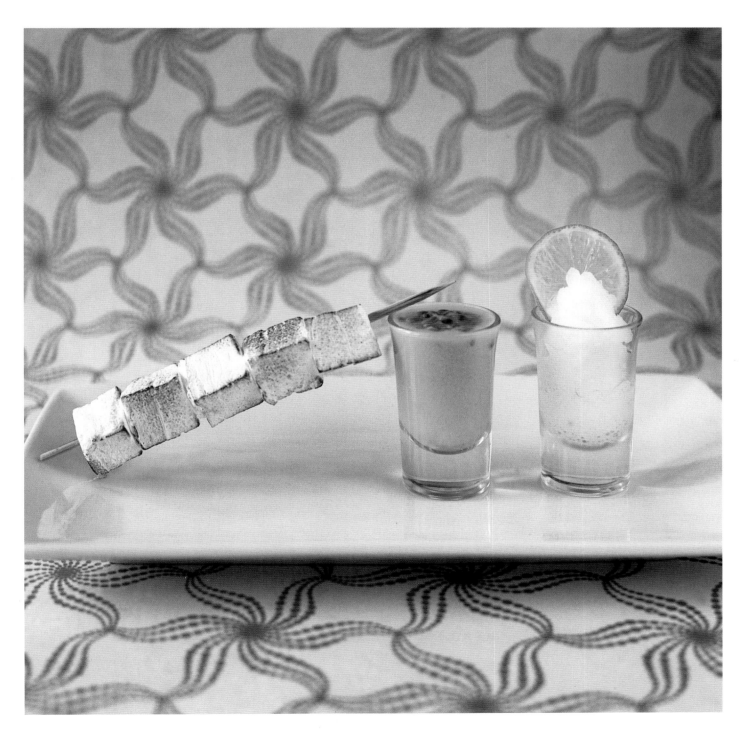

Windfall Apple Pie

{VEGAN}

bramley and cox's orange pippin pie served with calvados and clove ice cream and vanilla custard

There is great joy to be had picking apples yourself, although we don't often get the opportunity. The next best thing is a farm shop where you may be able to discover old and unusual varieties. For this recipe I have suggested Bramleys and Cox's Orange Pippins, which are easy to get hold of and good on flavour, but do have a go at experimenting with different varieties and taste combinations. Even a few crab apples plus liberal amounts of extra sugar will elevate the pie a notch or two. If you do use Bramleys, don't let them get too blowsy during cooking: you want them to keep their shape and have a bit of bite. Other fruit can be added to the cooled apple mix, maybe blackberries or raspberries, but be careful not to break them up as you stir them in.

There really is nothing more cheering than a filled to the rafters apple pie with golden crumbly pastry. It's a classic which really doesn't need to be tinkered with, so I've only done a bit of fine tuning and made it vegan and it's still an absolute corker.... And just in case you are umming and erring over the ice cream or custard dilemma, let me nudge you towards both! These two recipes are both so luscious, but the inclusion of Calvados in the ice cream makes it the ideal accompaniment to the hot apple pie – with just enough boozy sharpness to make a memorable mouthful – while the warm, comforting, vanilla custard is a vegan take on an old favourite.

serves 6-8

{windfall apple pie}

300g plain flour
50g icing sugar
a pinch of salt
150g vegetable pastry fat
½ teaspoon vanilla extract
150-170ml soya cream
caster sugar to sprinkle

for the apple filling
4 large Bramley apples, peeled, cored and cut into chunks
4 Cox's Orange Pippins apples, peeled, cored and cut into chunks
juice of ½ lemon
3 cloves
½ teaspoon ground cinnamon
6 tablespoons golden caster sugar

First make the apple filling. Put the apple chunks, lemon juice, cloves and cinnamon in a pan and cook on a medium heat for 7-8 minutes until the apples are slightly soft. Now add the sugar, cook for 1 minute more and turn the mixture out into a large shallow dish to cool down.

Next prepare the pastry. Sift the flour, icing sugar and salt into a bowl and rub in the fat until the mixture resembles breadcrumbs. Add the vanilla extract and 150ml soya cream and bind together with a fork, adding more soya cream if needed. The dough should be soft but not sticky.

Roll out two thirds of the dough into a circle, slide the rolling pin under it and lower into a 20cm plain loose based tart ring or pie dish, leaving an overlap of pastry. Make sure the pastry reaches into the corners, then fill the tart shell with the cold apple filling (first removing the cloves). Roll out the remaining one third of the pastry, lift as before on the rolling pin and lower gently on top of the filled

tart. Push the edges together to seal them. Cut off any excess pastry and crimp the sides together using either your fingers or a fork.

Brush the top of the pie with soya cream and sprinkle liberally with sugar. Pierce the top of the pie to allow steam to escape and decorate with leaves made out of the excess pastry. Place the filled tart on a lined baking sheet and bake at 180°C/Gas Mark 4 for 45-50 minutes until the pastry is golden brown and crispy on the edges. Allow to cool slightly before removing from the ring (if using a pie dish, leave in the dish).

{vanilla custard}

500ml rice milk
500ml soya milk
1 vanilla pod, split and scraped
½ teaspoon vanilla extract
80g cornflour
75ml water
75g caster sugar
100ml coconut milk
50ml soya cream

Place the rice milk, soya milk, vanilla pod and seeds, and vanilla extract in a pan and bring to the boil. Meanwhile, mix the cornflour with the water to make a runny paste. Once the milk mix has boiled, pour the cornflour paste into the pan, add the sugar and whisk immediately to ensure that all the ingredients are combined. Bring the liquid back to the boil and simmer for 1 minute, still whisking continuously.

Remove the pan from the heat, pour the custard into a bowl to cool, and stir with a whisk every 10 minutes to stop a skin forming and to help keep the mixture smooth. Once the custard is cool, add the coconut milk and soya cream and mix again. Put aside until needed.

{calvados and clove ice cream}

5 cloves
80g agave syrup
600ml organic vegan whipping cream
75ml Calvados (apple brandy)

Put the cloves, agave syrup and half the cream into a small pan and bring to the boil. Simmer for 1 minute. Allow to cool, then pass through a sieve. Add the remainder of the cream and the Calvados. Chill, then churn in an ice cream maker and freeze.

{to assemble}

This lovely pie is best served straight from the oven but can be reheated if made in advance. It is also delicious cold. Serve with some warm vanilla custard and a scoop of Calvados and clove ice cream.

Spaghetti Sweetie

chocolate spaghetti served with dark chocolate sauce, sweet walnut pesto, espresso granita and candied kumquats

The Italians have been at the sweet pasta lark forever but it's not caught on big time in the UK yet...and we think it should. Make these slippery chocolate strands the base of a mouthwatering combination, adding a rich chocolate sauce, a sprinkling of minty walnut pesto, an intense, slightly bitter coffee ice, and the sharp-sweet tang of barely cooked caramelized kumquats. Separately all classic flavours, but together they let rip!

While many foods have been labelled 'super' as a sneaky marketing ploy, walnuts truly are a superfood. They have the highest antioxidant activity of all nuts and are delicious too. They are also packed full of vitamin E, which is excellent for heart health, and are rich in cholesterol-lowering plant serums and omega 3 oils, which can help keep you jolly.

serves 6

{walnut pesto}

75g walnuts, toasted and chopped
50g mint leaves, chopped
grated zest of 1 orange

Put all the ingredients in a pestle and mortar (or mixer) and pound together. You do not want a paste, just a nice crumbly mix of the ingredients to sprinkle over the pasta.

{chocolate pasta}

250g '00' pasta flour
30g good quality cocoa powder
2 eggs, beaten
3–4 tablespoons cold water

Sieve the flour and cocoa together (either on to a work surface or into a large bowl). Make a deep well in the centre of the dry mix, and pour in the beaten eggs and 2 tablespoons of the water. Using a circular motion draw the dry mix into the centre and add another tablespoon of water. Mix with a fork until the mixture binds together (adding more water if necessary).

Bring all the mix together and start kneading with your hands to form a smooth ball of dough (this takes approximately 10 minutes). Cover the dough with clingfilm and refrigerate for 30 minutes.

Using a pasta machine, roll out one quarter of the dough at a time, in the same way as you would roll out any pasta, stopping at setting number 2 to make spaghetti.

Leave the strands to hang over a broom handle or similar to dry for at least 10 minutes. If you are not quite ready to cook them yet, layer the slightly dried out pasta in loose bundles between greaseproof paper and refrigerate in a sealed container.

Only cook the pasta just before you are ready to eat. Add a drop of olive oil to a large pan of water, bring to the boil and plunge in the pasta. Cook for 1 minute only, then quickly drain.

{candied kumquats}

200ml water
100g caster sugar, plus extra for dipping
½ vanilla pod, split and scraped
200g kumquats

Bring the water to the boil and add the sugar and vanilla pod and seeds. Gently simmer for 5 minutes until a syrupy consistency is reached.

Halve the kumquats lengthways. Bring a dry non-stick frying pan to medium heat. Dip the kumquats cut side down into a little caster sugar and place them face down in the frying pan, cooking until they are nicely caramelized. Now put them straight into the syrupy mixture, bring it back to the boil and simmer for 1 minute. Leave to one side until you are ready to assemble the dish.

{chocolate sauce}

300ml whipping cream
175g dark chocolate (70 per cent cocoa solids)

Bring the cream to the boil in a small pan and remove it from the heat. Add the chocolate and whisk well to make a smooth sauce. Once cooled, refrigerate until you are ready to use it.

{espresso granita}

100ml strong espresso coffee
400ml Sugar Syrup (see page 21)
¼ teaspoon vanilla extract
Mix all the ingredients together in a container and freeze. Fork through the mix every 30 minutes to form icy coffee crystals, then freeze until you are ready to use it.

{to assemble}

The pasta is best cooked just before serving (see recipe). Heat through the chocolate sauce in a pan. Twist the freshly cooked and drained spaghetti into portions, using a long pronged fork, and spoon a generous amount of the chocolate sauce over the top. Sprinkle with the walnut pesto and lay some kumquats to one side, drizzling the kumquat syrup over them. Serve the espresso granita in icy cups on the side of the plates.

Ladies of Seville

warm chocolate and hazelnut torte with bitter chocolate sauce, served with seville orange candy, orange salad and salt caramel ice cream

The sour punch of the magnificent and elusive plump Seville orange, when coupled with this fabulous tart, makes a great thing even better. Although delicious made with sweeter orange varieties, we guarantee that the sour Seville, salty-sweet ice cream and luxurious chocolate and hazelnut combination, will drive any savoury-toothed soul into a sweet foodie frenzy! It also goes without saying that chocolate really needs nothing to improve it, so the tart is fabulous on its own too.

It is worth taking advantage of the small window of seasonal availability of these pectin-packed little treasures that arrive on our shores between January and February. They are perfect for marmalade and a multitude of other dishes. The tart juice is a good alternative to lemon and the whole fruits will happily freeze so you can indulge in them at a later date.

serves 6

{chocolate and hazelnut torte (gluten free)}

175g dark chocolate (70 per cent cocoa solids)
175g unsalted butter
4 eggs
150g caster sugar
75g hazelnut flour
40g gluten free plain flour
a pinch of salt
1 teaspoon vanilla extract

Melt the chocolate and butter together in a bain-marie. Separate the eggs, putting the yolks in one large bowl and the whites in another. Mix the hazelnut flour, plain flour and salt together. Whisk the egg yolks with 75g of the sugar to the ribbon stage. Fold the chocolate and butter mix into the whisked egg yolks, and then fold in the hazelnut flour mix.

Whisk the egg whites until they form firm peaks, then whisk in the remaining 75g sugar. Fold this gently into the chocolate mix and pour into a lined 25cm cake tin. Cook at 180°C/Gas Mark 4 for about 20 minutes, until an inserted skewer comes out clean but with a few crumbly bits on. Allow to cool before cutting into slices.

{chocolate glaze}

100g liquid glucose
150ml water
200g dark chocolate (70 per cent cocoa solids)
15ml vegetable oil

Bring the glucose and water to the boil in a pan and instantly pour on to the chocolate. Stir well and add the oil. Allow to cool, then refrigerate.

{salt caramel crème fraîche ice cream}

400ml crème fraîche
100ml double cream
100ml whole milk
6 egg yolks
180g caster sugar

for the salt caramel sauce
300g granulated sugar
300ml double cream
a pinch of salt

Slowly bring the crème fraîche, cream and milk to the boil. Meanwhile whisk together the egg yolks and sugar until they reach a light and creamy ribbon stage. Once the crème fraîche mix has come to the boil, pour half of it on to the yolk mix, stir in well and return to the remaining crème fraîche mix in the pan. Now cook this on a low heat, stirring constantly, until the mixture coats the back of a spoon, taking care not to let it boil. Pour into a bowl and cool over iced water. Refrigerate and churn in an ice cream maker.

Meanwhile, make the salt caramel sauce. Bring the granulated sugar to the boil and cook until light golden brown. With a long handled whisk (do not have your hand over the pot) gradually whisk in the double cream to make a sauce. Finally add the salt and cool before using.

Once the ice cream is churned, spoon it into a tub, layering it with the salt caramel sauce to form a ripple effect. Refrigerate again.

(Continued on page 184)

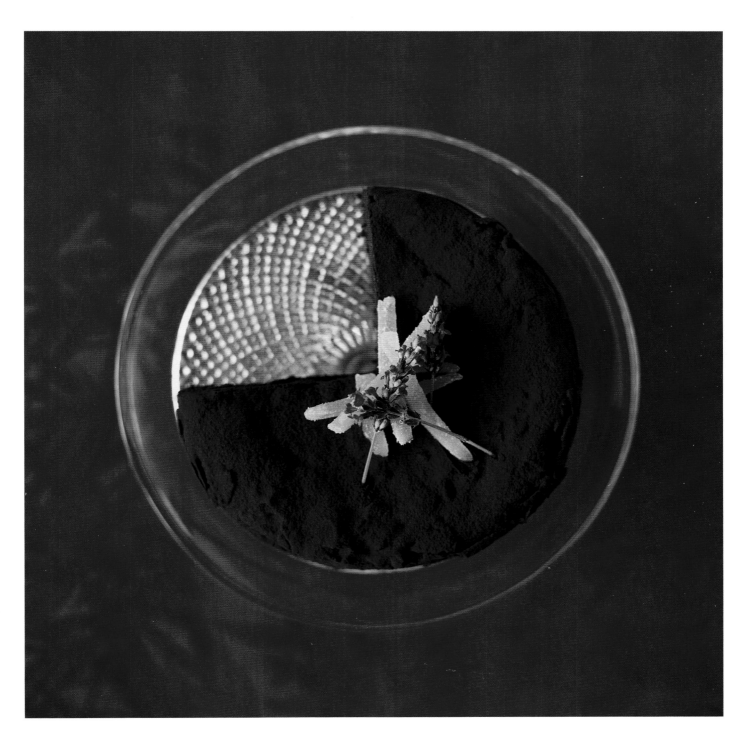

(Continued from page 182)

{sugared orange candy}

3 thick-skinned oranges (preferably
  Seville, but Navel or Valencia will do)
375g caster sugar
200ml water

Cut the tops and bottoms off the oranges
and score the remaining fruit into quarters,
cutting only into the skin, not into the
fruit. Cut the peel thinly off the oranges in
large pieces, then remove and discard the
pith. Liquidize the flesh of the oranges,
strain and reserve the juice. Cut the peel
into strips about 6mm wide. Put the peel
into a saucepan, cover with water and
bring to the boil. Once boiled, drain and
refresh under cold water. Repeat this twice
more. In a heavy based pan put the sugar
and water and bring to a simmer, making
a syrup. Now add the peel to the
simmering syrup, cooking gently for about
45 minutes until it becomes translucent.
Do not stir the peel when it is cooking as
this may cause the syrup to crystallize.
A little shake of the pan will do. Drain the
candied peel and save the syrup. Add the
reserved orange juice to the syrup, cool
and refrigerate. Roll the peel or 'candy'
in a little extra caster sugar and dry on
a cooling rack for 4-5 hours. Store in an
airtight container.

{to assemble}

1 sweet orange (Navel or Valencia)
good quality cocoa powder to dust
  (optional)

Remove the peel and pith from the orange
and, using a very sharp knife, cut into thin
segments. Warm the slices of torte in the
oven. This will take only about 5 minutes
at 160°C/Gas Mark 3. Meanwhile melt
the chocolate glaze gently over a bain-
marie. Put the torte slices on plates, then
spoon over the chocolate glaze to coat
them. Scoop out portions of salt caramel
crème fraîche ice cream on to the plates
and garnish with the fresh orange
segments, candied orange peel and bitter
orange syrup. If you want to, dust the
torte with a little cocoa powder.

Bananas and Custard

hot banana and custard turnovers, served with muscovado caramel rum ice cream, raisin relish and a dusting of allspice sugar

If only my school dinner puddings had been like this! There isn't much you can do to improve the banana and custard combo but here's our revamped version with reggae undertones. Hot oozy banana custard encased in golden pastry triangles muddles with the dark sultry flavours of muscovado caramel and plump sticky raisins. Allspice is the linchpin in this lovely dish, winding its spicy trail throughout – and with a good strong rum, it's a classic Caribbean line-up. Often thought mistakenly to be a blend of many spices, allspice is in fact a single berry also known as Jamaican pepper. The name derives from its complicated mix of flavours – cinnamon, nutmeg and cloves, to name just a few.

serves 6

{banana and custard turnovers}

400g Puff Pastry (see page 20)
2 ripe bananas
¼ quantity custard filling (see Custard Tarts, page 198)
1 egg, beaten
demerara sugar to sprinkle

for the raisin relish
100g raisins, roughly chopped
¼ pineapple (about 500g), peeled and finely diced
25g muscovado sugar
½ teaspoon ground cinnamon
¼ teaspoon ground ginger
2.5cm piece of fresh root ginger, peeled and grated
30ml dark rum

First prepare the raisin relish. Place the raisins and all the other relish ingredients in a pan, heat gently and simmer for 2 minutes. Remove from the heat, allow to cool and store in an airtight container. Preferably leave the relish to steep for several days before using.

To begin making the turnovers, roll out the pastry 5mm thick and cut into 6 discs. Layer these rounds on a plate between clingfilm or greaseproof paper and refrigerate. (Press the leftover scraps gently together and refrigerate so they can be re-used).

Chop up the bananas into small pieces and mix them with the custard filling. Place a generous heaped tablespoon of banana and custard into the centre of each pastry round and then spoon a couple of teaspoons of raisin relish on top of that. Brush around the edges of the pastry with the beaten egg then bring one side over the top of the banana mix and press down to seal. Crimp the edges with your fingers.

Brush the top of the pastry with more of the beaten egg, sprinkle with demerara sugar and make a couple of holes in the top with a knife to allow the steam to escape. Leave the turnovers in the refrigerator until you are ready to cook them.

Shortly before you are ready to eat, bake the turnovers in the oven at 180°C/ Gas Mark 4 for about 20 minutes, until they are golden brown and crispy.

{muscovado caramel rum ice cream}

300ml double cream
60g muscovado sugar
50ml dark rum
300ml whole milk
6 egg yolks
25g caster sugar

Put half the cream and the muscovado sugar in a heavy based pan and bring to the boil. Remove from the heat, then add the rum (it is important you do this off the heat or the rum might ignite). Put the pan back on the stove and boil for 1 minute,

then remove from the heat again. Now add the remaining cream and the milk, return to the heat and bring to the boil. Meanwhile, whisk the egg yolks and caster sugar together until they are light and creamy.

Once the cream mix has boiled, pour one third of it on to the egg and sugar mix, whisking in well until it is all incorporated. Return this mixture to the remaining cream mix in the pan and cook over a medium heat, stirring constantly, until the custard thickens and will coat the back of a spoon. Do not allow it to boil. When it is the right consistency, strain through a fine sieve and cool down quickly by pouring into a cool bowl over iced water or into a container with a large surface area. Leave overnight in the refrigerator before churning in an ice cream maker.

{to assemble}

2 teaspoons icing sugar
¼ teaspoon ground allspice

The banana and custard turnovers can be cooked in advance and then reheated, but it is better to serve them straight after cooking them. To make the allspice sugar, sift the icing sugar with the ground allspice. Place a turnover on each plate with a spoonful of raisin relish (there should be some left over), a scoop of muscovado caramel rum ice cream, and a liberal dusting all over of allspice sugar.

Coconut and Pistachio Wafers

{VEGAN}

coconut ice and pistachio wafers served with raspberry and rose water frappé

These snappy little pistachio loaded wafers are lovely to munch on their own (vegan, too), but are irresistible coupled with the cooling combination of luscious rose scented ruby raspberry crush and creamy rum spiked coconut ice.

As a member of the rose family, it's no surprise that the raspberry, when perfectly ripe, can have the most exquisite and perfumed flavour. English and Scottish raspberries are in full swing late June to early September, so it's worth raiding greengrocers and allotments for the plumpest, best tasting berries: their yearly visit is fleeting, so grab 'em while you can! At other times, using frozen is absolutely fine and dandy and indeed, to be recommended, as the berries are packed full of iron, potassium and vitamins A and C, to mention but a few of their fantastic properties. Made in Barbados, Malibu rum is flavoured with coconut extract, blending two of the Caribbean's most exotic flavours.

serves 4-6

{pistachio wafers (v)}

6 filo pastry sheets
100g soya margarine, melted
150g pistachio nuts, peeled and finely chopped

Line a baking tray with greaseproof paper. Lay a sheet of filo on the baking tray, brush with the melted margarine and sprinkle with the pistachios. Repeat this process three more times. After you have sprinkled on the last of the pistachio layers, lay a sheet of filo on the top, and brush with melted margarine. Then lay one more sheet of filo on top, also giving this final sheet a brush of margarine. Place a sheet of greaseproof paper over the pastry and flatten all the sheets together, smoothing them with your hands. Put a baking tray on top to weigh the pastry down and bake at 180°C/Gas Mark 4 for 25 minutes. While still hot, remove the top layer of paper and cut the pastry into required shapes – we like to cut ours into triangles. Store in an airtight container.

{raspberry and rose water frappé}

250g ripe raspberries
20ml rose water
icing sugar to taste

Put the raspberries and rose water in a mixing bowl, sprinkle with icing sugar and crush with a fork, leaving some of the fruit quite chunky. Refrigerate until needed.

{coconut glacé}

500ml Sugar Syrup (see page 21)
400ml coconut milk
100g creamed coconut
25ml Malibu rum

Warm the sugar syrup, coconut milk and creamed coconut in a saucepan until they blend together. Remove from the heat, add the Malibu rum and mix well. When cool, churn the mixture in an ice cream maker and freeze until required. Alternatively, if you do not have an ice cream maker, place the mixture in a container suitable for freezing and freeze until slushy. Remove the slushy ice mix from the freezer and whisk until the icy lumps are broken up and the mixture is smooth. Place back into the freezer and repeat this whisking and chilling process until the sorbet reaches the consistency required. Freeze ready to use.

{to assemble}

icing sugar to dust
crushed ice
50g coconut chips, toasted

Sprinkle the wafers with icing sugar and put under a hot grill for 20-30 seconds to give them a nice shiny glaze. Mix the rose water raspberries with some crushed ice, and place in frozen shot glasses. Serve the glazed pistachio wafers with little glasses of raspberry and rose water frappé and with scoops of coconut glacé sprinkled with toasted coconut chips.

Curdy Castles

hot lemon and almond sponge castles, stuffed with melting lemon curd, served
{WHEAT FREE}   with catalan creams and sherry grapes

This is really two puddings in one: you can of course divide them up and serve them separately but they are so wonderfully complementary, we recommend that you don't! Almond rich lemony castle cakes with soft curdy centres are perfect served warm with silky, quivering Catalan creams – vanilla set custards drenched in caramel, the Spanish version of crème caramel (crema catalana). Why would you prevent their mutual admiration?

The British have been making lemon curd since the early 19th century, and serving it at teatime. This recipe is very easy to make and there's enough left over for scones, toast, or just a spoonful every time you happen to open the refrigerator!

serves 6

{lemon and almond sponge castles (gluten free)}

2 lemons
175g ground almonds, plus extra to
    sprinkle
4 eggs
175g caster sugar
2 teaspoons gluten free baking powder

Boil the lemons for 2 hours, drain and cool. Cut into quarters, remove the insides and just leave the skins.

You will need six 100ml dariole moulds, buttered and sprinkled with ground almonds, and placed on a baking sheet. Put the eggs, sugar and lemon skins in a food processor (this is best done when the skins are still warm). Blend together. The mixture should become light in colour and texture. This will take 5-8 minutes.

Scrape the mix into a bowl and fold in the ground almonds and baking powder. Pour into your prepared moulds. Bake in the oven at 180°C/Gas Mark 4 for 15-20 minutes.

This pudding can also be made in one 20cm cake tin. Baking will take 30-40 minutes. (To test if the pudding is cooked, insert a skewer: it should be clean when withdrawn.)

{catalan creams}

500ml whole milk
500ml whipping cream
1 vanilla pod
1 teaspoon vanilla extract
8 eggs
400ml condensed milk

for the caramel
300g caster sugar
100ml water

Begin by making the caramel. You will need six 100ml dariole moulds. Put the sugar and water into a small, thick based pan. Bring to the boil and boil rapidly until the mixture changes colour to a dark golden brown. Do not shake or stir the pan as this could crystallize the mixture. Quickly pour caramel into the base of your moulds (about 1cm deep). Allow to cool and set.

To make the custard, put the milk, cream, vanilla pod and vanilla extract in a pan and bring to the boil. In a bowl beat the eggs with the condensed milk. Pour the hot milk mix into it and stir together. Remove the vanilla pod, and pour the custard up to the top of the moulds. Place the moulds in a deep sided roasting tin, fill the roasting tin with hot water to come three quarters up the sides of the moulds, and put in the oven at 160°C/Gas Mark 3 for 30–40 minutes. When ready, the custards will be slightly risen and soft and springy to touch. (If unsure, test with a skewer.) Cool down and refrigerate still in their moulds.

This pudding may also be made in a 1.5kg metal loaf tin, allowing 50 minutes' cooking time. Chill in the tin until ready to serve.

{lemon curd}

300ml lemon juice
grated zest of 6 unwaxed lemons
8 eggs
350g caster sugar
600g butter, diced

Put a pan of water to boil. Put the lemon juice, lemon zest, eggs and sugar in a bowl that will fit over the pan and whisk together thoroughly, using a balloon whisk. Now put the bowl on top of the boiling water (making sure it does not touch the water). You will need to continue whisking until the egg mix is hot and has thickened. It will look slightly wobbly in texture (this will take about 10 minutes). Remove from the heat, then whisk in the pieces of butter until they are incorporated. Strain the curd to remove any bits of lemon zest. Cool and refrigerate.

This is more than you will need to fill the Lemon and Almond Sponge Castles, so there will be lots left over for scones and toast. It will keep in the refrigerator for 2-3 weeks.

{sherry grapes}

300g seedless black grapes, halved
125ml cream sherry

Cover the grapes with the sherry and soak for at least 1 hour – ideally for as long as 48 hours – to allow time for the flavour to be fully absorbed.

{to assemble}

caster sugar to glaze (optional)

First fill the sponge castles. Take off the tops with a sharp knife and remove a cone shape from the middle of the bottom section. Fill with lemon curd, place the top back on, and warm slightly at 160°C/Gas Mark 3 for 5 minutes. (If you have made one large sponge, just spoon the curd generously over the top, omit warming, and cut into portions.)

Turn out the Catalan creams on to serving plates, preserving the lovely caramel. (Or turn out the single large custard.) If you like a crunchy texture, sprinkle the custard(s) with caster sugar and blast with a blow torch. (The large custard should now be cut into portions and placed on the serving plates.) Place a sponge castle (or sponge portion) on each plate. Add some sherry grapes for a finishing touch.

Alternatively, serve all the elements on separate dishes and invite everyone to dig in!

Bum

sweet sheep's milk cheesecakes crammed with sambuca-soaked sultanas, served with lemon rosemary syrup and warm walnut biscotti

Living in Brighton we like nothing more than a good bit of end-of-the-pier humour, so when we stumbled across this name for our Italian cheese tart, we quickly jumped on the ooo-err Mrs Carry-on bandwagon! The name doesn't do the tart justice, nor does it look like a bum, but it certainly is at the big end of flavour. Each creamy little cheesecake is crammed with the big boozy punch and subtle aniseed scent of sambuca-loaded sultanas. The flavours are drawn together by the warm taste tones of rosemary syrup with a lemony edge, and the snappy walnut biscuits provide the perfect host for smudging the whole lot on to.

serves 6

{walnut biscotti}

200g plain flour
200g caster sugar
½ teaspoon ground star anise
1 teaspoon baking powder
grated zest of 1 orange
grated zest of 1 lemon
grated zest of 2 limes
2 eggs and 2 yolks, beaten
150g walnuts, roughly chopped
½ teaspoon fennel seeds

Place the flour, sugar, star anise, baking powder, citrus zests and fennel seeds in a large mixing bowl and make a well in the centre. Pour in the beaten egg mix and work together to form a sticky dough. Mix in the walnuts and turn out on to a floured surface. Sprinkle a little flour on top of the dough, for ease of handling, and roll the mix into a sausage shape about 30cm long.

Place gently on a lined baking sheet, but do not worry if it breaks as it is easy to stick back together. Bake at 180°C/Gas Mark 4 for 20-25 minutes until golden

brown and set. The mix will spread and rise as it cooks. Remove from the oven, allow to cool for 15 minutes then place on a chopping board and gently cut with a serrated knife into 2cm slices. (There should be about 16 in all.)

Put the slices back on to a baking tray and dry out in the oven at 130°C/Gas Mark ½ for about 20 minutes. Cool down and store in an airtight container. The biscuits will keep for a couple of weeks.

{sweet sheep's milk cheesecakes}

400g soft sheep's milk cheese (Sussex Slipcote is ideal)
1 egg and 3 yolks, beaten
50g caster sugar
½ teaspoon vanilla extract
grated zest of 1 lemon
juice of ½ lemon
400ml double cream
6 rosemary sprigs
2 teaspoons olive oil

for the sambuca sultanas
about 45ml sambuca
100g sultanas

First prepare the sambuca sultanas. Pour sambuca over the sultanas to cover, and leave to marinate at room temperature for 24 hours.

You can make individual cheesecakes or one large round: choose 6 deep rings 7.5 x 5cm, or 1 deep spring-form tin 25 x 5cm. Crumble the cheese into a bowl and add the egg mix, sugar, vanilla, and lemon zest and juice. Mix with a spatula to form a smooth paste, then add the cream in 2 batches until combined. Stir in the soaked sultanas and mix well.

Now line your rings (this sounds more complicated than it is). For the small rings cut a 15cm square of greaseproof paper

and gently mould it into the rings, taking care not to tear it and leaving a slight overhang. (Use the same principle for the large ring mould.) Carefully fill the moulds with the cheese mix. Coat the rosemary sprigs in olive oil and push a sprig into the centre of each mould (or press all the sprigs into the large single mould). The rosemary will infuse into the cheese mix as it cooks.

Place the rings in a deep sided roasting tray and pour in hot water to come three quarters of the way up the sides of the rings. Bake at 160°C/Gas Mark 3 for 20 minutes. Once set, remove the rings from the bain-marie on to a flat tray and leave to cool. Refrigerate until needed.

{rosemary syrup}

200g caster sugar
200ml water
2 rosemary sprigs
zest of ½ lemon, cut into strips
juice of ½ lemon

Bring the sugar and water to the boil, then and add the rosemary and lemon zest. Simmer for 10 minutes. Allow to cool, then strain. Finally, mix in the lemon juice. Refrigerate until needed.

{to assemble}

Remove the rings from the cheesecakes and carefully peel off the greaseproof paper, then place on serving plates. Serve each cheesecake with a couple of warm biscotti (they can be heated gently at 180°C/Gas Mark 4 for just a few minutes) and some rosemary syrup drizzled over the top. A large, single cheesecake can be cut and served in a similar way.

Peachy Cheeks

{WHEAT FREE}

baked white peaches, layered with musky camomile jelly, muscat soaked
sponge fingers, almond custard and crunchy frumble topping

There is every reason why the word 'peachy' is used to describe fabulous things! A perfectly ripe peach will instantly catapult you back to long, baking summer days of childhood. Here the peaches are combined in lush layers with exceedingly complementary flavours – the musky cut grass perfume of camomile, and the sweet floral aroma of Muscat drenched vanilla fingers – all finished with sweet almond creamy custard and crunchy bites.

serves 6

{sponge fingers}

80g caster sugar
1 drop of vanilla extract
3 large eggs, whites and yolks separated
80g plain flour (or gluten free flour), sifted
icing sugar to dust

Line two baking trays with lightly oiled greaseproof paper. Add the sugar and vanilla extract to the egg yolks and whisk until light and creamy. Whisk the egg whites in a clean dry bowl until they form peaks. Fold the flour into the yolk mix and then gently fold in the beaten egg whites, taking care not to knock out any air.

Transfer to a piping bag with a 2.5cm nozzle. Pipe into 10-12cm lengths (about 18 fingers in all), dust with icing sugar and bake at 180°C/Gas Mark 4 for 10-12 minutes. Leave to cool down and store in an airtight container.

{almond custard}

300ml almond milk
300ml double cream
6 egg yolks
90g caster sugar
60ml almond liqueur (or a few drops of
   almond extract)

Bring the almond milk and cream to the boil in a heavy based pan. Meanwhile, beat together the egg yolks and sugar. Pour half of the boiling cream mix on to the egg yolks, beating in thoroughly, and return this mixture to the rest of the cream mix in the pan. Stir constantly over a low heat, until the mixture thickens and coats the back of the spoon. Add the almond liqueur or extract now. Pass the custard through a fine sieve and leave to cool. Refrigerate until you are ready to use it.

{baked peaches}

6 peaches, ripe but not too soft and
   preferably white
1 tablespoon caster sugar
1 tablespoon water

Preheat the oven to 180°C/Gas Mark 4. Place the peaches on a baking tray. Lightly score their tops with a sharp knife then sprinkle with the sugar and water. Bake for 10-15 minutes. The skin on the top will be just starting to come away from the peach. Allow to cool, then peel off and discard the skin.

{frumble topping}

200g gluten-free flour
1 teaspoon ground cinnamon
125g unsalted butter
100g demerara sugar
25g flaked almonds

Sift the flour and cinnamon into a bowl, then rub in the butter until the mixture resembles breadcrumbs. Stir in the sugar and almonds. Tip on to a lined and lightly oiled baking sheet and bake at 180°C/Gas Mark 4 for about 30 minutes until golden brown and crunchy, stirring every 10 minutes. Remove from the oven, stir again and leave to cool. Store in an airtight container.

{camomile jelly}

1 litre water
4 camomile tea bags
100g caster sugar
500ml Muscat wine
3½ teaspoons agar agar

Bring the water to the boil in a saucepan, remove from the heat and add the camomile tea bags, sugar and wine. Leave to infuse for 20 minutes. Remove the tea bags and squeeze out the liquid. Put the pan back on to the heat and bring up to the boil again. Turn down to a low simmer and sprinkle the agar agar on top. It is very important not to stir it in. Keep on a very low heat for 5-10 minutes, then bring to the boil again and boil for 2 minutes until all the agar agar crystals have dissolved. This mix can be used immediately or can be stored in the refrigerator once cooled. The jelly can easily be melted back down and reset.

{to assemble}

100g raspberries
125ml Muscat wine
mint or borage sprigs

Heat the jelly to melt it and put 4 or 5 raspberries at the bottom of a glass, pouring over a small quantity of jelly. Refrigerate to set. Break a few sponge fingers in half, place them in the glasses, sprinkle with a little wine and cover with more jelly. Set again in the refrigerator. Now lay some of the peach slices on top of this and pour in the remainder of the jelly. Set for a final time in the fridge.

Alternatively, you can assemble the dessert in one go; it looks slightly less impressive but is equally delicious.

Once set, spoon on some almond custard and sprinkle on a generous amount of frumble topping. Decorate with raspberries and sprigs of mint or borage.

Thai One On

deep fried lime rice ice cream served with hot palm szechuan pepper pineapple, and mango and lemon grass cooler

If you haven't been to the Far East yet, this pudding will at least give you a taste of the foodie delights awaiting you there: it's a fabulously fragrant collection of tropical tastes. Sizzling hot crumbly jackets encase rice ice puddings, creamy but still with little rice bites, and packed full of pungent lime leaf flavour. They're balanced by the sweet, slightly sharp succulent bites of hot pineapple, perky with punchy bursts of Szechuan pepper, and refreshing gulps of the chilled mango and lemon grass cooler.

Frying ice cream seems an unlikely thing to do until you try it, then it makes absolute   sense. The contrast of the hot crispy outside and the frozen centre is utterly addictive, and the coupling of the sweet pineapple with the kick of Szechuan pepper tantalizes your taste buds. There's nothing to be done but to submit to it…!

serves 6-8

{fried lime rice ice cream puddings}

500ml whole milk
3 long strips of unwaxed lemon rind
4 lime leaves
75g Arborio rice
salt
100g caster sugar
3 egg whites

for the coating
50g gluten free plain flour
2 eggs, beaten
100g panko (Japanese dry breadcrumbs) –
   or use any fine dry white breadcrumbs

to finish
sunflower oil for deep frying

In a thick based saucepan heat the milk, lemon rind and lime leaves over a medium heat and bring to the boil. Add the rice and a pinch of salt, turn down the heat and cook gently until the rice is tender, stirring frequently to prevent it sticking. Once the rice is cooked, stir in the sugar. Take the pan off the heat, then remove the lemon rind and lime leaves. In a food processor, blend the cooked rice for no longer than 1 minute, until the mixture is fairly smooth but still textured with some rice grains. Pour into a bowl to cool.

Once the rice is cold, whisk the egg whites with a pinch of salt to stiff peaks and gently fold into the rice mixture. Churn in an ice cream maker and freeze, preferably overnight.

Have ready a frozen, parchment lined tray. Scoop out balls of the ice cream on to the tray and place in the freezer for 2 hours.

Prepare the ice cream balls for frying by rolling them in the following order: first in flour, then in egg, then in panko, then in egg again and finally in more panko. Return the balls to the freezer for a minimum of 2 hours before you want to fry them.

Shortly before you are ready to eat, heat oil to 170°C in a deep fryer or deep pan. (If you do not have a thermometer, drop a small piece of bread into the oil: if it rapidly turns golden brown, the oil is hot enough). Now fry the ice cream balls for just 1-2 minutes, until golden and crispy. Drain on paper towels.

{caramelized pineapple}

½ large pineapple
30g caster sugar
¼ teaspoon ground star anise
¼ teaspoon ground Szechuan pepper
20g palm sugar, chopped (or dark
   muscovado sugar)

Peel and quarter the pineapple, removing the woody centre, and cut into 6mm thick pieces. Dip the pineapple pieces in the caster sugar, coating both sides, and put in a pan over a medium heat. Cook on one side until the sugar starts to caramelize, then turn over and sprinkle with the anise, Szechuan pepper and chopped palm sugar. Continue cooking until nicely caramelized. Serve immediately or set aside to be reheated when required.

{mango and lemon grass cooler}

2 ripe mangoes, peeled, stoned and cubed
   (about 300-350g prepared mango)
100ml coconut milk
½ lemon grass stick, chopped
1 lime leaf
¾ pint pineapple juice

Place all the ingredients in a jug blender and blend until smooth. Pass through a fine sieve and chill until required.

{to assemble}

2 passion fruits, halved

Pour mango and lemon grass cooler into glasses, top with a squeeze of passion fruit and keep cool in the refrigerator. Meanwhile, warm the pineapple slices in the oven at 180°C/Gas Mark 4 for about 5 minutes, or under a moderately hot grill. Once fried, serve the puddings immediately, with the mango and lemon grass cooler and the hot pineapple.

Taste of Honey

steamed buttermilk puddings, with warm baked pears and honey chestnuts, and bay cream custard

This autumnal combination is a fitting way to herald the arrival of the 'season of mists and mellow fruitfulness'. Perfectly ripe pears, with their soft subtly fragrant flesh, make a luscious liaison with delicious dribbles of honey drenched sweet nutty chestnuts, creamy aromatic bay custard, and lovely lofty puddings.

In the European tradition, bay more commonly appears in savoury dishes, so it's nice to show its versatility and subtle fragrance by using it in a pudding. And we like to use buttermilk often in our baking. It lends a refreshingly sour note to any bake and has fewer calories than milk or cream, despite its name. Can't be bad!

serves 6

{warm baked pears with honey chestnuts}

3 Packham or Comice pears, peeled
3 tablespoons lemon juice

for the honey chestnuts
18 chestnuts
1½ tablespoons runny honey

First prepare the honey chestnuts. Put the chestnuts into a pan of cold water and bring to the boil. Simmer for about 5 minutes. Drain, rinse under cold running water and peel while still hot. Allow to cool, then roast in the oven at 150°C/Gas Mark 2 for 25 minutes, to dry out. Put the honey in a pan, heat to boiling point and tip the chestnuts in, coating them well. Set aside until needed.

Halve the pears and cut out the cores and pips. Put face down into an ovenproof dish and spoon over the honey chestnuts and lemon juice. Cover the dish with foil and bake at 180°C/Gas Mark 4 for 30 minutes until the pears are tender. Keep warm until ready to serve.

{bay cream custard}

300ml whole milk
300ml whipping cream
3 small fresh bay leaves
5 egg yolks
125g caster sugar

Put the milk, cream and bay leaves in a heavy based pan and bring slowly to the boil to infuse the bay. Put the egg yolks and sugar in a bowl and whisk together until light and creamy. Remove the bay leaves from the hot milk mix and pour half of it on to the egg mixture. Stir well and return to the rest of the milk mix in the pan. Cook over a low heat, stirring constantly, until the custard thickens and coats the back of the spoon. Pour into a cold bowl to cool, and refrigerate until needed.

{buttermilk puddings}

75g plain flour
200g caster sugar
¼ teaspoon salt
4 eggs, whites and yolks separated
300ml buttermilk
2 teaspoons grated lemon zest
100ml lemon juice

Mix together the flour, sugar and salt in a bowl. In another bowl whisk together the egg yolks, buttermilk, lemon zest and juice. Make a well in the flour mix, pour in the egg yolk mixture and whisk together to form a smooth batter. Whisk the egg whites to soft peaks and fold one third of them into the batter to lighten the mix. Now gently fold in the rest of the egg whites. Spoon the mixture into six buttered ramekins and place in a bain-marie. Cook in a preheated oven at 180°C/Gas Mark 4 for 25-35 minutes. When cooked, the puddings will puff up and brown nicely on top, and they will feel springy to touch.

{to assemble}

The buttermilk puddings are best served straight from the oven, the ramekins set on to plates. To each pudding add a still warm pear with honey chestnuts, and serve a big jug of bay custard on the side. Alternatively, warm up the puddings at 160°C/Gas Mark 3 for 5 minutes, and serve accompanied in the same way.

Strawberry Lush

piping hot elderflower fritters with strawberry soup, served with pimms
gazpacho and cucumber and mint granita

{VEGAN}

Each mouthful of this light refreshing combination evokes the sounds and scents of a glorious British summer: the clinking of icy Pimms glasses on the freshly cut lawn, fragrant sun warmed strawberries ripening over straw in the borders, and the delicate fronds of creamy yellow elderflower heads above, dappling the sunlight. Every ingredient here shouts out that summer has arrived, even if you can't tell it from the weather! Fragrant elderflower fritters with big mouthfuls of crunchy fresh Pimms gazpacho; luscious slurps of sweet strawberry soup and icy cool as a cucumber mint granita.

Elderflower pollen is used by herbalists to relieve hay fever, so what better ingredient for a beautiful summer's day! Folklore has it that the flowers must be picked after the morning sun has warmed them, and then shaken – not washed – to dislodge stowaway bugs. The blooms start appearing in May and carry on into July; plenty of opportunity to gather them and make cordials and tisanes or these light and delicious fritters.

serves 6

{strawberry soup}

400g ripe strawberries
¼ teaspoon vanilla extract
about 1 tablespoon icing sugar
about 1 tablespoon lemon juice

Put all the ingredients into a blender (the amount of sugar and lemon juice will depend on how sweet the strawberries are) and blitz them until they reach a soupy consistency. Push the liquid through a sieve and refrigerate until you need it.

{cucumber and mint granita}

90g caster sugar
200ml water
1 cucumber, halved lengthways and deseeded
30g mint leaves

Bring the sugar and water to the boil and simmer for 2 minutes, then cool down. Roughly chop the cucumber and mint and blend them in a jug blender until smooth. Strain this liquid through a fine sieve and add to the cooled syrup. Freeze this mixture, stirring it with a fork every 30 minutes, until crystals form. Keep in the freezer until needed.

{elderflower fritters}

oil for deep frying
12 elderflower heads

for the tempura
85g plain flour
15g cornflour
200ml elderflower pressé

Make a tempura by putting the flour and cornflour in a mixing bowl and stirring in the elderflower pressé, mixing in well. Refrigerate until needed. Only start frying just before you are ready to serve. Preheat oil in a deep fryer or deep pan to 170°C,

dip the elderflower heads into the tempura and plunge them straight into the hot oil. Cook for about 1 minute until golden brown and crispy. Place the fritters on kitchen paper to drain.

{pimms gazpacho}

15 large firm strawberries
1 apple (preferably Braeburn or Cox), peeled and cored
100ml Pimms
grated zest and juice of ½ orange
5g mint leaves, finely chopped

Cut the stalk end off the strawberries and carefully slice the fruit into 2mm slices. Next, cut the slices into 2mm wide strips, then dice into tiny cubes. Put these into a small mixing bowl, being careful not to bruise them. Next, slice the apple into 2mm slices and make tiny cubes in the same way. Add these to the strawberries with the Pimms, the orange zest and juice, and the chopped mint. Refrigerate until you are ready to use.

{to assemble}

elderflower cordial to drizzle
20g mint leaves, finely chopped

Divide the elderflower fritters between the plates and drizzle some elderflower cordial over them. Ladle some of the strawberry soup into iced bowls and top this with a good spoonful of the gazpacho. Now mix the chopped mint into the granita and heap a little mound of this in the middle of the gazpacho. Place these colourful bowls next to the hot sticky fritters.

Pastéis de Nata

portuguese custard tarts, served with honey baked quince and kummel

Quite rightly an absolute customer favourite, these ridiculously delicious warm custardy pastries can be served with a mug of coffee in the morning or, with the addition of fragrant tender quince and a dash of caraway flavoured kummel, transformed into an autumnal sweet fest. This combination of tastes is guaranteed to convert the most intractable 'I don't eat puddings' customer. The main recipe makes about 12 tarts (it would hardly be worth baking less) and although you only need to serve six with the quince, the rest are likely to disappear fast.

Quince is one of my favourite fruits. The scent is heavenly, it's easy to grow and it has the most generous and beautiful blossoms. Until quite recently, it has been underrated and underused here in Britain but fortunately it is enjoying a bit of a come back. We always have quince on our menus when in season. The fruit itself does not appear all that promising in its raw form–it is hard, gritty and unpleasantly tart. But peeled, deseeded and baked with sugar, honey or maple syrup, it is transported to another level. A little quince goes a long way: a single fruit, added to a pile of cooking apples, will enhance the flavour of the resulting pie, crumble or compote.

We like to put quince with these Portuguese tarts, as the Portuguese have a long tradition of using the fruit which they call 'marmelo'. They make a delicious preserve or 'marmelada' from them, hence the origin of our own 'marmalade', which today is more often made with oranges.

serves 6

{custard tarts}

200g Puff Pastry (see page 20)
50g unsalted butter, melted

for the custard filling
500ml single cream
250ml whole milk
1 vanilla pod, split and scraped
grated zest of 1/2 lemon
8 egg yolks
225g caster sugar
40g cornflour

Take the pastry and roll it into a rectangle 15 x 12cm, then brush with the melted butter. Fold it in half, brush with butter again and roll up before wrapping in clingfilm. Chill for at least 1 hour, preferably overnight.

Next, prepare the custard filling. Place the cream, milk, vanilla pod and seeds, and lemon zest in a heavy based pan and cook over a low heat for 10 minutes without boiling. Put the egg yolks, sugar and cornflour in a bowl and whisk together until combined. Pour one third of the warm infused cream mix on to the egg and sugar mix. Quickly stir together and pour back into the remaining cream mix in the pan. Cook over a low heat, stirring constantly with a balloon whisk, until the mixture boils. Immediately remove from the heat and pour into a bowl to cool down. Remove the vanilla pod, giving it a squeeze to extract as much flavour as possible.

To make the tarts, use buttered non-stick muffin tins. Cut the roll of pastry into 1cm slices and roll these out into 7.5cm rounds. You should have about 12 rounds. Press these into the moulds and chill for 30 minutes before filling them.

Preheat the oven to 180°C/Gas Mark 4. Spoon the chilled custard mix into the chilled pastry cases, filling them almost to the top. Bake for 15-20 minutes until the pastry is golden brown and the tops of the tarts are starting to colour and rise up. Leave the tarts in the tins to cool, then carefully remove to assemble the dish.

{sticky baked quince}

2 large or 3 small quinces, peeled,
   quartered and cored
juice and grated zest of 1 lemon
200g caster sugar
4 tablespoons runny honey
500ml water

Place the quinces on a baking tray and coat them with the lemon juice. Sprinkle on the grated lemon zest and sugar and add the honey and water. Cover with foil and bake at 160°C/Gas Mark 3 for 1 hour, then remove the foil and bake for a further 15 minutes. If the quince looks a bit dry, add a little more water and carry on cooking until the fruit is a lovely deep red colour. Allow to cool.

{to assemble}

50ml kummel

If you made the tarts in advance, gently warm through the required quantity at 180°C/Gas Mark 4 for 5-10 minutes. Alternatively, once cooked, allow to rest in the tins for about 20 minutes before turning out. Arrange the tarts on dessert plates with some baked quince, drizzled with kummel, and spoon a little of the quince cooking syrup over the top.

Plum Pikelets

wild rice pikelets served with plum compote, umeboshi plum ripple ice cream and crystallized ginger custard

These are fabulous little treasures: the ground wild rice lends a nutty flavour to the delicious fried fluffy pancakes, which are just made for the mouthwateringly good velvety plum compote and luscious layered ice cream, rippled with the tang of sweet-sour umeboshi plum purée. Serve with abundant amounts of custard, peppered with moist, chewy chips of crystallized ginger – a sweet flavour with a little kick.

Traditional Japanese umeboshi purée is a versatile and zesty seasoning to have in the store cupboard. Although known as plum purée it is not in fact made from plums, but from a type of apricot. It has a multitude of uses and can be added to salad dressings, cooked vegetables, sauces and spreads. Here, it adds an interesting tang to the ice cream.

Crystallized ginger is as useful in the medicine cabinet as in the pantry: the pungent sweet root is used as a remedy to alleviate hot flushes, indigestion and the common cold – something for everyone then! We like it for the surprising heat – and texture – it gives to the otherwise smooth vanilla custard.

serves 8

{wild rice pikelets}

250g strong flour
50g caster sugar
80g ground wild rice
a pinch of salt
10g dried yeast
350ml whole milk
300ml crème fraîche
4 eggs, separated
olive oil and unsalted butter for frying

Sift the flour into a large bowl, then add the sugar, ground rice, salt and yeast. Put the milk and crème fraîche in a pan, then warm gently to body temperature. Dip your finger in to test. Stir this liquid into the flour mix and incorporate all the ingredients to form a smooth paste. Add the eggs yolks and mix well. Cover the bowl with clingfilm and allow the yeast mix to ferment and double in size. This should take about 20-30 minutes. Once the yeast mix has fermented, whisk the egg whites to stiff peaks and fold into the batter.

You can either fry the pikelets straight away or you can put the batter in the refrigerator to slow down fermentation until you are ready to cook them.

To cook, add a few drops of olive oil to a non-stick frying pan. Once hot, drop in 1 tablespoon batter for each pikelet, allowing room for the pancake to spread a little. Cook the pancakes on a medium heat and turn over once the first side is browned, adding a small knob of butter each time you turn them over. They will take about 2 minutes on each side. There is enough batter to make about 16 pikelets.

{umeboshi plum ripple ice cream}

2 teaspoons umeboshi purée (pickled plum)
1 quantity Vanilla Ice Cream (see page 21)

for the plum compote
500g slightly under-ripe plums
4 tablespoons runny honey
½ vanilla pod, split and scraped

First prepare the plum compote. Cut each plum into 8 pieces, removing the stones, and put in a heavy based pan with the honey, and vanilla pod and seeds. Cover and simmer gently for 10-15 minutes, stirring occasionally, until the plums start to break down and soften, and a nice syrup is forming. Remove from the heat and allow to cool, then remove the vanilla pod.

Reserve and refrigerate about three quarters of this compote for the final assembly. Blend the remaining quarter with the umeboshi purée until very smooth (add a splash of water if necessary to get the right consistency). Put this purée in the refrigerator to chill.

Once the vanilla ice cream is churned, layer it in a tub with the plum and umeboshi purée, a spoonful of ice cream followed by a layer of purée, and continue this layering until both mixes are finished. Freeze until you are ready to use.

{crystallized ginger custard}

300ml whole milk
300ml double cream
15g crystallized ginger, chopped
1 vanilla pod, split and scraped
6 egg yolks
175g caster sugar
1 tablespoon ginger wine

Put the milk, cream, ginger and vanilla pod and seeds in a heavy based pan and slowly bring to the boil to allow the vanilla to infuse. Whisk the egg yolks with the sugar until they are light in colour and creamy in texture, then pour in about one third of the hot milk mix and stir in well.

Return this mixture to the remaining hot milk mix in the pan. Place over a medium heat and stir constantly with a wooden spoon until the custard thickens and begins to coat the back of the spoon. Do not allow it to boil or the eggs will separate. Immediately take the pan off the heat and transfer the custard to a cool bowl. Remove the vanilla pod, giving it a squeeze to extract the last bit of flavour. Now add the ginger wine, mixing it in well. Chill.

{to assemble}

If possible, serve the pikelets straight from the pan. But if you have cooked them in advance, just place them on a baking tray, dot with tiny pieces of butter, cover with foil and warm in the oven at 180°C/Gas Mark 4 for about 5 minutes. Warm the ginger custard over a low heat, whisking: do not allow to boil. Serve the pikelets with a spoonful of plum compote, a scoop of umeboshi plum ripple ice cream, and plenty of ginger custard.

Vodka Cherry Chocolate Churros

sweet spice dusted doughnut batons served with warm sticky
dipping chocolate and vodka sozzled cherries

{VEGAN}

We have Spanish shepherds to thank for this centuries old dish. When their nomadic lifestyle high up in the mountains left them bereft of freshly baked staples, they came up with this sweet stick that could be cooked easily in a pan over an open fire. Originally churros were skinny, like breadsticks, but often curved and even coiled, and eaten plain or rolled in cinnamon sugar. They became a daily treat for the sweet toothed shepherds, too good a secret to keep quiet, and word got around. Their popularity spread and these irresistible snacks became a Spanish tradition.

Thankfully, their deliciousness spread further afield. Once they'd found their way to Terre à Terre, and after numerous tasting and slurping sessions involving chocolate dip and cherry vodka, they became a firm favourite. I think the shepherds would have approved too! Enjoy.

serves 4-6

{churros}

500g strong flour
¼ teaspoon salt
½ teaspoon caster sugar
50g soya margarine
5g dried yeast
280ml warm water sunflower oil for deep or shallow frying

for the cinnamon sugar
½ teaspoon ground cinnamon
40g caster sugar

Sift the flour, salt and sugar. Rub in the soya margarine. Stir the yeast into the warm water. Make a well in the flour and pour in the yeast and water mix. Mix to a smooth dough either by hand or with a hook attachment on a mixer. Once the dough has formed, knead for 5-6 minutes. Cut into quarters, cover with a damp cloth and leave for 5 minutes to allow the dough to puff up slightly.

Now divide each quarter into 3 pieces and roll each one into a 10cm long cigar shape. Place the churros on a lined baking tray, cover loosely with clingfilm and allow to prove for 1 hour. They do not need to double in size as they will expand when they are being fried. (Alternatively, if you are not ready to cook them, freeze them and remove from the freezer 1 hour before cooking.)

Prepare the cinnamon sugar just by mixing the cinnamon into the sugar. Finally, either deep fry the churros for 2-3 minutes, or shallow fry (turning regularly) until golden all over. While they are still hot, roll them in the cinnamon sugar.

{chocolate dip}

250g dark chocolate (70 per cent cocoa solids)
300ml soya cream
2 tablespoons hot water

Break the chocolate into pieces into a medium sized bowl. Bring the soya cream to the boil. As soon as it has boiled, pour on to the chocolate. Stir with a small balloon whisk until thoroughly combined, then add the hot water.

{vodka cherries}

300g fresh cherries, stoned
about 200ml vodka
1-2 teaspoons runny honey (optional)

Cover the cherries in vodka (add more if you dare), cover with clingfilm and leave to marinate overnight. Add a small amount of honey if you prefer things a little sweeter. Chill the vodka cherries until needed.

{to assemble}

Set the bowl of chocolate dip over a pan of simmering water and warm through without letting it boil, then pour into small bowls ready for dipping. Divide the chilled vodka cherries into cold glasses, adding cocktail sticks for spearing the fruit, and put these with the hot churros on to serving plates. The best bit is supping on very cold cherry scented vodka while dunking your churros into the warm chocolate. Roll up your sleeves and dig in!

MUDDLING

Here are a few liquid lovelies to whet your appetite and float your boat.

{measurements}

25ml = 1 shot
Many cocktails are based on multiples of this.

{glasses}

old-fashioned: short and chunky; often used for drinks served 'on the rocks'.
collins: tall, narrow tumbler with straight sides.
cocktail: the classic martini glass.

{techniques}

muddle: use a purpose-made muddler or similar blunt implement, such as a thin rolling pin or pestle. Place the ingredients in a thick, sturdy glass and push down on the muddler with a twisting action.

float: slowly pour the ingredient over the back of a teaspoon or cocktail spoon held close to the top of the drink, so that it floats on top.

{espresso martini}

serves 1

25ml organic vodka
35ml fresh espresso coffee
12.5ml organic coffee liqueur (we use Dwersteg Café Crème)
12.5ml agave syrup
a coffee bean

Shake all the ingredients except the coffee bean over ice and strain into a chilled cocktail glass. Float the coffee bean on the surface.

{elder bubble}

You can buy cucumber vodka. A couple of good makes are Blackwood's from Scotland and Square One (organic) from the USA. We prefer to infuse our own, using a large organic cucumber and a 750ml bottle of organic vodka. Slice the cucumber and place in a large glass container, such as a Kilner jar. Pour over the vodka and seal with a lid. Let it stand at room temperature for up to 2 weeks, giving it a gentle shake each day. Strain the vodka back into its original bottle and keep in the freezer or refrigerator until ready to use. This is also good used in a dry martini.

serves 1

12.5ml cucumber vodka (best if kept in the freezer)
12.5ml elderflower cordial
Champagne or Cava
a slice of cucumber
a mint leaf

Pour the vodka and elderflower cordial into a Champagne flute and stir. Top up with Champagne or Cava and garnish with the cucumber and mint leaf.

{basil blush}

serves 1

3 thin lemon slices
4 basil leaves
4 raspberries
25ml fresh raspberry purée
crushed ice
50ml Cointreau or Triple Sec
dash of Framboise (or other raspberry
    liqueur)

Place the lemon slices and 3 basil leaves
in an old-fashioned glass and muddle.
Add 2 raspberries and the raspberry purée
and muddle some more. Add crushed ice
and stir. Pour in the Cointreau or Triple
Sec and stir. Float the Framboise over the
top and garnish with the 2 remaining
raspberries and the remaining basil leaf.

{spiced dark and stormy}

serves 1

50ml spiced gold rum (we use organic
    Papagayo)
25ml lime juice
12.5ml agave syrup
ice
good quality ginger beer (we use Fentimans)
a lime wedge

Shake the first 3 ingredients with ice and
strain into a large ice-filled glass. Top up
with ginger beer, stir, then place the lime
wedge on the rim of the glass. Serve with
straws.

{sussex strawberry kir royale}

enough for 2 glasses

Breaky Bottom is Peter Hall's wonderful
vineyard. One of the pioneers of English
sparkling wine, Peter planted his vines on
the East Sussex Downs back in the 1970s
and is now one of England's premier
producers of quality sparkling wine.
He also produces a fine crème de cassis
for his Kir Royale bottling.

250g strawberries, halved
25g sugar
1 tablespoon crème de cassis (we use
    Breaky Bottom)
sparkling wine (again, we use Breaky
    Bottom)

Mix the strawberries and sugar together
in a bowl and leave to stand at room
temperature for 10 minutes, stirring
occasionally. Divide the strawberry
mixture between two Champagne flutes,
add a spoonful of cassis to each and top
up with Breaky Bottom fizz.

{frozen banana colada}

enough for 2 large glasses

100ml white rum (we use Utkins Fairtrade
   Single Estate)
100ml creamed coconut
250g fresh pineapple, peeled and diced
2 ripe bananas
a large glass of crushed ice (350ml)
2 slices of pineapple
ground cinnamon

Blend together all the ingredients, except
the pineapple slices and cinnamon, until
smooth. Pour into glasses, garnish with
the pineapple slices and dust lightly with
cinnamon.

{pomegranate cosmopolitan}

serves 1

25ml organic vodka
25ml Cointreau or Triple Sec
25ml organic pomegranate juice
$1/2$ teaspoon pomegranate molasses
12.5ml lime juice
ice
6 pomegranate seeds

Shake the first 5 ingredients with ice.
Strain into a chilled cocktail glass, garnish
with the pomegranate seeds and serve.

{mojito romano}

serves 1

11 mint leaves
25ml lime juice
4 large strawberries, plus 1 to garnish
2 teaspoons caster sugar
50ml organic Grappa di Chardonnay (we
   use Fasoli Gino)
crushed ice
soda water

Muddle 10 of the mint leaves in an old-
fashioned or Collins glass with the lime
juice, strawberries and sugar. Add the
Grappa, half fill the glass with crushed ice
and stir. Fill the glass to the top with more
crushed ice and stir again. Top up with
soda water, stir again, then garnish with
the remaining mint leaf and strawberry.
Serve with straws.

{margarita melons}

enough for 2 large glasses

1/2 ripe watermelon, peeled, deseeded and
    diced
50ml lime juice
50ml tequila
25ml Cointreau or Triple Sec
a large glass of crushed ice (350ml)
1/2 –1 tablespoon agave syrup (optional)
2 slices of lime

Blend the watermelon in a liquidizer until
smooth. Add the lime juice, tequila and
Cointreau or Triple Sec, top up with the
crushed ice and continue blending until
smooth. Add the agave syrup to taste, if
using. Tip into sugar-rimmed glasses and
garnish with the lime slices.

A non-alcoholic variation would be to
replace the tequila and Cointreau with
50ml bitter lemon, 50ml grenadine and
the juice of a blood orange.

{feeling fruity}
(non-alcoholic)

enough for 4–6 large glasses

400g strawberries
250g raspberries
100g redcurrants
100g blackcurrants
seeds of 1 pomegranate
juice of 2 oranges
2 ripe bananas
200ml organic apple juice
a large glass of crushed ice (350ml)

Blend together all the ingredients until
smooth, then strain and serve
immediately.

{muscat and melon}

enough for 2 large glasses

1 ripe honeydew melon, peeled, deseeded
    and diced
3 lemon balm leaves, plus extra to garnish
8 mint leaves, plus extra to garnish
25ml lime juice
200ml Muscat de Rivesaltes
a large glass of crushed ice (350ml)
balls of cantaloupe melon or slices of
    watermelon

Purée the melon flesh in a food processor
or blender with the lemon balm, mint,
lime juice and Muscat. Add the crushed
ice and continue blending until smooth.
Pour into tall glasses and garnish with
cantaloupe balls, lemon balm and mint.
Alternatively, a large wedge of
watermelon pushed on to the side of
each glass looks good.

For a refreshing non-alcoholic version,
omit the Muscat.

{passion mint}
(non-alcoholic)

serves 1

2 mint tea bags
a handful of mint leaves, plus a few to
   garnish
250g caster sugar
100ml pineapple juice
100ml orange juice
ice
pulp of 1 passion fruit

Put the mint tea bags and fresh mint in a
teapot, pour over 500ml boiling water
and leave to steep for 5 minutes. Add the
sugar and stir until dissolved, then strain
and leave to cool. Keep refrigerated in a
sealed container until required.

Shake the pineapple juice, orange juice
and 50ml of the mint syrup together, then
strain over ice in a large glass. Spoon over
the passion fruit pulp and garnish with
mint leaves.

{tom's lychee blush}
(non-alcoholic)

This is a great non-alcoholic thirst
quencher but also looks and tastes sophis-
ticated for those early-teen parties. What's
more, pomegranates are delicious and
packed with antioxidants and vitamins.

enough for 4–6 large glasses

400ml organic lychee juice
400ml organic lemonade (we use Duchy
   Originals, or you can make your own)
200ml organic cloudy apple juice (we use
   Oakwood Farm, a mix of Bramley and
   Fiesta)
50ml lime juice
crushed ice
seeds of $1/2$ pomegranate
100ml organic pomegranate juice

Stir the first 4 ingredients together in a
large jug. Fill each glass three-quarters
full with crushed ice, then pour the juice
to within 3cm of the rim. Add about
8 pomegranate seeds to each glass, stir
and top up with the pomegranate juice.
Garnish with more pomegranate seeds
and serve with straws.

{black and blue}
(non-alcoholic)

enough for 2 large glasses

We do not give precise measures overall:
the sweetness of the fruit determines how
much honey or lemon juice you may wish
to add.

blueberries
blackberries
about 1 tablespoon mild honey
lemon juice
250ml soda water
ice

Take a Collins or other large glass and fill
it two-thirds full with blueberries, topping
up with blackberries. Tip the berries into a
blender, add the honey, lemon juice and
soda water and blend until smooth. Strain
into 2 glasses, over ice, and garnish with
more blackberries and blueberries.

AND NOW
THE END
IS NEAR

PROVENANCE PLACE

A list of the very wonderful suppliers that we are proud to work with:

{Ashurst Organics}

Plumpton, East Sussex
01273 891219
ashurstveg@btinternet.com

{Bookham Fine Foods}

Cheeses, butter and pasta.
Arlington, East Sussex
www.bookhamcheese.co.uk

{Breaky Bottom}

Sparkling wine.
Lewes, East Sussex
www.breakybottom.co.uk

{Chef's Herbs Fresh Culinary Herbs}

Pulborough, West Sussex
01798 875020

{C.H. Mears & Sons}

Fruit and vegetables.
Brighton, East Sussex
01273 556888

{Chilli Pepper Pete}

Brighton, East Sussex
www.chillipepperpete.com

{Clearspring}

Organic/premium quality Japanese and European foods.
London
www.clearspring.co.uk

{Duggie Ainsley}

Stanmer Organics
Stanmer Park, Brighton, East Sussex.
07768770270

{Dunkertons}

Cider.
Hereford
www.dunkertons.co.uk

{Fundamentally Fungus}

Stockbridge, Hampshire
www.fundamentallyfungus.com

{Golden Cross Cheese Company}

Goat's and sheep's milk cheeses.
Whitesmith, East Sussex
www.goldencrosscheese.co.uk

{Hepworth and Company}

Organic ales and lager.
Horsham, East Sussex
www.hepworthbrewery.co.uk

{High Weald Dairy}

Organic cow's and sheep's milk cheeses.
Haywards Heath, West Sussex
www.highwealddairy.co.uk

{Infinity Foods}

Brighton, East Sussex
www.infinityfoods.co.uk

{Luscombe Organic Drinks}

Traditional soft drinks and juices.
Luscombe, Devon
www.luscombe.co.uk

{Mason & Mason Wines Ltd}

Chichester, West Sussex
sales@masonandmasonwines.co.uk

{Middle Farm Shop}

Firle, Lewes, East Sussex
www.middlefarm.com

{Neals Yard Dairy}

London
www.nealsyard.co.uk

{Nut Knowle Farm}

Goat's milk cheeses.
East Sussex
www.nutknowlefarm.com

{Oakwood Farm}

Organic juices, cider and perry.
Robertsbridge, East Sussex
01580 830 893.

{Red Roaster Coffee}

Brighton, East Sussex
www.redroaster.co.uk

{Secretts Farm}

Surrey/West Sussex
www.secretts.co.uk

{Sedlescombe Organic Vineyard}

Robertsbridge, East Sussex
www.english-wine.com

{Taj Mahal Stores}

Brighton, East Sussex
01273 325027

{The Garlic Farm}

Isle of Wight
www.thegarlicfarm.co.uk

{Turners Fine Foods}

Goodhurst, Kent
01580 212818

{The Seasons}

Organic fruit and vegetables.
Forest Row, East Sussex
01342 824673

{Vintage Roots}

Organic wines.
Heckfield, Hampshire
www.vintageroots.co.uk

{Wendy Taylor}

Decorative artist.
wendytayor1@hotmail.co.uk

{Watts Farm}

Soft fruit, herbs, baby leaves and vegetables.
Orpington, Kent
www.wattsfarm.co.uk

And a list of companies and organisations who think like we think:

{Big Barn}

www.bigbarn.co.uk

{Farmers' Markets}

www.farmersmarkets.net

{London Bio Packaging}

www.londonbiopackaging.com

{Magpie Recycling}

www.maypie.coop

{Raw Food Diet Advice and Courses}

www.therawlife.co.uk

{Soil Association}

www.soilassociation.org

{The Slow Food Movement}

www.slowfood.com

{Vegetarian Society}

www.vegsoc.org

{Vegan Voice}

www.viva.org.uk

INDEX

{m}

Macadamia mayonnaise 55
Mace bay cream 27

Mangoes
green mango salad, Rice noodle and 81
Mango and lemon grass cooler 194
Mango purée 167
Mangotango salad 122

Margarita melons 212
Marshmallow 176
masala, Yogurt 148
mashed potato, Creamy 20
mashed potato, Miso 96

Mayonnaise
Avocado lime mayonnaise 126
Lemon herb mayonnaise 133
Macadamia mayonnaise 55
Mayonnaise 18

Mellow mallow 176

Melon
Galia galliano smash 168
Margarita melons 212
Melon marble ab dab 168
Melon sorbet marbles 168
Muscat and melon 212

Meringue nests 167
merlot onions, Cinnamon 92
milk, Lentil and oregano 138
mille feuille, Lemon pickle, broad bean and mint 119

Mint
Cucumber and mint granita 197
Lemon pickle, broad bean and mint mille feuille 119
Mint oil 114
Mint tea granita 154
Minty mushy peas 91
Mojito romano 211
Passion mint 215

mirin dressing, Miso and 59

Miso
Miso and mirin dressing 59
Miso dauphinoise 97
Miso mashed potatoes 96
Miso pretty 127
Roast yellow pepper and miso dressing 127

Mojito romano 211
mousse, Broad bean 119
mousses, Cucumber 75
muffins, Turmeric and coriander rice 88
Muscat and melon 212

Mushrooms
Duxelles bun filling 143
Mixed mushroom duxelles 83
Mushroom ragout 139
Mushroom ragout puddings 141
Potsticker filling 100
shiitake sauce, Sherry and 72
Shimeji tat soi dry spice stir fry 144

mustard straws, Cheddar and 36

{n}

Nasturtium salad 75
No cocky big leeky 92

Noodles
Courgette noodle tangle 145
Rice noodle and green mango salad 81
Soba salad 58, 59
Yuba rolls 144

Nosy parkin pudding 161
Number seventy-one 34

{o}

oatmeal ice cream, Toasted 161

Oils
Dill and carraway oil 111
Herb oils 20
Lemon oil 131
Mint oil 114
Rocket oil 108
Turmeric and ginger oil 40

Olives
Deep fried olives 31
Green olive hash 136
Kalamata tapenade 130
Olive cassoulet 66
Olive, sultana and bulgur wheat salad 118

Onions
Caponata 125
Cinnamon merlot onions 92
Crazy onion salad 104
Horiatiki salad 131
Kitchen sink pickles 116
Pom toms 39
Soft spiced red onions 68

Orange, thyme and saffron dressing 125
orange candy, Sugared 184
oregano milk, Lentil and 138
Oregano mojo 47

{p}

pak choi, Stir fried 99
Parkin pudding 161
Parmesan doughnuts 27
Parmesan polenta sausages 83
(plantain fritters), Tostones 29

Parsley
Gremolata 130
Parsley liquor 96
Parsley purée 114
Pea and parsley pikelets 114
Salsa verde 145

Pasta
Between the sheets 145
Chocolate pasta 181

Pastéis de Nata 198

Pastry
Almond pastry cups 155
Banana and custard turnovers 185
Cheddar and mustard straws 36
Cigarillos 154
Lemon pickle, broad bean and mint mille feuille 119
Puff pastry 20
Suet crust pastry 141
Wrapped soufflés 110

Passion fruit curd 167
Passion mint 215
Passion shake 176
peaches, Baked 193
Peachy cheeks 192
peanut frizzle, Garlic, chilli and 81
pears, Riesling pickled 64
pears with honey chestnuts, Warm baked 195

Peas
Minty mushy peas 91
Pea and parsley pikelets 114
Pea purée 52
Pea shooter 52
Pea shooter soup 52

Peppers
Caponata 125
Cardamom and red pepper sauce 123
Marmara tapenade 125
Pickle pepper stingo 134
Poke mole 126
Roast yellow pepper and miso dressing 127
Shredded red peppers 97

Pernod terrine, Butternut and 136

Pestos
Edamame pesto 100
Rocket pesto 130
Soya bean pesto 143
Walnut pesto 181

Pickles
Kitchen sink pickles 116
Kohlrabi pickle 35
Lemony yemeni pickle 89
Piccalilli 105
Pickle pepper stingo 134
Pickled baby aubergines 143
Pickled chillies 148
Pickled lily pots salad 106

pineapple, Caramelized 194
pistachio wafers, Coconut and 187
Pistachio wafers 187
Plum compôte 156, 200
Plum pikelets 200
plum ripple ice cream, Umeboshi 200
plums, Whole roasted figs and 155
Podi spice 103
Poke mole 126

Polenta
Coca bread 130
Parmesan polenta sausages 83
Polenta plumps 66
Pomegranate cosmopolitan 211
Pomegranate, radish and fenugreek salad 63
Potager pickles 133

A NOTE FOR AMERICAN READERS

British and American cookbooks use different measuring systems. In the UK, dry ingredients are measured by weight, with the metric system increasingly replacing the Imperial one, while in the US they are measured by volume.

WEIGHT

7g	¼ ounce	200g	7 ounces
20g	¾ ounce	220–225g	8 ounces
25–30g	1 ounce	250–260g	9 ounces
40g	1½ ounces	300g	10½ ounces
50g	1¾ ounces	325g	11½ ounces
60–65g	2¼ ounces	350g	12 ounces
70–75g	2½ ounces	400g	14 ounces
80g	2¾ ounces	450g	1 pound
90g	3¼ ounces	500g	1 pound 2 ounces
100g	3½ ounces	600g	1 pound 5 ounces
110–115g	4 ounces	700g	1 pound 9 ounces
120–130g	4½ ounces	750g	1 pound 10 ounces
140g	5 ounces	800g	1¾ pounds
150g	5½ ounces	900g	2 pounds
175–180g	6 ounces	1kg	2¼ pounds

VOLUME

50ml	1¾ fl oz	300ml	10 fl oz
60ml	2 fl oz (4 tablespoons/¼ cup)	350ml	12 fl oz
75ml	2½ fl oz (5 tablespoons)	400ml	14 fl oz
90ml	3 fl oz (⅜ cup)	450ml	15 fl oz
100ml	3½ fl oz	475ml	16 fl oz (2 cups)
125ml	4 fl oz (½ cup)	500ml	18 fl oz
150ml	5 fl oz (⅔ cup)	600ml	20 fl oz
175ml	6 fl oz	800ml	28 fl oz
200ml	7 fl oz	850ml	30 fl oz
250ml	8 fl oz (1 cup)	1 litre	35 fl oz (4 cups)

LENGTH

5mm	¼ inch	8cm	3¼ inches
1cm	½ inch	9cm	3½ inches
2cm	¾ inch	10cm	4 inches
2.5cm	1 inch	12cm	4½ inches
3cm	1¼ inches	14cm	5½ inches
4cm	1½ inches	20cm	8 inches
5cm	2 inches	24cm	9½ inches
6cm	2½ inches	30cm	12 inches

A BIG THANK YOU

We are forever grateful to Absolute Press and the team who have managed to pull this book together despite numerous obstacles; but especially grateful for the dedicated focus, patience and brilliance delivered by Art Director and 'Chief Author Liaison Officer', Matt Inwood (who never did quite let the dogs out!); the unmatched talent and photo genius that belongs to Photographer Lisa Barber, whose vision delivered images that have raised the game for vegetarian cooking; and Diana Artley, my Editor, whose industry and intelligence provided the scaffold for this book and whose careful support and guidance ensured it kept going and reached its end. Many thanks.

But also to my publisher, Jon Croft, and his Commissioning Editor, Meg Avent, whose relentless pursual of me and the idea of a Terre à Terre book resulted in the wondrous thing you are now reading (and, I hope, about to cook from). To Claire Siggery for her committed and creative contribution to the design of the book and to Andrea O'Connor for her fine and functional index. And to Lucy Bridgers for her invaluable editorial assistance. To you all: many thanks.

Terre à Terre couldn't be what it is today without all those who have contributed to setting it up and tolerated the chaos that it caused (you all know who you are) and all those past and present who have given their heart, sweat and tears working with and for Terre à Terre (and thank you to the unfortunates – the partners and children – associated with them). The list seems endless, so I hope it's enough to give a sincere and heartfelt Thank You To All. Finally, a personal thanks to Paul Morgan, Lawrence Glass, Jan Gent, Charlotte Ricca-Smith, Lenny Butler and Elizabeth Osborne.

TERRE À TERRE | THE VEGETARIAN RESTAURANT | 71 EAST STREET | BRIGHTON | BN1 1HQ
01273 729051 | WWW.TERREATERRE.CO.UK